LONDON ALMANAC 2010

THE ONE-STOP RESOURCE: WHAT TO DO AND WHERE TO GO

Sarah Riches

NEW HOLLAND

Contents

Introduction

This book will tell you everything you need to know to make the most of London. You might be a tourist visiting for a week or two, maybe you've just moved here or perhaps you've lived here for years and have finally decided to branch out from your usual haunts. Well, you'll find all your favourites here – the British Museum (see p.136), ice skating at Somerset House (see p.16), or which cinemas have sofas (see p.154). And there are contact details for each, too, so if you need the phone number for your local bell-ringing club (see p.234), the website for the London Marathon (see p.27), or directions to Kew Gardens (see p.209), you know you've got it – all in your hand.

But this guide goes further. As well as the 'don't miss' art galleries (see p.122) and oldy-but-goody traditional pubs (see p.179), you'll find the best bits of London that even long-term residents haven't heard about. It's all here: floatation centres (see pp.226 and 229), beach volleyball (see p.228), zorbing (see p.229), and circus schools (see p.230) – as well as museums you've never heard of (see p.136), even though they're just 30 minutes' from your home. Plus, when I came across a little-known fact, spooky ghost story, something that made me chortle or basically anything that raised my eyebrows – I've passed it on to you, so there's a sprinkling of 'insider info' anecdotes throughout the guide.

You'll also spot a trend: London's going back in time. Across the city, you'll see women in their 20s knitting on the tube, groups of men tapping their feet to classic jazz or people dressed in the styles of the roaring twenties. And behind the scenes, burlesque is back. So, if you want to join a tea dance (see p.172), for instance, this guide will give you the contacts you need. You'll also find information on how you can learn basic knit and purl stitches (see pp.103, 117, 172), while dressed in vintage fashion your grandparents would envy (see pp.99, 106, 109, 114). You'll also be able to find out the best bars – from underground dives to upmarket joints – to listen to swing bands, banjo solos and sax jam sessions (see pp.169, 175, 188). And, ladies, you'll be able to find out how to do those all-important bump and grind, quiver and shimmy moves (see p.225), which are definitely not grandparent-friendly.

There's no need to waste your Saturdays Googling fun things to do or trawling through magazines' listing pages, because I've done the research for you – over 650 hours of research have gone into this book to enable you to make the most of your life. Just pick a page and go there.

Sarah Riches

CALENDAR
OF EVENTS

If your nights out follow the same routine – the cinema and a meal or a bar
then club – this chapter will inspire you for ideas to do something different.
As well as information on annual events, such as the London Marathon, the
BBC proms and even the Great Gorilla Run, this section highlights events
unique to 2010, including the Grace Kelly Style exhibition at the V&A. So
make 2010 your year.

*(N.B. At the time of writing the details below were correct, although some were
waiting to be confirmed – please call ahead to check.)*

ALPHABETICAL EVENT LISTINGS

Aegon Tennis Championships (Queen's)	Jun
Affordable Art Fair Autumn Collection	21–24 Oct
Affordable Art Fair Spring Collection	11–14 Mar
Alternative Fashion Week	19–23 Apr
Asian Bride Show, The	23–24 Jan
Aviva London Grand Prix	13–14 Aug
Banglatown Mela in Brick Lane	9 May
Battersea Contemporary Arts Fair	14–16 May
BBC Proms	16 Jul–11 Sep
Big Dance, The	3–11 Jul
Blackheath Funfair	3 Apr
Boat Race, The – Oxford and Cambridge	3 Apr
BP Portrait Award	17 Jun–26 Sep
Brands Reunited	22 Sep 2009–31 Mar 2010
British Animation Awards, The	Mar
Cabinet War Rooms Anniversary	4 Apr 2009–30 Apr 2010
Camden Crawl 2010, The	17–18 Apr
Camille Silvy	8 Jul–24 Oct
Ceremony of the Keys	Daily (*see* p.28)
Changing of the Guards	Daily (*see* p.28)
Chelsea Flower Show	25–29 May
Chinese New Year Celebrations	14 Feb
Christmas Carols at Hampton Court	Late Dec

Events Calendar

Jazz Plus	1–20 Jul
Liberty Festival, Trafalgar Square	Aug
London International Boat Show, The	9–18 Jan
London Art Fair	13–17 Jan
London Burlesque Festival	1st week of Apr
London Design Festival	18–26 Sep
London Duathlon, The	Sep
London Edge and London Central	31 Jan–2 Feb
London Fashion Week: Autumn/Winter Collections	Late Feb
London Festival of Architecture	19 Jun–4 Jul
London Gathering	Sep
London International Mime Festival	16–31 Jan
London Literature Festival	Jul
London Marathon	25 Apr
London Mela	15 Aug
London Open House	18–19 Sep
London to Brighton Veteran Car Rally	7 Nov
London Triathlon, The	7–8 Aug
Lord Mayor's Show	13 Nov
Lovebox Weekender	Jul
Maharajas: The Splendour of India's Royal Courts	10 Oct 2009–17 Jan 2010
Master Tennis, The	7 Dec
Mayor's Thames Festival	11–12 Sep
Meltdown Festival	Jun
Mid Century Show	28 Mar
Mind Body Spirit Festival	26–31 May
New Year's Day Parade	1 Jan
New Year's Day Swim	1 Jan
Notting Hill Carnival	29–30 Aug
Olympia International Art and Antiques Fair	4–13 Jun
Olympia Musicmania	23 Jan
One New Change	Dec
Open Garden Squares Weekend	12–13 Jun
Originals	18–28 Feb
Photomonth	1 Oct–30 Nov
Playtex Moon Walk London 2010, The	15 May
Portobello Film Festival	Sep
Quilts: Innovation and Tradition	20 Mar–4 Jul
Race for Life	Mid May–Jul
Raindance Film Festival	29 Sep–10 Oct
Red Bull Air Race World Championship	Aug

Regent Street Spanish Festival	Sep
Royal Academy Summer Exhibition	Early Jun–Aug
Royal Ascot	15–19 Jun
Royal Parks Foundation Half Marathon	10 Oct
Run to the Beat – Musical Half Marathon	26 Sep
Sci Fi London 9	23–25 Oct
Scoop, The	Mid May–Oct
Scottish Military Tattoo	Around 21 Apr
Shakespeare's Birthday Celebrations, London	23–25 Apr
Shoreditch Festival	July
Sit Down: Seating for Kids	6 Feb–summer
South West Four 2010 London	29 Aug
The Spitalfields Show and Green Fair	12 Sep
Spitalfields Winter Festival	1 week in Dec
St Patrick's Day Parade and Festival	Around 17 Mar
State Opening of Parliament	Nov/Dec
Stratford and East London Music Festival	8–21 Feb
TS. Eliot Prize, The	18 Jan
Taste of Christmas	Early Dec
Taste of London Festival	Jun
Taylor Wessing Photographic Portrait Prize	11 Nov 2010–20 Feb 2011
Thai Festival	14–15 Aug
Thomas Lawrence Exhibition	21 Oct 2010–23 Jan 2011
Times BFI London Film Festival, The	Oct
Trafalgar Parade and Service	24 Oct
Trafalgar Square Christmas Carols	Early Dec
Trooping of the Colour	12 Jun
Turner Prize 2009, London	6 Oct 2009–16 Jan 2010
Turner Prize 2010, London	5 Oct 2010–early Jan 2011
Turning on the Lights	Last week of Nov
Twickenham Festival	Mid Jun
Underage Festival 2010, London	Aug
Venice: Canaletto and His Rivals	13 Oct 2010–16 Jan 2011
Waitangi Day	6 Feb
Wimbledon	21 Jun–4 Jul
Wine Show, London	4 days in Oct
Winter Fine Art and Antiques Fair	Nov
Winter Wonderland	Nov–Jan 2011
Wireless Festival	3–4 Jul
Wise Words	11–31 Mar

▼ JANUARY

 NEW YEAR'S DAY PARADE 1 JAN

- ❶ *Parliament Square, Westminster, SW1A 0AA*
- ⊕ *Tel: 020 8566 8586 (organizers); www.londonparade.co.uk*
- ◉ *Westminster, Piccadilly Circus, Charing Cross, Green Park*
- ❹ *FREE*

This year, London will celebrate its 24th New Year's Day Parade, which is the biggest outdoor parade in Europe. As usual, when Big Ben chimes 12 midnight, the parade will begin at Parliament Square, continue through Whitehall and skirt past Trafalgar Square. It will then head up Regent Street, before turning left at Piccadilly and finishing, three hours later, at Green Park. An audience of 550,000 is expected to turn out to see over 10,000 performers from 20 countries cover the 1.6-km route; expect to see clowns, charity floats, marching bands and perhaps the odd elephant.

 NEW YEAR'S DAY SWIM 1 JAN

- ❶ *Serpentine Lake, Hyde Park, W2 2UH*
- ⊕ *Tel: 01344 291 578 (Serpentine Swim Club); www.serpentinelido.com*
- ◉ *Hyde Park Corner, Marble Arch, Knightsbridge*
- ❹ *FREE*

Why would anyone want to jump into the Serpentine mid-winter? Still, it does make fantastic entertainment for the 150 spectators who go along to watch. The swim take place in a lido, a 100 metre by 30 metre space on the south bank of the lake, which is 1.5 metres at its deepest point. To participate, you have to be a Serpentine Swim Club member; they swim every day, so they're used to icy water.

 THE LONDON INTERNATIONAL BOAT SHOW . 9–18 JAN

- ❶ *ExCeL Exhibition Centre, One Western Gateway, Royal Victoria Dock, E16 1XL*
- ⊕ *Tel: 0844 209 0333; www.londonboatshow.com*
- ◉ *Custom House DLR*
- ❹ *£15 on door; £12.50 in advance; concessions: £10; children under 15: FREE with an adult*

Each year, over 150,000 are drawn to this major marine event, which was opened by the lovely Kelly Brook in 2009. You have the chance to gaze upon classic boats, test new products and try your hand in rowing competitions, while a fashion show and interactive games ensure there is something for all the family.

LONDON ART FAIR   **13–17 JAN**

- ❶ *Business Design Centre, 52 Upper Street, Islington, N1 0QH*
- ☏ *Tel: 020 7288 6272 (venue), 020 7288 6736 (event); www.londonartfair.co.uk*
- ⊕ *Angel*
- ❹ *£15 on door; £25 five-day pass*

Mingle with art collectors and novices at this fair, which displays the work of 1,500 promising and established artists. The exhibits are mostly paintings, but there will also be sculpture, photography, prints, video and installation art. There will also be areas dedicated to emerging talent, photography and lectures.

 LONDON INTERNATIONAL MIME FESTIVAL   **16–31 JAN**

- ❶ *Various venues. Office: 35 Little Russell Street, WC1A 2HH*
- ☏ *Tel: 020 7637 5661; www.mimefest.co.uk*
- ❹ *£10–£25*

This annual mime festival has grown and grown since its conception in 1977. In venues across central London, emerging contemporary visual artists will perform acrobatics, puppetry, dance and comedy for 20,000 spectators. As well as live performances, there will be a host of talks and workshops.

 THE T.S. ELIOT PRIZE   **18 JAN**

- ❶ *South Bank Centre, Belvedere Road, SE1 8XX*
- ☏ *Tel: 020 7833 9247; www.poetrybooks.co.uk*
- ⊕ *Waterloo*
- ❹ *Price tbc*

If you're a poet, a publisher or simply someone who wants to discover the next big name in poetry, then join the 1,000-strong audience at the South Bank Centre. Here, the Poetry Book Society will announce which of the 250 poets present will be awarded the coveted £15,000 prize for the best poetry book of 2009.

<table><tr><td>23
JAN</td></tr></table> **THE ASIAN BRIDE SHOW**   **23–24 JAN**

- ❶ *Wembley Stadium, Wembley, Greater London, HA9 0WS*
- ☏ *Tel: 020 8786 9988; www.theasianbrideshow.com*
- ⊕ *Wembley Park, Wembley Central*
- ❹ *£10 adults; £18 couples; £25 family*

Brides, this is a groom-friendly event, so tell him he's got no excuse! As well as fashion shows, celebrity appearances and makeovers, the 25,000 expected visitors will have a chance to sample complementary cocktails and whisky.

OLYMPIA MUSICMANIA 23 JAN

- *Olympia, Hammersmith Road, W14 8UX*
- *Tel: 020 7385 1200 (venue), 0116 277 1133 (event); www.vip-24.com*
- *Kensington (Olympia)*
- *Price tbc*

Been hunting for a B-side track from Chesney Hawkes' *Buddy's Song* album? Or perhaps you've been trawling second-hand vinyl shops for Barry Mann's 1961 one-hit wonder, 'Who Put the Bomp (in the Bomp, Bomp, Bomp)'? Well, this fair has everything music-related that you could wish for – but be prepared to admit your music tastes face to face with 400 stallholders to find what you're after. As well as new and second-hand CDs, videos and 'tapes', here you can pick up autographed posters, rare band T-shirts and old concert programmes from any genre or era. About 2,500 visitors attend from Europe, the US and as far as Japan. The event also occurs on 24 April, 18 September and 13–14 November.

 HOLOCAUST MEMORIAL DAY 27 JAN

- *Various venues*
- *Tel: 0845 838 1883; www.hmd.org.uk*
- *Various*

Since 2001, the horrors of the Holocaust and the strength of human spirit it engendered have been marked on this day by events organized by councils, museums and community groups throughout the capital. Past events have included film screenings, candlelit vigils and photography exhibitions – check the website above for this year's programme.

 LONDON EDGE AND LONDON CENTRAL 31 JAN–2 FEB

- *Olympia, Hammersmith Road, W14 8UX, W14 8UX*
- *Tel: 0116 289 8249; www.londonedge.com*
- *Kensington (Olympia)*
- *£5 (includes free catalogue and gifts)*

If you're looking for studded collars, glow sticks or board shorts, these combined exhibitions are for you. Since 2000, over 220 companies have attended these annual events to showcase alternative clothes and accessories for the gothic, punk, surf, club and biker scene. As well as stalls selling urban fashion, boho clothes and club wear, there'll also be DJs, a skate ramp and dancers showing off their break-dance and hip hop moves. Make sure you take a break to do some people-watching – no matter how outrageous you think your outfit is, someone is sure to outdo you. The event will also occur in September (the date will be released in 2010).

ONGOING EVENTS

See these exhibitions and events, which started towards the end of 2009, before they finish.

 TURNER PRIZE 2009, LONDON   6 OCT 2009–16 JAN 2010

---

❶ *Tate Britain, Millbank, Pimlico, SW1P 4RG*
⊕ *Tel: 020 7887 8888; www.tate.org.uk*
⊖ *Pimlico*
❹ *FREE*

Catch the end of the most talked about art exhibition in the country, which exhibits the work of the four artists nominated for the 2009–10 Turner Prize. This year's nominees are Roger Hiorns, best known for his work *Seizure*, where he poured copper sulphate into an ex-council flat, which then crystallized; Lucy Skaer, who creates sketches and statues based on photojournalism; Enrico David, who embroiders portraits onto canvas; and Richard Wright, who draws delicate, geometric patterns.

 MAHARAJAS: THE SPLENDOUR OF   10 OCT 2009–17 JAN 2010
INDIA'S ROYAL COURTS

---

❶ *V&A, Cromwell Road, South Kensington, SW7 2RL*
⊕ *Tel: 020 7942 2000; www.vam.ac.uk*
⊖ *South Kensington*
❹ *£11*

This three-month exhibition explores the era of India's maharajas, from the 18th century to the end of British rule in 1947. Over 250 artefacts are on display, including textiles, costume, jewellery, rare film footage, photography and furniture. Highlights include an Indian royal procession display and an ivory sedan chair that was presented to the Prince of Wales in 1876.

 ECO HOME   13 OCT 2009–7 FEB 2010

---

❶ *Geffrye Museum, 136 Kingsland Road, E2 8EA*
⊕ *Tel: 020 7739 9893; www.geffrye-museum.org.uk*
⊖ *Old Street, then bus 243*
❹ *FREE*

This exhibition will look at the growing interest in eco living, exploring how to save energy in the home, sustainable design and eco-friendly behaviour. Learn how you can reduce the toxins you release into the environment by using chemical-free products or by making small changes to the way you decorate your home.

JACOB EPSTEIN, HENRI GAUDIER-BRZESKA AND ERIC GILL 24 OCT 2009–24 JAN 2010

🛈 *The Royal Academy, Burlington House, Piccadilly, W1J 0BD*
☎ *Tel: 020 7300 8000; www.royalacademy.org.uk*
⊖ *Piccadilly Circus, Green Park*
💲 *FREE permanent collection; £8–£12 temporary collections*

This exhibition brings together some of the most exciting works from the revolutionary modern British sculptors Epstein, Gaudier-Brzeska and Gill. Many of the pieces have never before been displayed in London.

 BRANDS REUNITED 22 SEP 2009–31 MAR 2010 (MAY BE EXTENDED)

🛈 *Museum of Brands, Packaging and Advertising, 2 Colville Mews, Lonsdale Road, W11 2AR*
☎ *Tel: 020 7908 0880; www.museumofbrands.com*
⊖ *Notting Hill Gate, Ladbroke Grove, Westbourne Park*
💲 *£5.80*

Remember C&A, Aztec chocolate bars, Kellogg's Puffa Puffa Rice and Smith's Crisps? Well, you can take a trip down memory lane at this exhibition, which celebrates long-gone brands from the past 50 years. As well as reminiscing, you can learn about why some brands disappear while others stick around, which brands are still popular elsewhere in the world and the power of the people in bringing back the Wispa chocolate bar (*see* p.149).

CABINET WAR ROOMS ANNIVERSARY 4 APR 2009–30 APR 2010

🛈 *Churchill Museum and the Cabinet War Rooms, Clive Steps, King Charles Street, SW1A 2AQ*
☎ *Tel: 020 7930 6961; cwr.iwm.org.uk*
⊖ *Westminster*
💲 *£12.95 museum entry, exhibition included*

For the next few months a series of events, activities, screenings and lectures will continue to commemorate the 70th anniversary of the Cabinet War Rooms, which became operational the week before war was declared in 1939. Through oral accounts and photographs, an exhibition will explore the experience of those who worked in this secret underground site during World War II.

OUTDOOR WINTER ICE SKATING

You can ice skate all year round, but it's much more fun out in the open air and when you can't feel your fingers anymore. There are temporary winter ice rinks all over London. We've listed the best ones below. Remember, most are open for over six weeks, so if you want to go when it's a bit quieter, avoid December. You can book anytime online and in person at the ice rinks, subject to availability.

| TOWER OF LONDON | 21 NOV 2009–10 JAN 2010 |
| | (2010–11 LIKELY TO BE SIMILAR) |

ⓘ *HM Tower of London, Tower Hill, Tower Hamlets, EC3N 4AB*
⊕ *Tel: 0844 482 7777; www.toweroflondonicerink.com*
⊖ *Tower Hill*
❹ *£10 off-peak; £12 peak*

New York wins points for its rink in Central Park, but London has one inside the moat of the Tower of London, which, for beauty and romance, is hard to beat. The imposing brick walls of the tower, which dates from 1078, are transformed by twinkling lights in the evening sessions. It's advisable to book in advance. If it's raining, the skating still goes ahead.

| KEW GARDENS | 1 NOV 2009–31 JAN 2010 |
| | (2010–11 LIKELY TO BE SIMILAR) |

ⓘ *Royal Botanic Gardens, Kew Road, Kew, Richmond, Surrey, TW9 3AB*
⊕ *Tel: 020 8332 5655; www.kewgardensicerink.com*
⊖ *Kew Gardens*
❹ *£13*

Go at night and you'll see the gardens eerily lit up with discreet spotlights. The ice rink is in front of the stunning Temperate House, the world's largest Victorian glasshouse, built in 1859. During the day, if you're lucky, a light mist will descend on the rink and the spindly trees around it – magical.

| HAMPTON COURT | 21 NOV 2009–10 JAN 2010 |
| | (2010–11 LIKELY TO BE SIMILAR) |

ⓘ *Hampton Court Palace, East Molesey, Surrey, KT8 9AU*
⊕ *Tel: 0844 482 7777; www.hamptoncourticerink.com*
⊖ *Hampton Court BR*
❹ *£15 on door; £12.50 in advance*

Whether you're doing loops around the rink or grabbing on to the side, don't forget to admire your surroundings: Henry VIII's grand Tudor palace. The palace dates from the 11th century, and the red brick turrets, stone crosses and flag make a majestic backdrop to the rink in front of its main entrance. Don't forget your camera.

| **SOMERSET HOUSE** | NOV 2009–JAN 2010;
24 NOV 2010–27 JAN 2011 |

🚇 *The Strand, Westminster, WC2R 1LA*
☎ *Tel: 020 7845 4600 (recorded information), 020 7845 4613;*
   www.somersethouse.org.uk
🚇 *Temple*
💷 *£10.50*

Every winter, over 25,000 visitors attend the ice skating sessions at
Somerset House, including a few celebrities – *Harry Potter*'s Emma Watson
(Hermione Granger) has been spotted here. For groups, DJs will get you
in the mood to dance; couples, there are torch-lit late-night sessions.
A 7-metre-high Christmas tree overlooks the ice rink in the courtyard,
which is surrounded by marquees for those who want to watch.

| **WINTER WONDERLAND** | 21 NOV 2009–3 JAN 2010
(2010–11 LIKELY TO BE SIMILAR) |

🚇 *Off South Carriage Drive, Serpentine Road,*
   Hyde Park, Westminster, W2 2UH
☎ *Tel: 084 4847 1771; www.hydeparkwinterwonderland.com*
🚇 *Hyde Park Corner*
💷 *£10*

If you can't get enough of the festive spirit, visit London's largest outdoor
rink in Hyde Park's Winter Wonderland. It's a favourite with celebrities
and is in a corner of the park dedicated to Christmas, so you can also
enjoy a toboggan snow slide, or mosey around the German Christmas
market afterwards.

| **NATURAL HISTORY MUSEUM**
ICE RINK AND CHRISTMAS FAIR | 1 NOV 2009–31 JAN 2010
(2010–11 LIKELY TO BE SIMILAR) |

🚇 *Natural History Museum, Cromwell Road, SW7 5BD*
☎ *Tel: 020 7942 5000; www.nhm.ac.uk*
🚇 *South Kensington*
💷 *FREE; £13 ice skating*

With the museum illuminated in the background, romantic types won't be
able to resist ice skating under the stars at this 1,000-square-metre
outdoor rink. And there's plenty of entertainment even if you're not loved
up, from the cafe/bar in the tent overlooking the ice rink. From there you
can sip mulled wine or hot chocolate as you get into the Christmas spirit,
watching people fall over, or, better still, wobble backwards and forwards –
classic comedy. As well as the main rink, there's one for children, too, and
sessions are set aside for wheelchair users. Elsewhere in the gardens
there are 38 huts selling festive food, Christmas decorations, candles and
hand-crafted presents.

▼ FEBRUARY

📅 WAITANGI DAY 6 FEB

- ℹ️ Venue tbc (Central London)
- ☎️ Tel: 020 7930 8422 (New Zealand High Commission), 07957 424 004 (New Zealand Society); www.nzsociety.co.uk
- 💷 Around £65–£80

Organized by the New Zealand Society, this black-tie dinner celebrates the signing of the Treaty of Waitangi, which founded modern-day New Zealand. Enjoy classic dishes – lamb served with kumara, mussels and boysenberry pavlova – and only wine and beer from New Zealand will be served. You can also watch a Maori cultural performance and find out the winner of the grand title of New Zealander of the Year. Ticket prices include all food and drink and are sold through the society's website.

📅 SIT DOWN: SEATING FOR KIDS 6 FEB–SUMMER

- ℹ️ Museum of Childhood, Cambridge Heath Road, E2 9PA
- ☎️ Tel: 020 8983 5200; www.vam.ac.uk
- 🚇 Bethnal Green
- 💷 FREE

This interactive exhibition, aimed at families, will explore British and European trends in children's furniture. A diverse range of designs will be on display – anything from potties, a high chair from 1920 and contemporary classroom chairs to rocking horses and seesaws. Some of the pieces date back to 1680, though the exhibition will focus on designs from the past 200 years. The closing date is still to be released at the time of writing.

📅 STRATFORD AND EAST LONDON MUSIC FESTIVAL 8–21 FEB

- ℹ️ Redbridge Music Service, John Savage Centre, Fencepiece Road, Hainault, Ilford, Essex, IG6 2NB
- 🚇 Fairlop
- ℹ️ St Mary's Parish Church, Woodford High Road, Woodford, Essex, E18 2PA South
- 🚇 South Woodford
- ☎️ Tel: 020 8491 7691; www.stratfordmusicfestival.org.uk
- 💷 £1 per event

This English music festival has been running since 1882, making it the longest established festival of its kind. This year, about 1,250 contestants will compete in a series of competitions based around categories such as speech, drama, musical instrument recitals, solo singing, duets and ensembles. Genres range from opera and jazz to wartime songs and modern ballads, as well as Shakespeare, solo acting and storytelling. The finale is the best night to attend.

CHINESE NEW YEAR CELEBRATIONS   **14 FEB**

- 📍 *Trafalgar Square, SW1Y; Leicester Square, WC2H; Chinatown, W1D; Shaftesbury Avenue, WC2H*
- ☎ *Tel: 020 7851 6686; www.chinatownchinese.co.uk*
- 🚇 *Charing Cross, Leicester Square, Piccadilly Circus*
- 💷 *FREE*

See in the Year of the Tiger with cries of '*Gung Hei Fat Choi!*' ('Wishing you happiness and prosperity!'), lions and dragons dancing to Chinese music, drumming, nimble acrobats and a fireworks closing display. A colourful parade will travel down the Strand, Charing Cross Road and Shaftesbury Avenue.

 THE GREAT SPITALFIELDS PANCAKE RACE   **16 FEB**

- 📍 *Old Truman Brewery, 91–5 Brick Lane, Spitalfields, E1 6QL (venue tbc)*
- ☎ *Tel: 020 7375 0441 (organizers); www.alternativearts.co.uk*
- 🚇 *Aldgate East*
- 💷 *FREE*

Bring along a frying pan, join a team of four, grab a floppy pancake and you're off! Each year, Alternative Arts hosts the Great Spitalfields Pancake Race, a fun, free, family event watched by about 2,000 people. Apply in advance or turn up before 12.30pm to join in the relay on the day. Help raise money for charity and celebrate Shrove Tuesday by donning a pancake costume – if you're voted the best-dressed team, you'll win a prize. But it's the first prize that everyone's after – a highly coveted engraved frying pan. For the losers, the E Team clowns and the Lost Marbles string band will cheer you up, and you can scoff as many pancakes as you can from the crêperie.

 IRVING PENN PORTRAITS   **18 FEB–31 MAY**

- 📍 *National Portrait Gallery, St Martin's Place, Westminster, WC2H 0HE*
- ☎ *Tel: 020 7306 0055; www.npg.org.uk*
- 🚇 *Charing Cross*
- 💷 *£10*

See the work of American fashion photographer Irving Penn (born 1917), whose assignments included his first *Vogue* cover in 1943.

 ORIGINALS   **18–28 FEB**

- 📍 *Mall Galleries, The Mall (near Trafalgar Square), SW1*
- ☎ *Tel: 020 7930 6844; www.mallgalleries.org.uk*
- 🚇 *Charing Cross*
- 💷 *£2.50*

A panel of artists, collectors and academics have put together this exhibition, which showcases only original, contemporary prints (no reproductions). About 2,500 people are expected to attend.

📅 FEB LONDON FASHION WEEK: AUTUMN/WINTER COLLECTIONS   LATE FEB

- 📍 Somerset House, the Strand, Westminster, WC2R 1LA
- ☎ Tel: 020 7845 4600; www.londonfashionweek.co.uk, www.somersethouse.org.uk
- Ⓔ Temple
- 💷 Various

Organized by the British Fashion Council, LFW aims to promote British fashion through a series of catwalks and an exhibition, which will be held in Somerset House for the first time this year. You can expect to see all your favourite designers as well as some new names – watch out for this year's New Gen, a collection of emerging designers who receive mentoring and up to £10,000 to put towards their show costs, exhibition space and use of the catwalk tent – previous participants have included Alexander McQueen.

📅 FEB FACSHION   LATE FEB

- 📍 Old Truman Brewery, 91–5 Brick Lane, E1
- ☎ Tel: 07946 121 043; www.facshion.co.uk
- Ⓔ Aldgate East
- 💷 FREE

Some 2,500 hipsters will attend this two-day event for its cool catwalk shows and stalls selling eco-friendly clothes and one-off designs. There are three catwalk shows each day, and up to 50 stalls which also sell accessories and treatments, such as manicures and facials. The event is aimed at a mainstream audience – so you should be able to pay with cash, not credit card.

📅 FEB DEUTSCHE BÖRSE PHOTOGRAPHY PRIZE EXHIBITION   LATE FEB–APRIL

- 📍 The Photographers' Gallery, 16–18 Ramillies Street, W1F 7LW
- ☎ Tel: 0845 262 1618; www.photonet.org.uk
- Ⓔ Oxford Circus
- 💷 FREE

This is the international photography exhibition of the year, where four artists, chosen for their contribution to photography over the past 12 months, display their work. The winner will be announced in March, and will bag £30,000. Over 400,000 visitors are expected to attend this annual event.

LAST CHANCE TO BOOK

These popular events require a good deal of forward planning, as tickets sell out far in advance. Here is are some tips to keep you one step ahead.

CHELSEA FLOWER SHOW

• Tickets go on sale around Nov 2009. If you want to choose your day and time, it's best to buy then. Royal Horticultural Show members' days (25 and 26 May 2010) and Saturday 28 May 2010 sell out first. Daytime tickets and evening tickets also sell out early on. There will still be some evening tickets, most likely the Friday, left by early May 2010. It's best to buy early to avoid disappointment.

ROYAL ASCOT

• Tickets go on sale from November 2009. The Thursday and Saturday sell out first, usually by the end of April.

WIMBLEDON

• Most of the tickets for Centre Court and Courts 1 and 2 are sold in advance via a public ballot. To enter the 2010 ballot you need to request an application and send it to the following address by 31 December 2009: Ticket Office, AELTC, P.O. BOX 98, London SW19 5AE.
• You can also buy tickets on the grounds. Around 500 tickets for Courts 1 and 2 are reserved for sale on the day; however, you'll need to get up early and be prepared for a long queue and you still might be disappointed. You can also buy ground passes for the day and try your luck with the ticket resale kiosk inside the venue for resold tickets (again, expect to queue).
• Tickets can be bought through affiliated tennis clubs, tour packages and corporate hospitality or debenture seat holders (stakeholders).
• There are also a limited number of online tickets that can be bought on the evening before play on www.ticketmaster.co.uk.

THE PROMS

• General booking will open in May but availability is limited. Tickets for the last night are likely to be sold out, although there may be returns available.
• Weekend promming passes and season tickets can be booked in advance. If you want to buy advance tickets for the last night, a 'five concert rule' applies – you have to book five concerts in the same seating area at the Royal Albert Hall in the 2010 season before you can buy one ticket for the last night.
• There is also a last-night ballot, where 100 tickets are allocated by ballot. To apply you need to send an official ballot form to: BBC Proms Ballot, Box Office, Royal Albert Hall, London SW7 2AP.
• You can buy tickets on the door – up to 1,400 standing tickets and over 500 arena and gallery tickets are on sale at the door. Last night standing tickets are available, but there is a good deal of competition and people even sleep out the night before to ensure a good spot.

▼ MARCH

◻ 1 MAR   WISE WORDS   1–31 MAR

- ❶ *Various venues; office: Top Studio, Montefiore Centre, Hanbury Street, E1 5HZ*
- ⊕ *Tel: 020 7375 0441; www.alternativearts.co.uk*
- ❸ *Various, many events FREE*

Each year, international poets, artists, storytellers, comics and musicians gather in various East End venues to celebrate women's writing. As usual, all sorts of events will be hosted, so expect anything from gritty documentaries, plays and book readings to talks by leading female authors about their own lives or latest novel. Bring tissues, because if you're not brought to tears by a poignant memoir, then you'll be crying with laughter at the tales of a stand-up comedian. You'll also have the chance to tell your own story in writing workshops, where you can pick up tips on how to write your first comedy.

◻ 1 MAR   EAST FESTIVAL   1–31 MAR

- ❶ *Various venues in East London*
- ⊕ *Tel: 08701 566 366; www.visitlondon.com/events/east/*
- ❸ *Various prices, some events are FREE*

Now in its fourth year, East Festival continues to celebrate East London's art scene, multi-ethnicity and history. Sounds like any excuse for a party. Activities take place over six days in venues from churches to nightclubs, as well as the usual East End suspects – Bethnal Green Working Men's Club, Rich Mix and Whitechapel Art Gallery. Previous events have included a treasure hunt, classical quartet and jazz band performances, a chance to meet a Pearly Queen and a mystery history bus, which offered tours of the area. Most events are suitable for all ages.

INTERNATIONAL WOMEN'S WEEK   6–14 MAR

- ❶ *Various venues: Office: Top Studio, Montefiore Centre,*
  Hanbury Street, E1 5HZ
- ⊕ *Tel: 020 7375 0441; www.alternativearts.co.uk*
- ❸ *FREE*

Women's groups across Tower Hamlets are organizing a variety of events themed around the 2012 Olympics. Activities in previous years have included watersports in the local docks, storytelling, handicrafts, photography exhibitions, as well as line dancing and Bollywood dance shows. International Women's Day itself is held on 8 March every year.

AFFORDABLE ART FAIR SPRING COLLECTION   11–14 MAR

- ❶ *Battersea Park, SW11 4NJ*
- ⊕ *Tel: 020 8246 4848; www.affordableartfair.com*
- ❷ *Battersea Park BR*
- ❸ *£12 on door; £10 in advance*

The Affordable Art Fair was set up in 1999 to give Londoners the chance to buy original contemporary art on a budget. None of the pieces sell for more than £3,000, with many on sale for as little as £50 – perfect for a first home, present or investment. Today, over 22,500 visitors come to browse the paintings, sculpture, photography and original prints on display, which are created by graduates as well as well-known artists such as Sam Taylor-Wood, Bridget Riley and Anthony Micallef, best known for his eerie sketches of angels and gun-wielding cherubs. Free drawing workshops, sculpture demos, installations and hands-on printmaking for kids mean this is no stuffy art fair for avid collectors – even first-time buyers whose last purchase was a print from Athena will enjoy having a look around.

 THE INDIAN PORTRAIT: FROM   11 MAR–20 JUN
PRE-MUGHAL TO BRITISH RAJ

- ❶ *National Portrait Gallery, St Martin's Place, Westminster, WC2H 0HE*
- ⊕ *Tel: 020 7306 0055; www.npg.org.uk*
- ❷ *Charing Cross*
- ❸ *Price tbc*

This collection of 70 paintings will be organized by theme and cover topics from the Mughal rulers and courtiers to holy men and the East India Company. The exhibition will look at the influence of Iran, Europe and local Hindu and Muslim traditions on Indian culture; and, through the pieces of art, visitors will be able to see how Indians saw themselves, as well as how they wished to be seen.

 ST PATRICK'S DAY PARADE AND FESTIVAL   AROUND 17 MAR

- ❶ *Various locations*
- ⊕ *Tel: 020 7983 4000; www.london.gov.uk*
- ❸ *FREE*

The highlight of this all-day family event is a parade of floats, performers in costumes, stilt walkers and a marching band. The route begins on Park Lane, heads towards Hyde Park Corner, down to Piccadilly Circus and on to Regent's Street, before ending up in Trafalgar Square. Events continue all day from noon until 6pm in Trafalgar Square, Leicester Square and Covent Garden, where there will be performances of traditional and modern Irish music. Listen to pipers, harpists, flutists and musicians on the fiddle – as well as Ireland's latest boy band – take part in a ceilidh, watch Irish folk dancing or find out the best place to visit on the Emerald Isle. Go on – paint your face with stripes of green, white and orange and jig your way there.

📅 20 MAR IDEAL HOME SHOW   20 MAR–5 APR

- ❶ *Earl's Court, Warwick Road, SW5 9TA*
- 🌐 *Tel: 020 8515 2000 (organizers); www.idealhomeshow.co.uk*
- ◉ *Earl's Court, West Brompton*
- ❶ *Price tbc*

Attracting 250,000 visitors each year, this lifestyle show has been running since 1908 and is the biggest and oldest of its kind in Britain. Over 15,000 exhibitors will host events on interior design, DIY and the garden, helping you make your home more homely. There'll also be cooking demonstrations and stalls selling health and beauty products. Last year's [2009] exhibitors included Global Nomadic Carpets, known for its Kashmir hand-knotted rugs; Nia's World of Art & Design, popular for its bold print fabric; and the aptly-named Very Interesting Water Features and Landscape Company. Design teams will be on hand to teach you how to make the most of your home, too, offering tips on ways to save energy and space – without spending a fortune.

📅 20 MAR QUILTS: INNOVATION AND TRADITION   20 MAR–4 JUL

- ❶ *V&A, Cromwell Road, South Kensington, SW7 2RL*
- 🌐 *Tel: 020 7942 2000; www.vam.ac.uk*
- ◉ *South Kensington*
- ❶ *Price tbc*

Whoever knew the UK tradition of quilting could be so exciting? Well, 85,000 visitors can't all be wrong. The exhibition explains the social significance behind the patchwork quilts on display, as each one tells a story – some of them are 300 years old. You can also find out about different techniques used to create quilts, the skills required to make them and the meanings behind their patterns.

📅 24 MAR COUNTRY LIVING SPRING FAIR   24–28 MAR

- ❶ *Business Design Centre, 52 Upper Street, Islington, N1 0QH*
- 🌐 *Tel: 020 7359 3535 (info), 0844 848 0169 (bookings); www.wineshow.co.uk,*
- ◉ *Angel*
- ❶ *£15 on door; 11.50 in advance*

This popular fair, run by *Country Living* magazine, brings the products of small and independent craftmakers and designers from around Britain to Islington's Business Design Centre. Expect to find plenty of sumptuous treats as well as household goods and accessories.

HEAD OF THE RIVER RACE   **27 MAR**

- *Mortlake, Richmond, SW14 to Putney, Wandsworth, on the River Thames*
- *Tel: 01932 220 401; www.horr.co.uk*
- *Mortlake BR*
- *FREE*

This year, 420 professional crews from around the country and further afield will compete to win this rowing race, which dates back to 1926. The race begins at around 1pm at Mortlake Stone, a marker 60 metres below Chiswick Bridge, and continues down the 6.8-km route towards Putney. A record time of 16 minutes and 37 seconds was set in 1989 by the Great Britain National Squad, but on average, it takes about 20–1 minutes for a boat to finish. Still, the event lasts about two hours from the first boat setting off to the last boat finishing, so it's worth the trek even if you don't live nearby. If you want a good view, the best spots are from the Surrey bank above Chiswick Bridge, near the start, or on the north side of Hammersmith Bridge, which is roughly halfway. Check in advance that the bridge isn't closed, though, and check the website, too, as the race is cancelled in bad weather.

 MID CENTURY SHOW   **28 MAR**

- *Dulwich College, Dulwich Common, SE21 7LD*
- *Tel: 020 8761 3405; www.modernshows.com*
- *West Dulwich BR*
- *£6*

This event, attended by 70 dealers and designers such as People Will Always Need Plates, celebrates interior design and home antiques. Browse and buy decorative chests, rocking chairs or antique candlestick holders, as well as modern ceramics, wallpaper and textiles. Prices range from £10 up to £5,000. There will also be an autumn show on 14 November.

THE BRITISH ANIMATION AWARDS (BAA)   **MAR**

- *BFI Southbank, Belvedere Road, South Bank, SE1 8XT*
- *Tel: 020 8430 4563; www.britishanimationawards.com*
- *Waterloo*
- *Price tbc*

The public have the chance to vote for new talent and big names at this event, which celebrates the British animation industry. The BAA consider all types of animation, from adverts and music videos to children's TV programmes and short films created by students – screenings are shown at the BFI Southbank. The winners receive artwork created by fellow animators, all of which have some connection to sheep...

▼ APRIL

 THE BOAT RACE – OXFORD AND CAMBRIDGE 3 APR

❶ *Thames Rowing Club, Putney Embankment, SW15 1LB*
⊕ *Tel: 020 8971 9241; www.theboatrace.org*
◉ *Putney Bridge, Ravenscourt Park, Hammersmith*
❹ *FREE*

Ever since Cambridge first challenged Oxford in 1829, the two universities have held a boat race in the spring. At the time of writing, the score was Cambridge 79, Oxford 74. This year will be the 156th race, and 250,000 spectators are expected to watch the amateur oarsmen battle it out to finish before the 16.19-minute record (set by Cambridge, in 2008). The 6.8-km route starts at Putney Bridge and passes Fulham Football Club, then Hammersmith Bridge, just before the Surrey Bend around the halfway mark. It continues past Barnes Bridge before the grand finale at Chiswick Bridge. If you want a good view, get there early and head for Putney Bridge or Bishop's Park near the start, or Dukes Meadows near the finish. If all you can see is a river of heads, then there are big screens at Bishops Park in Fulham and Furnival Gardens in Hammersmith.

 BLACKHEATH FUNFAIR 3 APR

❶ *Circus Field, Shooters Hill Road, Blackheath, SE3*
⊕ *Tel: 01784 461 805 (organizers); www.showmensguild.com*
◉ *Blackheath BR, then bus 53, 54, 89, 380*
❹ *Price tbc*

Every Easter, May and August bank holiday, a funfair takes over the common in this otherwise sleepy village. Have a family day out on the dodgems, merry-go-round and carousel – or try your hand on those catch-a-fish games.

 LONDON BURLESQUE FESTIVAL 1ST WEEK OF APR

❶ *Various venues*
⊕ *www.londonburlesquefest.com*
❹ *Various*

For the fourth year running, 150 British and international performers will strip across the city, celebrating the resurgence in burlesque. Expect high quality performances of slapstick comedy, saucy cabaret, showgirl dances and jazz, swing and big band tunes sung in husky tones. You can watch performers whip the crowd into a whistling frenzy as they pull off silk gloves with their teeth, unclip suspenders and peel off stockings before their nipple tassel finale. Turning up in retro attire is encouraged, but not required. Full details of London Burlesque Festival 2010 will be released by 31 December.

GRACE KELLY STYLE 17 APR–26 SEP

❶ *V&A, Cromwell Road, South Kensington, SW7 2RL*
⊕ *Tel: 020 7942 2000; www.vam.ac.uk*
◉ *South Kensington*
❸ *Price tbc*

This exhibition displays the elaborate wardrobe of Grace Kelly, including hats, jewellery and haute couture gowns by Dior, Givenchy and Yves St Laurent. Highlights include the original Hermès 'Kelly bag', the lace outfit she wore for her wedding to Prince Ranier and the gown she wore when accepting her Oscar in 1955.

 THE CAMDEN CRAWL 2010 17–18 APR

❶ *Various venues around Camden*
⊕ *Tel: 020 7403 3331 (tickets); www.thecamdencrawl.com*
◉ *Camden*
❸ *£32.50 single-day pass; £55 for a two-day pass*

Camden has the atmosphere of a carnival on a quiet day, so imagine it during this annual festival, which sees over 150 bands playing in venues around the area. During the day, you can take part in events from theatre workshops, bingo, music quizzes and karaoke, or watch stand-up comedians, street performers and short films. Then, later on, listen to unsigned bands and household names such as Amy Winehouse, Noah and the Whale and Madness – who performed in an open-top bus last year [2009]. Many of the venues taking part include Camden institutions, ranging from the Jazz Cafe (5 Parkway, NW1 7PG) and The Hawley Arms (2 Castlehaven Road, NW1 8QU) to Electric Ballroom (184 Camden High Street, NW1 8QP), Koko (1a Camden High Street, NW1 7JE) and the Roundhouse (Chalk Farm Road, NW1 8EH).

 ALTERNATIVE FASHION WEEK 19–23 APR

❶ *Spitalfields Trader's Market, Crispin Place, Brushfield Street, E1 6AA*
⊕ *Tel: 020 7375 0441; www.alternativearts.co.uk*
◉ *Liverpool Street*
❸ *FREE*

While London Fashion Week is an exclusive event for top fashion houses, Alternative Fashion Week gives 60 emerging designers the chance to showcase original work in daily fashion shows, which start at 1.15pm. There's also a Fashion Market around the catwalk, which runs between 11am and 5pm everyday, with stalls selling clothes, textiles and accessories.

SCOTTISH MILITARY TATTOO **AROUND 21 APR**

- ❶ *Royal Albert Hall, Kensington Gore, SW7 2AP*
- ⊕ *Tel: 0845 401 5040; 01722 332 233; www.thescottishtattoo.com*
- ❷ *South Kensington, High Street Kensington*
- ❹ *£14–£24 – tickets available from the Royal Albert Hall box office*

Whether you're a Scot or not, you'll be swept away by the infectious enthusiasm for Scottish culture at this annual festival. So, don a kilt and get into the party spirit – join in with a Highland jig or Irish country dancing, hum along to Celtic tunes played on the bagpipes and listen to the drums of military bands.

 SHAKESPEARE'S BIRTHDAY CELEBRATIONS, LONDON **23–25 APR**

- ❶ *Shakespeare's Globe Theatre, 21 New Globe Walk, Bankside, SE1 9DT*
- ⊕ *Tel: 01789 204 016 (Birthday Celebrations Committee); www.shakespeare.org.uk*
- ❷ *Mansion House, London Bridge*
- ❹ *FREE events outside the globe*

Celebrate William Shakespeare's 446th birthday in and around Shakespeare's Globe. Watch performers in period costume dance, sing and play traditional instruments in an annual parade or try folk dancing.

 LONDON MARATHON **25 APRIL**

- ❶ *Route: from Blackheath, Greenwich, SE3 to Pall Mall, Westminster, SW1*
- ⊕ *Tel: 020 7902 0200; www.virginlondonmarathon.com*
- ❷ *Blackheath BR, Victoria, Green Park*
- ❹ *FREE for spectators*

Now in its 30th year, the Marathon will be sponsored by Virgin for the first time. About 1 million spectators cheer on 36,000 runners along the 42.2-km route, making it one of the world's five most significant marathons. The course starts on Blackheath and winds around southwest London to finish in central London at Pall Mall. This year there will be a major post-Marathon party (venue tbc).

 EAST END FILM FESTIVAL **END OF APR**

- ❶ *Various East End venues; office: Brady Arts Centre, 192–6 Hanbury Street, E1 5HU*
- ⊕ *Tel: 020 7364 7917; www.eastendfilmfestival.com*
- ❹ *Various*

Since 2001, this week-long film festival has given local filmmakers the chance to show their work to the public. As well as film screenings, there will be live bands and talks and debates with well-known directors and composers. In previous years, composer Michael Nyman and director Danny Boyle have taken part.

DAILY EVENTS

London has so much history and tradition, but it's easy to forget that on the daily commute. Take a day off and go to see the changing of the guards, or get organized and plan a trip to the Tower of London for the ceremony of the keys (below), both of which occur daily. You'll see what draws 27 million tourists to the city every year.

CEREMONY OF THE KEYS

- ❶ *HM Tower of London, Tower Hill, EC3N 4AB*
- ☎ *Tel: 0870 950 4466, 0870 756 6060; www.hrp.org.uk*
- ❸ *Tower Hill*
- ❹ *FREE*
- ▬ *9.53pm daily*

The ritual of locking the tower to ensure no intruders get in dates back 700 years; these days, the process of getting hold of a ticket does the same job. The ceremony begins at 9.53pm each evening, and lasts seven minutes. The chief yeoman warder, dressed in a red Tudor watchcoat, carries a candlelit brass lantern in one hand and the tower keys in the other. He is greeted silently by a guard, who takes the lantern from him as he locks the wooden gates. On their return they are stopped by a sentry and a brief exchange takes place as the sentry checks the identity of the warder, who then continues on to the Queen's House. These days, the ritual of locking the tower is largely symbolic, although still important because the tower is home to the crown jewels (*see p.220*).

(N.B. Tickets must be applied for in writing at least two months in advance, or three months from Jun–Aug. Applications must be accompanied by a self-addressed envelope and a postage stamp.)

CHANGING OF THE GUARDS

- ❶ *Horse Guards Parade, Horse Guards Road, SW1A 2AX*
- ☎ *Tel: 020 7766 7300; www.army.mod.uk*
- ❸ *Embankment*
- ❹ *FREE*
- ▬ *11.30am daily from May to the end of July; alternate days the rest of the year*

This 40-minute ceremony takes places in the courtyard of Buckingham Palace. The two sentries at the front of the palace change over, accompanied by guards and a marching band. The old guard then marches back to the army barracks.

▼ MAY

 INTERNATIONAL DAWN CHORUS DAY **2 MAY**

- ℹ️ *Tower Hamlets Cemetery Park, Southern Grove, Bow, E3 4PX*
- ☎️ *Tel: 020 8252 6644, 07904 186 981 (liaison officer); www.towerhamletscemetery.org*
- Ⓜ️ *Mile End*
- 💷 *FREE*
- ▨ *4.30am*

No, you don't have to sing... This Sunday, for one day only, bird lovers will congregate in Tower Hamlets Cemetery Park as the sun rises to join in with a worldwide celebration of birdsong.

 COVENT GARDEN MAY FAYRE AND PUPPET FESTIVAL **9 MAY**

- ℹ️ *St Paul's Church Gardens, Bedford Street, WC2E 9ED*
- ☎️ *Tel: 020 7375 0441; www.alternativearts.co.uk*
- Ⓜ️ *Covent Garden*
- 💷 *FREE*

This annual, nationwide festival celebrates the art of puppetry and the first Punch and Judy show ever held in England, which was mentioned in Samuel Pepys's diary in May 1662. Over 60 different Punch and Judy shows will run from 10.30am to 5.30pm, as well as puppet-making workshops, folk music and maypole dancing.

 BANGLATOWN MELA IN BRICK LANE **9 MAY**

- ℹ️ *Brick Lane, Tower Hamlets, E1; Weavers Fields, Tower Hamlets, Vallance Road, E1; Allen Gardens, Buxton Street, Tower Hamlets, E1*
- ☎️ *Tel: 020 7364 7905; www.towerhamletsarts.org.uk*
- Ⓜ️ *Aldgate East*
- 💷 *FREE*

While this is the first year this event has been held, it has grown out of the annual Baishakhi Mela, which has been celebrated around Brick Lane since 1997. The festival is held in celebration of the Bengali New Year and is attended mostly by the Bengali community. But everyone is welcome and up to 80,000 people are expected to attend from all over the UK and Europe – making it the biggest Bengali festival outside Bangladesh. As well as live music and both contemporary and traditional dancing on the main stage in Weavers Fields and on a smaller stage in Allen Gardens, there will be Bengali food stalls, exhibitions by local and international artists and a 1-km street parade running between Allen Gardens, Brick Lane and Weavers Fields.

BATTERSEA CONTEMPORARY ARTS FAIR   **14–16 MAY**

❶ *Battersea Arts Centre, Lavender Hill, SW11 5TN*
✆ *Tel: 020 7223 6557; www.bcaf.info*
◉ *Clapham Junction BR*
❶ *Price tbc*

If you're looking to replace that ugly vase that your grandma gave you for your birthday, then head to this fair, where 350 exhibitors will display over 150 pieces of artwork. Browse or buy photographs, prints, sculptures and glasswork. Past exhibitors have included Glaswegian-based Bill Millett, known for his stunning, ethereal photographs; Jennifer M. Taylor, who creates collages of stilettos using scraps of vintage cloth and buttons; and Claire Harrison's watercolours of flowers and geometric forms.

 THE PLAYTEX MOON WALK LONDON 2010   **15 MAY**

❶ *Hyde Park, W2 2UH*
✆ *Tel: 014 8374 1430; www.walkthewalk.org*
◉ *Hyde Park Corner, Marble Arch*
❶ *Price tbc*

Union Jack ones, fluffy pink ones or the frilly variety – turn up to this charity night-time power walk and you'll see 15,000 men and women marching through London wearing every type of bra imaginable. Now in its 13th year, Walk the Walk continues to raise awareness and funds for breast cancer research charities such as Breakthrough Breast Cancer. Starting at midnight in Hyde Park, participants donned in bras, wigs, feather boas and tutus stroll the 26-mile route through the city under the moonlight, egged on by crowds as well as performers on stage.

 THE SCOOP – FREE EVENTS   **MID MAY–OCT**

❶ *The Scoop, The Queens Walk, SE1 2AA*
✆ *www.morelondon.com/scoop.html*
◉ *London Bridge, Tower Hill*
❶ *FREE*

If only London had more places like The Scoop, an open-air venue along the South Bank. The sunken amphitheatre, which seats around 800, is between London Bridge and the Tower of London, outside City Hall. The Scoop runs a varied programme of free events, including music concerts, street theatre, dance and cult film screenings. Past events have included an early morning boot camp, performances by soul singers, craft, art and design stalls, and a cabaret. You can usually just turn up to the free events without pre-booking, which means even passers-by can get involved, but check ahead just in case. Oh, yes, and bring a cushion – the stone steps make your bottom go numb after a while.

RACE FOR LIFE MID MAY–JUL

- *Various venues*
- *Tel: 087 1641 2282; www.raceforlife.org*
- *Price tbc*

This women-only event has been held since 1994, with the aim of raising money for Cancer Research. The women who take part can run, jog, walk or skip their way through 5-km routes across the UK. In London, races will be held on Hampstead Heath and Blackheath, in Regent's, Hyde and Battersea parks, and in Richmond, the City, Crystal Palace, Croydon and Enfield. You can enter up to one week before the event.

 CHELSEA FLOWER SHOW 25–29 MAY

- *Chelsea Royal Hospital, Royal Hospital Road, SW3 4SR*
- *Tel: 020 7881 5200 (venue); www.rhs.org.uk*
- *Sloane Square*
- *From £20*

The show began in 1862, albeit under a different name – the Great Spring Show – and was originally held in the Royal Horticultural Society Garden in Kensington. It moved to its current site in 1912, and this year's show will be the 88th to be held in the Royal Hospital grounds. As in previous years, the 64-acre site showcases plants and flowers grown by over 600 professional gardeners and amateurs. The event is popular with celebrities – Paul McCartney, Paul Smith, Ringo Starr and Michael Caine have all been spotted admiring the latest trends in blooms in the show gardens and listening to the live music in the bandstand. The great pavilion, which is big enough to park 500 London buses, hosts the most popular exhibition, so head there first.

 MIND BODY SPIRIT FESTIVAL 26–31 MAY

- *Royal Horticultural Halls, 80 Vincent Square, Victoria, SW1P 2PE*
- *Tel: 020 7371 9191; www.mindbodyspirit.co.uk*
- *St James's Park*
- *£6–£9*

Since it was established in 1977, the MBS festival has been a Mecca for those interested in alternative healing and spiritual development. The event promotes a peaceful and healthy lifestyle through talks and workshops. Topics range from colour therapy and yoga to alternative medicine such as reiki, an ancient Japanese healing technique in which the whole body is treated. You can also learn about astrology, the power of positive thinking and how to use crystals, have a henna tattoo or watch a capoeira performance. Over 100 exhibitors will attend the event, which is held over six days.

SPORTS IN 2010

	JANUARY	FEBRUARY	MARCH	APRIL	MAY
FOOTBALL PREMIER LEAGUE					
RUGBY UNION GUINESS PREMIERSHIP					
RUGBY UNION RBS SIX NATIONS CHAMPIONSHIP					
COUNTY CRICKET CHAMPIONSHIP SEASON					

ESSENTIAL LONDON SPORTING EVENTS

Football

FA Cup Final	15 May	
League Cup Final	28 Feb	
FA Community Shield	9 Aug	

RUGBY

Six Nations, England vs Wales	6 Feb	
Six Nations, England vs Ireland	27 Feb	

Marathons, runs and endurance events

London Marathon	25 Apr	see p.27
London Triathlon	7–8 Aug	see p.46
London Duathlon	Sep	see p.51
Run to the Beat – Musical Half Marathon	26 Sep	see p.52
Royal Parks Foundation Half Marathon	10 Oct	see p.54

JUNE	JULY	AUGUST	SEPTEMBER	OCTOBER	NOVEMBER	DECEMBER

Rowing

The Boat Race – Oxford and Cambridge	3 Apr	*see p.25*
Henley Royal Regatta	30 Jun–4 Jul	*see p.39*
Doggett's Coat and Badge Race	Late Jul	*see p.44*
Great River Race	18 Sep	*see p.51*

Athletics

Aviva London Grand Prix	13–14 Aug	*see p.46*

Tennis

Wimbledon	21 Jun–4 Jul	*see p.38*
Masters Tennis	7 Dec	*see p.60*
Aegon Tennis Championships (Queen's)	Jun	*see p.34*

N.B. Please note that all dates are preliminary and subject to change

▼ JUNE

📅 HAMPTON COURT FESTIVAL   1–15 JUN

- **❶** Hampton Court Palace, East Molesley, Surrey, KT8 9AU
- **☎** Tel: 084 5658 6971; 084 4847 1638 (tickets); 084 4811 0050 (picnic orders); www.hamptoncourtfestival.com
- **◉** Hampton Court BR
- **❹** £42.50+

Now in its 18th year, this spectacular music festival is still as popular as ever, with an audience of 3,000. Each year hosts different musicians – Russell Watson, the Royal Philharmonic Orchestra and James Morrison have all featured in previous years – followed by a firework finale. The grounds open at 5.30pm, so you can have a picnic beforehand – you can take your own or treat yourself to a Carluccio's one, which has to be pre-ordered. If you really want to splurge, opt for a dinner and concert package, which also includes canapés and champagne. After dinner take a seat in the stands in the palace courtyard, only part of which is undercover. Umbrellas aren't allowed, so you'd better pray it doesn't rain...

OLYMPIA INTERNATIONAL ART AND ANTIQUES FAIR   4–13 JUN

- **❶** Olympia, Hammersmith Road, W14 8UX
- **☎** Tel: 020 7385 1200 (venue), 020 7370 8211 (event); www.olympiaartsinternational.com
- **◉** Kensington (Olympia)
- **❹** £14 on door; £10 in advance

Over 34,000 private buyers, interior designers, curators and dealers gather at this annual fair, now in its 37th year. The event attracts celebrities – Dustin Hoffman, Piers Morgan and Tamara Beckwith were spotted browsing in the grand hall last year. Over 260 galleries exhibit Chinese silk tapestries, art deco jewellery, Renaissance paintings and furniture, which are all vetted for authenticity by a team of 200 international experts. Even if you're intending just to look, or go just for the lectures and art tours, chances are you'll come home with an armchair and an Italian bust or two.

ROYAL ACADEMY SUMMER EXHIBITION   EARLY JUN–AUG

- **❶** Royal Academy of Arts, Burlington House, 50–2 Piccadilly, London Haymarket, W1J 0BD
- **☎** Tel: 020 7300 8000; 084 4209 1919 (tickets); www.royalacademy.org.uk/events
- **◉** Piccadilly Circus, Green Park
- **❹** £9

The first Summer Exhibition was held in 1769 – a year after the academy was founded by George III (*see p.126*) – and it has been held every year since its conception. It's open to amateur and rising artists as well as celebrated ones such as Anish Kapoor, known for his enormous stainless steel *Cloud Gate* sculpture, and the woodblock printer, Utagawa Kuniyoshi. It now receives 150,000 visitors each summer, and is popular with celebrities – Stella McCartney, David Hockney, Agyness Deyn and Tracy Emin have all been spotted browsing here. Each year, the paintings, sculpture and photographs on display in the main galleries are linked by a common theme, such as man-made, light and printmaking. Last year [2009] a room of film and video art saw a shift towards displaying diverse works of art side by side. Most of the work is for sale.

 TROOPING OF THE COLOUR   **12 JUN**

- ❶ *Horse Guards Parade, Whitehall, Westminster, SW1A 2AX*
- ⊕ *Tel: 020 7414 2357; www.trooping-the-colour.co.uk*
- ◉ *Embankment, Charing Cross*
- ❹ *£20.00 tickets by ballot (held end of Feb)*
- ▦ *10.30am–12pm*

Steeped in history, this quintessentially British event dates back to 1700, and has been held on the Queen's official birthday since 1805 (her actual birthday is 21 April). The parade, which sees decorative flags paraded in front of troops, was originally deemed necessary so troops could familiarize themselves with their unit's flag and assemble around it during battle. Nowadays, the gloriously pompous parade is attended by 13,000, and watched by 100 million on TV worldwide. If you've only ever seen it on the telly, make 2010 the year you wave your Union Jack in front of the Queen and Duke of Edinburgh in their horse-drawn carriage. As well as the parade, which marches down the Mall from Buckingham Palace to Horse Guards Parade, Whitehall and back again, there is a marching band, a national anthem singalong and a spectacular RAF show. To apply for tickets, write to: Brigade Major, Household Division, Whitehall, London SW1A 2AX. Apply early 2010.

AEGON TENNIS CHAMPIONSHIPS (QUEEN'S)   **JUN**

- ❶ *The Queen's Club, Palliser Road, West Kensington, W14 9EQ*
- ⊕ *020 7386 3400; www.aegonchampionships.com*
- ◉ *Baron's Court, West Kensington*
- ❹ *£15–£85*
- ▦ *Gates open 10.30am; play starts noon Mon–Fri, 1.30pm Sat, 2pm Sun*

Ever since it began in 1979, this annual tennis event has attracted over 55,000 spectators. Held in the run up to Wimbledon, the championships tend to be overshadowed to a degree – but that's not to say it's not an exciting sporting fixture. Limited centre court and ground admission tickets are available to buy on the day – go early to beat the queues, especially if it's a hot day. The event runs for seven days, with matches taking place on four of the grounds' 28 courts. Half-price ground admission tickets are sold from 5.30pm each evening, Monday–Thursday. *Insider info: in 1985, Boris Becker became the youngest-ever winner, aged 17 and 207 days.*

📅 15 JUN   ROYAL ASCOT   15–19 JUN

- ❶ Ascot Racecourse, Ascot, Berkshire, SL5 7JX
- ☎ Tel: 0870 722 7227; www.ascot.co.uk
- 🚉 Ascot BR
- 💰 From £15

While not strictly in London, Ascot has been the place to mingle with London's well-to-do since Queen Anne saw its potential in 1711. These days, over 275,000 people attend the races, which are held on the notoriously challenging 2.8-km track, over five days. Within the 179-acre grounds, there are three enclosures: the Silver Ring, Grandstand and the Royal Enclosure. From the silver ring you may be able to glimpse the track, but most of the action can be seen only from big screens. It's in the Royal Enclosure that you'll see ladies competing with the maddest hats, and a strict dress code is enforced. As well as the races, there's an exclusive fashion show in the Bessborough restaurant – last year, Vivienne Westwood and Steven Jones showcased their collections on the catwalk. Tickets go on sale at the end of October. Thursday (also known as 'Ladies' Day') is the first day to sell out, usually by the end of January. The royals attend each day, in a grand procession of horse-drawn carriages. If it's serious racing you're after, and not just a jolly flutter over a glass of Pimms, then attend on the first day, when three of the event's seven Group One races – the races of the highest standard – are held.

📅 JUN   MELTDOWN FESTIVAL   JUN

- ❶ Centre, Belvedere Road, South Bank, SE1 8XX
- ☎ Tel: 0871 663 2500; 020 7833 9247; meltdown.southbankcentre.co.uk
- 🚉 Waterloo
- 💰 Various prices, some shows FREE

Imagine choosing your all-time favourite artists, past and present, and getting them to sing for you – even if it means they have to re-form their band. Well, every year, an influential musician gets to do just that. Since 1993, a legendary musician has been chosen to direct Meltdown and choose which singers perform. In the past, Massive Attack, David Bowie and Morrissey have each directed the festival. The New York Dolls reunited for Morrissey; Jeff Buckley played his final UK show for Elvis Costello; and Nick Cave, Grace Jones and Pete Doherty sang Disney songs with Jarvis Cocker. Who would you pick?

OPEN GARDEN SQUARES WEEKEND 12–13 JUN

- *Various venues*
- *Tel: 020 7839 3969; www.londongardenstrust.org, www.opensquares.com*
- *Various*
- *£6.75 in advance; £8 from gardens*

For one weekend only, over 190 historic squares, prison gardens, allotments and churchyards which are usually closed to the public throw open their doors. Discover gardens you didn't even know existed, or visit the ones whose locked gates you pass everyday. The London Parks and Gardens Trust, the organizers behind the event, also hold fêtes, plant sales and live music in many of the spaces, as well as tours of the gardens. They offer guided walks between the sites, too; if you'd rather explore alone, visit the website for recommended self-guided walks. Highlights in previous years have included Lincoln Inn's garden in the City, with its well-tended lawns surrounded by 15th-century buildings; Eastbury Manor House Walled Gardens and Herb Garden in Barking; Cable Street Community Gardens in Tower Hamlets; Sutton Ecology Centre, for its butterfly gardens; St Michael's Convent in Richmond, for its four acres; and Thrive Battersea, which is tended to by members of a blind gardeners' club.

 FRANCIS ALŸS EXHIBITION 16 JUN–19 SEP

- *Tate Modern, Bankside, SE1 9TG*
- *Tel: 020 7887 8888; www.tate.org.uk*
- *London Bridge, Southwark*
- *Price tbc*

Born in Antwerp, Belgium, in 1959, Alÿs now lives in Mexico City. His drawings, paintings, films and photography have reached an international audience, but he is best known for his performance art. This exhibition shows a range of his work.

LONDON FESTIVAL OF ARCHITECTURE 19 JUN–4 JUL

- *Various venues*
- *Tel: 020 7636 4044; www.lfa2008.org*
- *FREE*

Over 35,000 are expected to attend this biennial event, which will host temporary, open-air sculpture exhibitions, interactive installations, dance performances and film screenings across the city. Join one of the organized walking or cycling tours, and your guide will make you see London in a new light: you'll be taken past some of the capital's most iconic buildings, as well as structures you might have passed everyday, which, until now, you've never stopped to think about. There will also be conferences, seminars and debates. This year's theme is the 'welcoming city'.

BP PORTRAIT AWARD

17 JUN–26 SEP

- *National Portrait Gallery, St Martin's Place, Westminster, WC2H 0HE*
- *Tel: 020 7306 0055; www.npg.org.uk*
- *Charing Cross, Leicester Square*
- *FREE*

From now until September, the gallery is hosting its prestigious annual BP Portrait Award exhibition, which displays contemporary portrait paintings. Last year [2009], the first prize was awarded to Peter Monkman for *Changeling 2*, which was part of a series of portraits of his daughter, Anna, as she grew up.

 WIMBLEDON

21 JUN–4 JUL

- *The All England Lawn Tennis Club, Church Road, Wimbledon, SW19 5AE*
- *Tel: 020 8944 1066; www.wimbledon.org*
- *Wimbledon*
- *£29–£100 show court tickets; £5–£20 ground tickets*

The history of Wimbledon goes back to 1877 – although in those days it wasn't quite the international grand slam tournament it is today. Back then, there were no 'cyclops' or infrared beams to determine whether the ball was in or out. No, in 1877 the event had much more of a summer garden party feel to it, and few guessed it would morph into an event attended by 511,000 over a two-week period. For information on booking, *see p.20. Insider info: in 2009, 54,200 Slazenger balls were used during the fortnight.*

 TASTE OF LONDON FESTIVAL

4 DAYS IN JUN

- *Outer Circle, Regent's Park, NW1 4NR*
- *Tel: 087 1230 7132; www.tastefestivals.com*
- *Regent's Park, Great Portland Street*
- *£12–£95*

This four-day outdoor food and drink festival is now well established on the foodie scene, popular for its mix of wine-tasting stalls, cooking demonstrations and opportunities to pick up speciality ingredients. Expect cook-offs by TV celebrity chefs, barbecues, champagne masterclasses and mixologists making their signature cocktail. Sample your way around the fair, browsing food stalls such as Fudges, Paul A. Young Fine Chocolates (*see* p.106) and Rachel's Organic. If you want to buy the food on offer, you'll need to stock up on crowns, the festival's currency. Each crown is worth 50p, and a typical dish will cost about eight crowns. When you've had your fill, sit by the bandstand to watch live bands playing, or wander round the stands showcasing cuisine prepared by the likes of Hugh Fearnley-Whittingstall and Angela Hartnett.

TWICKENHAM FESTIVAL   MID JUN

- ❶ *Church Street, Twickenham, TW1*
- ⊕ *Tel: 020 8891 7410; www.twickenhamtown.co.uk*
- ◉ *Twickenham BR, or bus 110*
- ❹ *FREE*

This year the 14th Twickenham Festival will descend on and around Church Street. Highlights include a lively tug of war, usually held on the first day of the 10-day festival, and a dragon boat race, in which 14 boats compete – one year two boats collided and everyone fell in the Thames. Live bands and a carnival provide further entertainment for the 10,000 people expected to attend. If you're feeling peckish, there's a barbecue and a continental farmer's market.

CITY OF LONDON FESTIVAL   25 JUN– 8 JUL

- ❶ *Fitz Elwyn House, 25 Holborn Viaduct, EC1A 2BP*
- ⊕ *Tel: 020 7583 3585; www.colf.org*
- ◉ *Chancery Lane*
- ❹ *100 events FREE; 50 ticketed concerts – prices vary*

Since 1962, this annual festival has provided London with a calendar of arts events throughout the year. The highlight of the festival is a three-week programme that uses the city's outdoor spaces for live music shows, visual arts performances, films, organized walks and talks. Some events require a ticket – check the website for details – but most of the outdoor events are free. Each year is different; last year's events [2009] included a duo performing a drumming show on reclaimed materials on the steps of St Pauls, puppet shows, acrobatics, a mass ceilidh and pianos scattered around the City for anyone to play on.

HENLEY ROYAL REGATTA   30 JUN–4 JUL

- ❶ *Starting point: Temple Island, Henley-on-Thames, Oxfordshire, RG9 2LY*
- ⊕ *Tel: 014 9157 2153; www.hrr.co.uk*
- ◉ *Frequent trains from Paddington (one hour one-way) to Henley-on-Thames BR*
- ❹ *FREE view from towpath; £12–£20 inside regatta enclosure*

We're breaking the rules: while the regatta is not in London per se, this historic event is popular with Londoners, and the royal family, who make the day trip to the quaint village of Henley for its annual rowing race. When the first regatta was held in 1839, it was a single day event; these days it takes place over five days. The races begin close to Temple Island, named after the island's elegant summerhouse, a former fishing lodge built in 1771. Go along to watch teams of oarsmen and women race the 2,112-metre course downstream, past rolling meadows to the finishing point at Poplar Point, just before Henley Bridge. Up to 300 races are held each year.

▼ JULY

 HARD ROCK CALLING FESTIVAL 1–5 JUL

- ❶ *Hyde Park*
- ☎ *Tel: 020 7195 2133; 020 7428 1799 (customer service); www.hardrockcalling.co.uk*
- ❷ *Marble Arch*
- ❸ *£45*

Over 45,000 attend this annual rock fest, which has been going strong since its conception in 2006. Previous performers have included Aerosmith, Eric Clapton, The Police and The Kooks. Last year's [2009] line-up included The Killers, Neil Young and Bruce Springsteen, who performed on the main stage in the middle of the park.

 JAZZ PLUS 1–20 JUL

- ❶ *Victoria Embankment Gardens, Villiers Street, WC2N 6NE*
- ☎ *Tel: 020 7375 0441; www.alternativearts.co.uk*
- ❷ *Embankment, Charing Cross*
- ❸ *FREE*

Musicians from across the country come to play at these open-air lunchtime concerts, held on a stage in Victoria Embankment Gardens along the Thames. Up to six artists play in each concert. So, if it's a sunny day, don't sit at your desk with your wilting sandwich; have your lunch outside instead, listening to contemporary jazz.

 EAT YOUR ART OUT 1–31 JUL

- ❶ *Kingsland Road, Hackney, E8*
- ☎ *Tel: 020 7375 0441; www.alternativearts.co.uk*
- ❷ *Hackney Central BR, then bus 26, 55, 67, 149, 242, 243*
- ❸ *FREE*

For the first time, over 100 restaurants, bars and cafes on Kingsland Road will exhibit the work of 100 contemporary artists this month.

 LONDON LITERATURE FESTIVAL JUL

- ❶ *Southbank Centre, Belvedere Road, SE1 8XX*
- ☎ *Tel: 087 1663 2501; www.southbankcentre.co.uk*
- ❷ *Waterloo*
- ❸ *Events vary in price*

For two weeks, London will once again celebrate classic fiction, poetry, lyrics and comic books on the South Bank. A host of activities are set to take place, including storytelling, writing workshops, debates and performances of classic stories. Last year's events included a talk given by the astronaut 'Buzz' Aldrin about his moon walk, and Shakespeare's sonnets set to music.

📅 3 JUL   WIRELESS FESTIVAL   3–4 JUL

- ❶ *East side, Hyde Park (near Park Lane) – main entrance will be north of the site*
- ☎ *Tel: 020 7009 3484; 020 7195 2133; www.wirelessfestival.co.uk*
- ◉ *Marble Arch*
- ❹ *£45 day ticket; £80 weekend ticket*
- ▨ *Noon–10.30pm; music starts at 2pm*

Since 2005, 30,000 festival-goers have flocked to Hyde Park for its annual Wireless Festival. In previous years, The White Stripes, Basement Jaxx and Kelly Rowland have performed, as well as Dépêche Mode and Counting Crows. This year, as well as stages headlining 2010's biggest acts, there will be displays of performance art, dance shows, a catwalk, funfair and stalls selling international food and drink, plus chill out zones with cushions and bean bags.

📅 16 JUL   BBC PROMS   16 JUL–11 SEP

- ❶ *Royal Albert Hall, Kensington Gore, SW7 2AP*
- ☎ *Tel: 084 5401 5040; www.bbc.co.uk/proms*
- ◉ *South Kensington, High Street Kensington*

- ❶ *Cadogan Hall, 5 Sloane Terrace, Chelsea, SW1X 9DQ*
- ◉ *Knightsbridge, Sloane Square*

- ❶ *Royal College of Music, Prince Consort Road, SW7 2BS*
- ◉ *South Kensington, High Street Kensington*
- ❹ *From £5 prom tickets*

The first Proms concert was held in the summer of 1895. This spectacular music festival, which hosts some 75 performances of opera, percussion, jazz, gospel, folk and stage musicals, largely takes place in the Royal Albert Hall. Opened in 1871, the hall was specially designed for large audiences – it has a capacity for 6,000. Smaller performances are held in Chelsea's Cadogan Hall. The Royal College of Music hosts Proms Plus – a new addition to the Proms calendar of events – which includes pre- and post-concert events, such as interviews and workshops that complement the main concerts held at the Royal Albert Hall. Proms in the Park (Hyde Park) is another relatively new event; since 1996, tribute bands, international singers and choirs have been entertaining an audience of 30,000, and big screens linked to the live performances in the Royal Albert Hall mean that everyone can sing along to classics, including the national anthem on the last night of the Proms. Ticket prices range enormously. The cheapest tickets mean you have to stand – which is tradition at the Proms, but this does not necessarily mean the worst view. There are 500 of these tickets available on the day – just get there early (*see p.20 for further ticket information*). (*N.B. The proms have an informal dress code, but on the last night most people tend to wear evening dress.*)

 GREENFORD CARNIVAL   3 JUL

- ❶ *Ravenor Park, Ruislip Road, Greenford, UB6*
- ☎ *Tel: 020 8825 6640; www.ealing.gov.uk*
- ◉ *Greenford*
- ❹ *FREE*

Over 8,000 are expected to attend this festival, which will have a local, community feel to it. The carnival will be largely divided into four arenas: a stage for dance, a stage for acoustic performances, a sports area and a space for families. Children will particularly enjoy the arts and crafts stalls.

 THE BIG DANCE   3–11 JUL

- ❶ *Various venues*
- ☎ *Tel: 020 7983 4071; www.london.gov.uk, www.londondance.com*
- ❹ *Price tbc*

Love dancing? This festival celebrates all types of dance, from folk and hip hop to tap and barn. Over 500 events take place in venues all over London, with an impressive dance finale in Trafalgar Square. In 2008, 500,000 people participated and world records were broken for the biggest Bollywood dance class (278 participants) and the most 'kip-ups' – a break-dance move involving flipping from your back onto your feet – in one minute (22).

 HAMPTON COURT PALACE FLOWER SHOW   6–11 JUL

- ❶ *Hampton Court Palace, East Molesey, Surrey, KT8 9AU*
- ☎ *Tel: 084 4209 1810; www.rhs.org.uk*
- ◉ *Hampton Court BR*
- ❹ *£27, 10am–7.30pm; £17, 3pm–7.30pm*

The palace gardens are worth a visit at any time of the year, but they really come alive during this six-day horticultural show. As well as gardening, cookery and flower-arranging demonstrations, a range of organized and informal talks are planned so you can find out more about growing your own food, gardening in a changing climate and making the most of a small garden. You can also pick up tips on composting, which has never been so sexy. Visitors will also get the chance to see temporary gardens designed by leading garden landscapers, exotic plants and flowers awarded gold, silver or bronze by judges from the Royal Horticultural Society.

🗓 8 JUL | CAMILLE SILVY   8 JUL–24 OCT

- ❶ National Portrait Gallery, St Martin's Place, Westminster, WC2H OHE
- ☎ Tel: 020 7306 0055; www.npg.org.uk
- ◉ Charing Cross, Leicester Square
- ❻ £5

This exhibition will showcase the work of Silvy (1834–1910), a French photographer who was one of the leading portrait photographers in London in the 1800s. He is known for his portraits of the British royal family and aristocracy.

🗓 16 JUL | EALING SUMMER FESTIVALS   16 JUL– 2 AUG

- ❶ Walpole Park, Mattock Lane, W5
- ☎ Tel: 020 8825 6640; www.ealing.gov.uk
- ◉ Ealing Broadway, South Ealing
- ❻ £1 Greenford, blues, jazz and global; from £10 opera; from £15 comedy

Expect this 1,200-person venue to be packed for over two weeks as it hosts, in turn, festivals celebrating comedy (16–17, 21–23 Jul), blues (24 Jul), world music (25 Jul) and jazz (28 Jul–2 Aug). Both local and international artists form the line-up at all the events. The music festivals will also have children's activities and entertainment, and arts and crafts. Tickets can be bought on the door.

🗓 JUL | EALING OPERA IN THE PARK   JUL

- ❶ Walpole Park, Mattock Lane, W5
- ☎ Tel. 020 8825 6640; www.ealing.gov.uk
- ◉ Ealing Broadway, South Ealing
- ❻ Price tbc

Join an 800-strong audience to listen to opera in Walpole Park in this annual event, which is now in its third year. Previous performances include *The Barber of Seville* and *Carmen* by Opera A La Carte.

🗓 JUL | YOUNG PEOPLE'S CARIBBEAN CARNIVAL   JUL

- ❶ Walthamstow Town Hall, Forest Road, E17 4JA
- ☎ Tel: 020 8496 3000; www.walthamforest.gov.uk
- ◉ Walthamstow Central
- ❻ FREE

This annual carnival sees colourfully dressed members of local schools and community groups dance from Walthamstow Town Hall to the town square, where they are met with live music from reggae, pop and soul singers. Last year's line-up included Mica Paris, Qmar and Peter Hunningale. The town square will also be filled with stalls selling Caribbean food and other world cuisines, plus there are plenty of activities including workshops and bouncy castles. Each year sees a different theme for costumes – 2009's was 'Myths and Legends' – so expect to see creative costumes.

 CONTEMPORARY ARCHITECTURE   **SUMMER**

- ❶ V&A, Cromwell Road, South Kensington, SW7 2RL
- ☎ Tel: 020 7942 2000; www.vam.ac.uk
- ◉ South Kensington
- ❹ Price tbc

If looking at pictures of Battersea Power Station, the CN Tower or Dubai's Atlantis The Palm hotel inspires you, then you'll enjoy this exhibition devoted to modern architecture. The images on display are a mix of iconic structures from around the world, as well as lesser known buildings. How many can you name?

 SHOREDITCH FESTIVAL   **JULY**

- ❶ Shoreditch Park, New North Road, N1 6TA
- ☎ Tel: 020 7324 5117; www.shoreditchfestival.org.uk
- ◉ Old Street
- ❹ Price tbc

This six-day annual event is a mixed bag, with something for the skinny jeans type, wartime grannies and the under 10s. Each day hosts different events, including sports and games, dance and dog shows and films shown in the park's amphitheatre. Elsewhere in the park, catch the Royal Philharmonic Orchestra or the English National Ballet perform live on stage, or stroll around the craft, fashion and food stalls. Active types can try bouldering, dressing up in the 1920s area or taking part in a swinging tea dance. Go on the last day to watch the firework finale.

GREENWICH BEER AND JAZZ FESTIVAL   **5 DAYS IN JUL**

- ❶ King Charles Lawn, Old Royal Navy College, Greenwich, SE10 9LW
- ☎ Tel: 020 8241 9818; www.greenwichbeerandjazz.com
- ◉ Cutty Sark DLR
- ❹ £7–£20
- ▦ Noon–11pm

For many, this outdoor festival will combine your two favourite things: beer and jazz. The beers on offer change daily, so if you go for more than one day (and why not?) you'll get to sample a mix of light ales, rich stouts and bottled beers such as Brecon county ale, Pilsner, raspberry wheat beer and

British Bulldog. All the drinks are labelled weak, average or strong to encourage responsible drinking, but no one's going to mind if you get a bit tipsy... Cocktails, wine and Pimms are also available, and to help soak up the booze you can indulge in hearty British favourites: fish 'n' chips and pies. As for the music, jazz, blues, funk and Latin performers will provide entertainment throughout the day.

LOVEBOX WEEKENDER   2 DAYS IN JUL

- *Victoria Park, 360 Victoria Park Road, Hackney, E9 7BT*
- *Tel: 084 4847 2436, 087 1230 2200 (info); www.lovebox.net*
- *Mile End*
- *£42.50 per day; £75 for the weekend*
- *10am–10pm*

Riding on the success of their London-based club, Groove Armada, Andy Cato and Tom Findlay set up Lovebox in 2005. The event proved so popular it was moved from its original location on Clapham Common to its current site, Victoria Park, and is now held over two days, instead of one. This year, over 25,000 are expected at the dance festival, which, naturally, headlines Groove Armada among its top acts. As well as stages hosting dance acts, revellers can listen to funk, soul, reggae, indie and pop. The festival is also likely to host yoga and Tai Chi classes, a funfair, a farmer's market, a massage tent and chill out zone.

DOGGETT'S COAT AND BADGE RACE   LATE JUL

- *Watermen's Company, 16 St Mary-at-Hill, EC3R 8EF*
- *Tel: 020 7285 2373; www.watermenshall.org*
- *London Bridge*
- *FREE*
- *12.30pm*

Possibly the oldest boat race in the world, this event dates back to 1715, when Thomas Doggett, an Irish actor and manager of the Drury Lane Theatre, organized it to commemorate the first anniversary of the crowning of George I. The race has been held every year since then, with the exception of WWII, and little has changed. The 7,400-metre route remains the same, starting at London Bridge and finishing at Albert Bridge, Chelsea. However, the race is now rowed with the tide, whereas traditionally, before 1873, it was rowed against it. On average it takes 30 minutes to complete, although Bobby Prescott set a record in 1973 when he finished in 23 minutes, 22 seconds. The prize is a scarlet coat with a large silver badge. The date changes each year depending on the tide – check the website nearer the time for details.

▼ AUGUST

📅 THE LONDON TRIATHLON   7–8 AUG

- 📍 ExCeL London, One Western Gateway, Royal Victoria Dock E16 1XL
- ☎ Tel: 020 8233 5900; www.thelondontriathlon.co.uk
- 🚈 Custom House DLR
- 💷 £35–£78 to compete; FREE to watch

Over 4,000 compete in this triathlon, which involves a 1,500-metre swim, 40-km bike ride and 10-km run. Spectators can watch participants throughout the course, although the best place to watch the swimmers is from Dockside. To see the cyclists, stand near ExCel's west entrance (in front of the car park), the walkway from Custom House DLR to ExCel or Fox Bar. The bike and run sections both require laps, so if you're looking for your mate, you may get to glimpse them more than once. The finish line is indoors.

📅 AVIVA LONDON GRAND PRIX   13–14 AUG

- 📍 Crystal Palace National Sports Centre, Ledrington Road, SE19 2BB
- ☎ Tel: 020 8778 0131 (venue); 080 0055 6056 (tickets); www.uka.org.uk
- 🚈 Crystal Palace BR

Watch and cheer as the world's best athletes, including Olympic champions such as Jamaican Usain Bolt, compete in this track and field event. Categories include 100-m and 200-m sprints, hurdles, long jump and shot put, among others. The third day is a new addition to the event, and will focus on races for people with disabilities.

📅 THAI FESTIVAL   14–15 AUG

- 📍 Bandstand field, Greenwich Park, Blackheath Gate, Charlton Way, SE10 8QY
- ☎ Tel: 0870 608 2000 (Greenwich Tourist Information Centre); www.amthai.co.uk/festival
- 🚈 Greenwich DLR
- 💷 £5 on door; £3 in advance

This annual festival, sponsored by the Thai Festival Organisation, combines Thai food and culture for an indulgent day out for the 20,000 expected visitors. Expect to find restaurants showcasing classic Thai dishes and exotic fruit and stalls selling food, clothes, accessories and household items. For entertainment, Thai dancers will parade across the park and there will be classical and contemporary dance displays along with traditional music on the main stage.

LONDON MELA 15 AUG

- ❶ *Gunnersbury Park, Pope's Lane, Acton, W3*
- ⊕ *Tel: 020 8825 6640, 020 73871203; www.ealing.gov.uk,*
  www.londonmela.org
- ⊖ *Acton Town, then bus E3*
- ❶ *FREE*

Over 75,000 are expected to attend this carnival, where visitors are encouraged to get involved with their local community (*mela* is Sanskrit for gathering, or 'to meet'). The festival has an Asian flavour, so you can expect Bollywood dance shows and film screenings, as well as DJs playing bhangra, drum and bass and desi beats – a fusion of Indian and Western tunes. Throughout the day there will also be plenty of family-friendly activities such as face-painting, crafts, storytelling and Punch and Judy shows, as well as performances of acrobatics and visual arts on an outdoor stage.

 RED BULL AIR RACE WORLD CHAMPIONSHIP AUG

- ❶ *Location: East Parkside, Greenwich, SE10; office: Red Bull Air Race GmbH,*
  Petersbrunnstrasse 17, 5020 Salzburg, Austria
- ⊕ *+43 662 65820 (Austria); www.redbullairrace.com*
- ⊖ *North Greenwich*
- ❶ *£15*

This international aviation race was designed to challenge the world's best pilots – each race is marked on speed, precision and skill. The pilots must manoeuvre an aerial racetrack, zigzagging between inflatable pylons at speeds of up to 370km per hour. The quickest pilot with the fewest penalties wins the race. Since 2001, this event has been held over the section of the Thames closest to the O2. You can watch for free, but if you want to really see what's going on, you'll need a ticket – you can book right up until the day of the race. At the time of writing, the 2010 event was unconfirmed, so check the website for further details.

 LIBERTY FESTIVAL, TRAFALGAR SQUARE AUG

- ❶ *Trafalgar Square, SW1Y*
- ⊕ *Tel: 020 7983 4100; www.london.gov.uk*
- ⊖ *Charing Cross*
- ❶ *FREE*

Inspired by the European Year of Disabled People in 2002, this festival for people with disabilities is Europe's largest disability rights festival. Many of the performances – mime, aerial acrobatics, circus acts and comedy – are performed by disabled artists on stage. Theatre workshops, live music, dance and cabaret shows will also be performed throughout the day, and there will be food stalls, films and displays of street art around the square. With its carnival atmosphere, the festival will appeal to everyone, and is accessible to all, with BSL interpretation, induction loops at information points and a wheelchair loan service. The event programme will be available in large print, Braille and tape formats, and there will be free parking nearby for blue badge holders.

AUG GREAT BRITISH BEER FESTIVAL   AUG

- ❶ Earl's Court, Warwick Road, SW5 9TA
- ⊕ Tel: 017 2786 7201; www.camra.org.uk
- ❷ Earl's Court, West Brompton
- ❹ £8–£12; £12 beer-tasting tutorials

With over 450 real ales from 200 British breweries, including Fuller's, Jersey, Theakston's, and Wells and Young's, it's no wonder this beer fest has been dubbed a 'liquid feast'. Over the festival's five days, visitors can sample a selection of tangy ciders, ginger ales and beers flavoured with herbs, spices and fruit. As well as regional varieties from around Britain, punters can try beers from Germany, Belgium, the Czech Republic and the US. You'll also be able to quench your thirst with organic and coeliac-friendly beer, as well as vegetarian beer (the casks are made without animal products). But the day is not just about downing as many pints as you can, though – heaven forbid – you can also sign up for tutored beer tastings, where you'll learn about the history of beer, how it's produced and the subtleties in smell, colour and taste; or take part in an auction to win a trip to a brewery. If all that leaves you peckish, kick back with a Cornish pie, sausage roll or curry from one of the food stalls, or snack on a bag of pork scratchings while listening to live music. Then top off your dream day out with a round of darts.

AUG UNDERAGE FESTIVAL 2010 LONDON   AUG

- ❶ Victoria Park, 360 Victoria Park Road, Hackney, E9 7BT
- ⊕ Tel: 020 7364 7907; www.underagefestivals.com
- ❷ Mile End
- ❹ £26.50

For the past three years, London's teenagers have finally had a music festival to call their own – although whoever came up with the idea could surely have thought of a more inspiring name. Still, 14–18 year olds love it, as they get to see over 60 different bands and solo singers in a single day. Past performers have included indie band the Mystery Jets, duo Blood Red Shoes and London-based rock group, Video Nasties. The 10,000 teens who attend will be delighted to know that no parents or guardians are allowed, but if you're a parent, you needn't panic – there's more protection here than at a high-security prison. Food and non-alcoholic drinks stalls are available.

🗓️ NOTTING HILL CARNIVAL   29–30 AUG

- ❶ *Westbourne Grove, Notting Hill, W11; Ladbroke Grove, Kensington, W11; Great Western Road, Westminster, W11*
- 🌐 *Tel: 020 7727 0072; www.nottinghillcarnival.biz*
- ◉ *Ladbroke Grove, Westbourne Park, Latimer Road, Holland Park, Notting Hill Gate*
- ❶ *FREE*

If you've never been before, then psych yourself up for the largest, and possibly the loudest, street festival in Europe. This massive al fresco party, which grew out of the Trinidad Carnival of 1964, brings together all the cultures within London. Over 2.5 million spectators will be entertained by 50,000 performers dressed in elaborate costumes – some so wide they sweep the width of the road. As well as a 5.6-km parade of dancers and steel pan bands, DJs play Caribbean-inspired music such as soca, reggae, jazz, soul, hip hop, house and garage. Street stalls sell a range of ethnic food, including jerk chicken and Jamaican patties. Unfortunately, with a carnival of this size (second only to Rio de Janeiro), expect pickpockets, ringing ears and exploding rubbish bags piled high.

🗓️ SOUTH WEST FOUR 2010 LONDON   29 AUG

- ❶ *Clapham Common, SW4 0AA*
- 🌐 *Tel: 077 9885 2208; www.southwestfour.com, www.metroweekender.com*
- ◉ *Clapham Common*
- ❶ *Price tbc; tickets on sale on the day*

Since 2005, Clapham Common has hosted South West Four, a dance, trance and electronic music marathon with DJs like Sasha and Pete Tong revving up a crowd of 20,000 on Saturday, and Get Loaded in the Park (*see below*) is held the following day.

🗓️ GET LOADED IN THE PARK 2010 LONDON   30 AUG

- ❶ *Clapham Common, SW4 0AA*
- 🌐 *Tel: 077 9885 2208; www.getloadedinthepkar.com, www.metroweekender.com,*
- ◉ *Clapham Common*
- ❶ *Price tbc; tickets on sale on the day*

This one-day music festival sees 20,000 revellers enjoying indie bands on Sunday, following the South West Four dance festival the day before.

▼ SEPTEMBER

 EID IN THE SQUARE 10 SEP

- Trafalgar Square, SW1Y
- Tel: 020 7983 4000; 0845 2626 786; www.eidinthesquare.com
- Charing Cross
- FREE

Join the 30,000-strong throng celebrating Eid al-Fitr, a festival marking the end of Ramadan. After a month of fasting, Muslims gather in Trafalgar Square to party – so expect Islamic art exhibitions, food stalls galore and live Asian music from the likes of rapper Muslim Belal and Pearls of Islam, a duo known for playing traditional hand drums such as the dumbek and djmebe.

 MAYOR'S THAMES FESTIVAL 11–12 SEP

- Venue: Along the River Thames, between Westminster Bridge and Tower Bridge
- Tel: 020 7928 8998, www.thamesfestival.org
- Westminster, Embankment, Waterloo, Blackfriars, Tower Hill, London Bridge
- FREE
- Noon–10pm

This spectacular festival will make you feel proud to be a Londoner, and jealous if you're not. Ever since its launch in 1997, with a jaw-dropping high-wire walk across the Thames, the Mayor's Thames Festival has surpassed itself year on year. This festival of the arts is held on and around the river's banks, bridges and roads, which close for the day so that the 500,000 expected to attend can celebrate. In previous years, events have included a tango workshop, trapeze acts, Chinese dragon dancing and parkour displays, as well as hay fights, street theatre, IMAX film screenings and children's film-making classes. As dusk falls, the party continues, culminating in a night carnival. Dance in the streets to live music as you watch dancers performing in glittering costumes and masks, illuminated by pyrotechnics. And the best news? It won't cost you a penny.

 THE SPITALFIELDS SHOW AND GREEN FAIR 12 SEP

- Allen Gardens, Buxton Street, Tower Hamlets, E1 5AR;
  Spitalfields City Farm, Buxton Street, Tower Hamlets, E1 5AR
- Tel: 020 7375 0441; www.alternativearts.co.uk
- Aldgate East
- FREE

Stalls sell flowers, handicrafts and homemade produce from 12pm to 5pm at this annual horticultural show, held inside a marquee. Organic, healthy food and Fairtrade tea and coffee are available to sample and buy. You can also try your hand at traditional crafts, such as spinning and weaving, have a massage or try reflexology, find out how to grow your own food and take part in a raffle.

 ## THE GREAT RIVER RACE   18 SEP

- ℹ️ *Starts from: The riverside end of Ham Street, Ham, Richmond, TW10 7RS*
- ⊕ *Tel: 020 8398 9057; www.greatriverrace.co.uk*
- ⬤ *Ham BR, then bus 65, 371*
- 💷 *FREE*
- ▬ *11.25am start*

Since 1988, boat crews have taken to the Thames in a 35.4-km race from rural Richmond to the Docklands in Greenwich. Also known as London's River Marathon, this event is a fun day out for spectators and racers alike. It's an anything-goes type of race, so you may see both serious competitors planning their team strategy in a tight huddle, and groups just in it for a laugh, larking around in ridiculous costumes with their faces painted. Over 300 international boat crews take part, and you can watch them from the bridges of Richmond, Hammersmith, Wandsworth, Battersea, Westminster, as well Tower Bridge.

 ## LONDON OPEN HOUSE   18–19 SEP

- ℹ️ *Various locations; Office: Open House, 44–46 Scrutten Street, EC2A 4HH*
- ⊕ *Tel: 020 3006 7008; www.londonopenhouse.org*
- 💷 *FREE; book ahead – see website for details*

If you pass a spiral staircase on your way to work each day, but don't know where it leads, or if you've glimpsed the old tube carriages off Great Eastern Street, and wonder why they're raised in the air, then London Open House was designed for you. Since 1993, this annual architectural festival has given Londoners access to over 700 buildings across 31 boroughs. As well as meeting with the architects and design teams who construct and regenerate London, you'll have the chance to listen to talks and debates on sustainable design, learn how London is coping with its rising population and take part in walks across the capital – like the mass night hike held last year [2009].

LONDON DESIGN FESTIVAL   18–26 SEP

- ℹ️ *Various venues; Office: London Design Festival Ltd, 60 Frith Street, W1D 3JJ*
- ⊕ *Tel: 020 7734 6444; www.londondesignfestival.com*
- 💷 *Price tbc*

Aimed at both consumer and trade visitors, this festival looks at how design – in the form of fashion, architecture, photography, textiles or interiors – can change our life for the better. British and international designers will showcase their latest work and ideas at 200 events held over 10 days throughout the city – venues range from Trafalgar Square and the Southbank Centre to the V&A and Somerset House, as well as a number of museums, shops and universities. Each of the participating venues host cultural and commercial events, so whether you want to find out the latest news in the industry, join in with talks or just get inspired, there's an event to suit your taste. Expect design competitions, product launches, private viewings and the unveiling of commissions.

 DIAGHILEV AND THE BALLET RUSSES 1900–1939   **18 SEP 2010–16 JAN 2011**

- ❶ *V&A, Cromwell Road, South Kensington, SW7 2RL*
- ☏ *Tel: 020 7942 2000; www.vam.ac.uk*
- ◉ *South Kensington*
- ❸ *Price tbc; can buy on the door*

This exhibition looks back upon the 20-year history of the Ballet Russes, the Russian ballet company Serge Diaghilev established in Paris in 1909. With the help of original costumes, old programmes and first-hand accounts, the exhibition explores the company's origins, its sensational popularity, financial problems and how its innovative approach changed the direction of ballet.

 GREAT GORILLA RUN   **25 SEP**

- ❶ *Starting and finishing point: London Underwriting Centre, 3 Minster Court, Mincing Lane, City of London, EC3R 7DD*
- ☏ *Tel: 020 7916 4974; www.greatgorillas.org*
- ◉ *Monument, Tower Hill, Aldgate*
- ❸ *FREE for spectators*

Gorillas skipping through London? No, you're not going bananas. They're taking part in an annual 7-km race, which is organized by the international non-governmental Gorilla Organization to raise money to help save gorillas from extinction. The event has grown since its conception in 2003; now, over 1,000 people each year dress as gorillas to run, walk or dance in tutus over Tower, London and Southwark bridges and through Blackfriars. A new world record was even set in 2004 for the largest gathering of people in gorilla suits. It's probably the silliest event of the year, and definitely one of the most fun – one year, 10 gorillas turned up in Borat-style mankinis, and they didn't know each other. If you want to join in, you have to pay a £80 registration fee and commit to raising £400; you can register up until the day before the race. Or just go along and beat your chest in support.

RUN TO THE BEAT – MUSICAL HALF MARATHON   **26 SEP**

- *Starting and finishing point: O2, East Parkside, Greenwich, SE10*
- *Tel: 020 8233 5900; www.runtothebeat.co.uk*
- *North Greenwich*
- *£33*

Leave your iPod at home for this race, as live music will be played along its 13.1-mile course. Both live and recorded music will play at 16 different points throughout the route to rally the participants, because, according to Dr Costas Karageorghis, a reader in sport psychology at Brunel University, upbeat music can improve a runner's performance. And Costas should know, as he's spent the last 20 years looking into the effects of listening to music during exercise. The event attracts 12,500 runners, and it's now in its third year. Most of the music is pop, rock, dance and urban, and last year's musicians included Olli Collins, a DJ for the Ministry of Sound; A Human, known for their electro rock and Black Cat Blues Band, a rhythm and blues group – saved for the after race massages, we imagine. The race begins and ends at the O2. First it heads towards the Thames Barrier, before cutting through Woolwich Common around the halfway point. At the 9-mile mark, runners reach Greenwich Park, passing the Royal Observatory, National Maritime Museum and Old Royal Naval College, before finding themselves on the home stretch.

 RAINDANCE FILM FESTIVAL   **29 SEP–10 OCT**

- *Various venues tbc*
- *Tel: 020 7287 3833; www.raindance.co.uk*
- *Various*

When set designer Elliot Grove founded this indie festival in 1993, even he didn't realize just how big it would grow. Now, 17 years on, the festival is the first to discover new talent, screening anything from controversial documentaries and low-budget films to 15-second shorts designed for mobiles. Successful premieres have included *The Blair Witch Project*, *Memento* and *In Search of a Midnight Kiss*.

 LONDON GATHERING   **SEP**

- *Inner Temple Gardens, EC4Y 7HL*
- *scot@thelondongathering.com; www.thelondongathering.com*
- *Temple, Blackfriars*
- *Price tbc; tickets available on the day*

The London Gathering is an event for all homesick Scots in London – and anyone else who wants to experience Scottish culture. The festival takes place in the Inner Temple Gardens, a modest three-acre space close to Fleet Street. All your home comforts will be there, with a farmer's market offering whisky tastings and samples of Arbroath Smokie and stovies – the Scottish take on bubble and squeak. With the sound of bagpipes filling the air, browse Scottish brands along a mock-up of Edinburgh's Princes Street, take part in a Q&A session with Scottish authors or listen to comedians who've fine-tuned their material at the Edinburgh Festival. Alternatively, roll up your sleeves and join in with a ceilidh, tug of war or a scaled-down version of the Highland Games.

SEP **REGENT STREET SPANISH FESTIVAL**   SEP

- ❶ *Regent's Street, Westminster, W1B*
- ✆ *Tel: 020 7486 8077*
- Ⓢ *Oxford Circus, Piccadilly Circus*
- ❹ *FREE*

Every year, for one day only, Regent's Street is the site of a lively fiesta, organized by the Spanish Tourist Office. As well as flamenco dancing and Spanish music, there will be world-record attempts, face-painting and local handicraft demonstrations. The shops, too, are keen to get involved with the carnival, and many organize fashion shows and wine tasting. Street stalls serve food from all of Spain's 14 regions.

SEP **THE LONDON DUATHLON**   SEP

- ❶ *Start and finish point: Roehampton Gate, Richmond Park, Richmond, SW15 5JR*
- ✆ *Tel: 020 8233 3900; www.thelondontriathlon.com*
- Ⓢ *Richmond, then bus 65, 371*
- ❹ *£52 individual entry; £99 team entry*

For one day only, Richmond Park closes to cars for this sports event, which takes over the whole park. Participants begin the duathlon in the park's north-east corner, at Roehampton Gate. From there they run 9km around the north of the park, return to the starting point to grab a bike, then cycle two laps (20km) clockwise around the park before ending the course with a 5-km sprint. With over 4,000 participants, the London Duathlon is the world's largest, so spectators should get there early to secure a good view near the gate.

SEP **PORTOBELLO FILM FESTIVAL**   SEP

- ❶ *Various venues*
- ✆ *Tel: 020 8960 0996; www.portobellofilmfestival.com*
- ❹ *FREE*

This alternative film festival has gone from strength to strength since it began in 1996. Back then, an audience of 1,000 turned up to watch screenings in parks, tents, theatres and bars; now, 15,000 come along. It pledges to show all film submitted, giving new film-makers a chance to show off their work. The quality varies, but some go on to screen in Cannes, Venice and Macau.

▼ OCTOBER

 PHOTOMONTH 1 OCT–30 NOV

- 🛈 *Various East End venues*
- ☎ *Tel: 020 7375 0441; www.photomonth.org, www.alternativearts.co.uk*
- 🎟 *Price tbc*

This two-month photography festival showcases the work of new artists alongside well-known names in over 100 galleries across east London.

 TURNER PRIZE 2010, LONDON 5 OCT 2010–EARLY JAN 2011

- 🛈 *Tate Britain, Millbank, Pimlico, SW1P 4RG*
- ☎ *Tel: 020 7887 8888; www.tate.org.uk*
- ⊖ *Pimlico*
- 🎟 *FREE*

Be one of the first to see the work of the four British artists nominated for the 2010–11 Turner Prize.

 ROYAL PARKS FOUNDATION HALF MARATHON 10 OCT

- 🛈 *Queen Elizabeth Gate, Rotten Row, Hyde Park, W2 2UH*
- ☎ *Tel: 020 7298 2065; www.royalparkshalf.com*
- ⊖ *Hyde Park Corner*
- 🎟 *FREE; £39*

You can raise money and sightsee at the same time with this half marathon, which passes through four of London's eight royal parks. The route, which starts and finishes in Hyde Park, covers 13.1 miles. Participants swing by Buckingham Palace and cut through St James's Park, before passing the Houses of Parliament and the London Eye. The runners then continue through Green Park and under Wellington Arch, before looping around Hyde Park and Kensington Gardens – the home stretch is parallel to the Royal Albert Hall. For those left behind, there will be food and drink stalls, activities and live music in Hyde Park.

 VENICE: CANALETTO AND HIS RIVALS 13 OCT 2010–16 JAN 2011

- 🛈 *National Gallery, Trafalgar Square, WC2N 5DN*
- ☎ *Tel: 020 7747 2885; www.nationalgallery.org.uk*
- ⊖ *Charing Cross, Leicester Square*
- 🎟 *Price tbc*

Take advantage of this chance to see the works of Giovanni Antonio Canal (1697–1768), best known as Canaletto. Many of his paintings portray extravagant Venetian ceremonies. Paintings by his peers are also on display.

FRIEZE ART FAIR   14–17 OCT

- 📍 Regent's Park, Outer Circle, NW1 4NR
- ☎ Tel: 020 3372 6111 (info), 087 1230 7159 (tickets); www.frieze.com, www.seetickets.com,
- 🚇 Regent's Park, Great Portland Street
- 💷 £15 Thur, Fri before 1 Oct; £20 after (tours extra); £15 Sat, Sun before 1 Oct; £25 after (tours extra); £40 Thur–Sun before 1 Oct; £60 after 1 Oct (tours extra)

Over 60,000 curators, artists, galleries and members of the public are drawn to this contemporary art fair each year, which features the work of living artists from over 150 international galleries. In previous years, Berlin's Contemporary Fine Arts, London's White Cube and New York's Broadway 1602 have taken part. The fair is held in a temporary structure within the park.

 AFFORDABLE ART FAIR AUTUMN COLLECTION   21–24 OCT

- 📍 Battersea Park, SW11 4NJ
- ☎ Tel: 020 8246 4848; www.affordableartfair.com
- 🚇 Battersea Park BR
- 💷 £12 on door; £10 in advance

The autumn collection of affordable art. See p.22 for further details.

 THOMAS LAWRENCE EXHIBITION   21 OCT 2010–23 JAN 2011

- 📍 National Portrait Gallery, St Martin's Place, Westminster, WC2H 0HE
- ☎ Tel: 020 7306 0055; www.npg.org.uk
- 🚇 Charing Cross, Leicester Square
- 💷 Price tbc

At the tender age of six, rather than making mud pies or play-fighting with sticks, Thomas Lawrence (1769–1830) started his career as a portrait artist. At 18, he went on to study at the Royal Academy of Arts, and later became one of Britain's greatest early 19th-century artists. He was knighted in 1815 and became president of the Royal Academy in 1820. This exhibition celebrates his work.

 SCI FI LONDON 9   23–25 OCT

- 📍 Apollo West End Cinema, Piccadilly Circus, 19 Lower Regent Street, SW1Y 4LR
- ☎ Tel: 020 3239 9277, 020 7451 9944; www.sci-fi-london.com
- 🚇 Oxford Circus
- 💷 Price tbc

Over 4,000 sci-fi lovers are expected to attend this annual science fiction and fantasy film festival, which is now in its ninth year. As well as special screenings of classics such as *Labyrinth*, *ET*, *Ghostbusters* and *Harry Potter*, cinema-goers will be able to see the latest documentaries, premieres and short films. They'll be chance to meet with leading sci-fi script writers and directors, too, in a series of writing workshops aimed at budding film-makers keen to discover how to write for a younger audience or make a budget sci-fi film. A host of conferences and talks will also be held.

🗓 TRAFALGAR PARADE AND SERVICE 24 OCT

- ❶ Trafalgar Square, Westminster, SW1Y
- ⊕ Tel: 020 7928 8978
- ⊖ Charing Cross
- ❹ FREE

Ever since Admiral Lord Nelson won the Battle of Trafalgar on 21 October 1805, he has been remembered in this annual celebration. The victory was all the more spectacular because all of Britain's fleet survived. However, Nelson died after taking a direct hit from a canon ball. This march to Trafalgar Square remembers the hero, and wreaths are laid at the foot of Nelson's Column.

🗓 WINE SHOW, LONDON 4 DAYS IN OCT

- ❶ Business Design Centre, 52 Upper Street, Islington, N1 0QH
- ⊕ Tel: 020 8948 1666; www.wineshow.co.uk
- ⊖ Angel
- ❹ £12.50–£55

With both wine connoisseurs and amateurs in mind, this wine fair gives you a chance to ask everything you ever wondered about wine. Wine experts will be on hand to guide you around the venue, offering tips on wine tasting and recommending bottles to suit your taste and budget. You'll be able to try wine from your favourite regions within France, Italy and the US, and sample new wines from China, India and Slovenia – countries which are rapidly developing their own wine-producing areas. There's a home delivery service if you get carried away and buy more than you promised you would.

🗓 THE TIMES BFI LONDON FILM FESTIVAL OCT

- ❶ Various venues
- ⊕ Tel: 020 7815 1440; www.bfi.org.uk
- ❹ Vary from FREE to £25 for opening and closing galas

For film buffs, this is the highlight of the year. For two weeks, you can watch premieres of documentaries, shorts and full-length films from every imaginable genre produced by film-makers from around the world. As well as the BFI Southbank Centre, screenings are held in the ICA, Ritzy, Curzon Mayfair and the Tricycle, among other locations across London. Big screens will also be erected outdoors.

▼ NOVEMBER

📅 DIWALI ON THE SQUARE · 5 NOV

- ⓘ *Trafalgar Square, SW1Y*
- ☎ *Tel: 020 7983 4813; www.diwaliinlondon.com*
- Ⓔ *Charing Cross*
- 💷 *FREE*

Witness Trafalgar Square transform from a grey, stone square into a glowing space lit by lanterns, with floating candles in its fountains. The square is one of many sites across London celebrating Diwali, or the festival of light. Each year, Hindus, Sikhs and Jains all over the world celebrate the triumph of good over evil and light over darkness at this festival, which represents a new beginning and a time to reflect and forgive. As well as light displays, lasers and fireworks, there will be traditional dance performances, live bands and a Sikh martial arts display on the main stage. You will also find storytellers, henna tattooists, dance lessons, vegetarian food stalls and a demonstration on how to wear a sari (it's more difficult than it looks). The event, which is organized by the Greater London Authority and the Diwali in London Committee, runs throughout the day till 8pm – over 25,000 people are expected to attend.

📅 LONDON TO BRIGHTON VETERAN CAR RALLY · 7 NOV

- ⓘ *Route: from Queen Elizabeth Gate and Apsley Arch, Hyde Park, W2 2UH to Preston Park, Brighton, East Sussex, BN1*
- ☎ *Tel: 013 2785 6024; www.lbvcr.com*
- Ⓔ *Hyde Park Corner, Marble Arch*
- 💷 *FREE*

Ever since a law was passed in 1896 raising the speed limit from 4mph to 14mph, and a man waving a red flag was no longer required to walk in front of each vehicle, there's been a ceremonial drive from London to Brighton. These days, vintage cars crawl the 60-mile route at 20mph in pairs, leaving Hyde Park at sunrise (around 6.55am). The route putters through Westminster, Lambeth and Norbury, arriving in Croydon around 7.30am. It continues through Redhill and Gatwick before reaching the halfway point, Crawley, around 8.10am. The procession then travels via Cuckfield, Burgess Hill and Clayton Hill, before its official finish in Brighton's Preston Park. The cars continue on to Madeira Drive, on the seafront, for a ceremonial finish beginning at 10am – where plenty of honking is guaranteed. Over 300,000 fans of early examples of Rover, Ford, Vauxhall, Cadillac, Benz and Mercedes from around the world enjoy watching the 500-strong procession – you'll also get to see rare electric and steam cars, driven by drivers in period costume. The cars are also displayed the day before, in Regent Street. *Insider info: Nick Mason of Pink Floyd fame is an avid car collector, and regularly participates in his own cars.*

TAYLOR WESSING PHOTOGRAPHIC　　**11 NOV 2010–**
PORTRAIT PRIZE　　**20 FEB 2011**

❶ *National Portrait Gallery, St Martin's Place, Westminster, WC2H 0HE*
⊕ *Tel: 020 7306 0055; www.npg.org.uk*
◉ *Charing Cross, Leicester Square*
❹ *FREE*

This annual competition displays the work of well-known professionals, up-and-coming photographers – both photography students and talented amateurs – and, of course, the prize winners. Entrants come from around the world, so expect to see a broad range of portraits, including artworks commissioned by magazines, portraits used in advertising, fine-art images and spontaneous and intimate photos that capture the artists' friends and family. Many of the portraits are previously unpublished.

 LORD MAYOR'S SHOW　　**13 NOV**

❶ *Route: Mansion House, EC4N 8LB, to the Royal Courts of Justice, then back to Mansion House via Victoria Embankment*
⊕ *Tel: 019 0830 0106 (grandstand tickets); www.lordmayorsshow.org*
◉ *Mansion House*
❹ *FREE; £27 grandstand tickets*
▦ *11am–5pm*

The Lord Mayor's Show dates back to 1215, when King John allowed the public to elect their own mayor for the first time. Since then, every year the new Lord Mayor parades through the city to the Royal Courts of Justice, where they take an oath of allegiance to the Queen. Unlike the Mayor of London (Boris Johnson), the Lord Mayor is an unpaid, apolitical ambassador for one year only. This year, the day begins at 11am with an RAF flypast. The Lord Mayor then travels from Mansion House to St Paul's Cathedral, arriving at the courts around noon. At 1pm the procession continues its 3-mile loop via Victoria Embankment, returning to Mansion House at 2.30pm. Over 500,000 turn up to watch the procession's marching bands, decorative floats, acrobats and puppeteers – if you want to ensure a decent view, book a grandstand seat outside the cathedral. The day ends at 5pm with a firework finale over the Thames, between Blackfriars and Waterloo bridges. Tickets go on sale in June; only 2,300 are available, so you need to book at least four weeks ahead.

 TURNING ON THE LIGHTS　　**LAST WEEK OF NOV**

❶ *Regent Street, W1; Oxford Street, W1*
⊕ *www.westminster.gov.uk*
◉ *Marble Arch, Bond Street, Oxford Circus, Piccadilly Circus*
❹ *FREE*

Events Calendar – November

Shop windows may have displayed festive decorations since October, but it never really feels like Christmas until the lights get turned on. Every year, scores of people swarm to the West End to watch the celebrity of the day switch on the Christmas lights. Yes, it's crowded, and yes, it's so cold you can't feel your toes anymore, but it's still worth it for the carols sung by gospel choirs and DJs playing cheesy Christmas tunes. If you're not already in the Christmas vibe and/or panicking about Christmas presents, then you will be after tonight.

 WINTER FINE ART AND ANTIQUES FAIR   **NOV**

- ❶ *Olympia, Hammersmith Road, W14 8UX*
- ⊕ *Tel: 020 7385 1200 (venue), 020 7370 8211 (event); www.olympia-antiques.co.uk*
- ◉ *Kensington (Olympia)*
- ❹ *£13 on door; £10 in advance*

Over 20,000 art enthusiasts, antique aficionados, collectors and dealers have been flocking to this fair every year since 1991. The 230 exhibitors sell a range of art, including fine furniture, jewellery, china and old maps. Antique specialists are on hand to offer free guided tours of the fair and answer your queries.

 WINTER WONDERLAND   **NOV–JAN 2011**

- ❶ *Off South Carriage Drive, Serpentine Road, Hyde Park, Westminster, W2 2UH*
- ⊕ *Tel: 084 4847 1771; www.hydeparkwinterwonderland.com*
- ◉ *Hyde Park Corner*
- ❹ *£10*

If you can't get enough of the festive spirit, visit Hyde Park's Winter Wonderland – a corner of the park dedicated to Christmas. There are plenty of stalls, plus a toboggan snow slide and ice rink (*see* p.16).

 STATE OPENING OF PARLIAMENT   **NOV/DEC**

- ❶ *House of Lords, Westminster, SW1A 0PW*
- ⊕ *Tel: 020 7219 3107; www.parliament.uk*
- ◉ *Westminster*
- ❹ *FREE*

The Queen formally opens each new parliamentary session by reading the Queen's Speech from her throne in the House of Lords. The tradition dates back to the 16th century, yet the ceremony of today began in 1852, with the reopening of Westminster following the fire of 1834. The Queen's Speech outlines the Government's game plan for the year ahead – but it's not written by the Queen herself. Following the announcement of the proposals, both houses debate them.

BONFIRE NIGHT – 5 NOVEMBER

While London's firework displays may not compete with the opening ceremonies of the 2008 Beijing Olympics or Dubai's Atlantis The Palm hotel, the capital does show some amazing firework displays – many of which are free. A selection of the best is below – check the websites for the date of the fireworks, as they're not all held on 5 November.

★ ALEXANDRA PALACE, NORTH

- ✪ Alexandra Palace Way, Wood Green, N22 7AY
- ☎ Tel: 020 8365 2121; www.alexandrapalace.com
- ⊖ Wood Green, then bus W3
- ✪ Voluntary donation

★ BLACKHEATH, SOUTH

- ✪ Blackheath Hill, SE3 9LE
- ☎ Tel: 020 8856 2232; www.greenwich.gov.uk
- ⊖ Blackheath BR
- ✪ FREE

★ BROCKWELL PARK, SOUTH

- ✪ Herne Hill, Lambeth, SE24 0NG
- ☎ Tel: 020 7926 6283; www.brockwellpark.com
- ⊖ Herne Hill BR
- ✪ FREE

★ BATTERSEA PARK, SOUTH

- ✪ Albert Bridge Road, SW11 4NJ
- ☎ Tel: 020 8871 7534; www.batterseapark.org
- ⊖ Battersea Park BR, Queenstown Road BR
- ✪ £6

★ VICTORIA PARK, EAST

- ✪ Victoria Park Road, E9 7BT
- ☎ Tel: 020 7364 7907; www.towerhamletsarts.org.uk, www.walktheplank.co.uk
- ⊖ Mile End
- ✪ FREE

★ RAVENSCOURT PARK, WEST

- ✪ Ravenscourt Park, Hammersmith, W6 0UA
- ☎ Tel: 084 5337 0314; www.lbhf.gov.uk
- ⊖ Ravenscourt Park
- ✪ £6
- ▦ 6 Nov

★ BISHOP'S PARK, WEST

- ✪ Bishop's Park, Fulham, SW6 6EA
- ☎ Tel: 084 5337 0314; www.lbhf.gov.uk
- ⊖ Putney Bridge
- ✪ £6

▼ DECEMBER

📅 THE MASTERS TENNIS   7 DEC

- 🛈 *Royal Albert Hall, Kensington Gore, SW7 2AP*
- ☎ *Tel: 020 7070 4404, 020 8233 5880 (box office); www.themasterstennis.com*
- ⊖ *South Kensington, High Street Kensington*
- 💷 *£17.50–£95*

A tennis tournament, in December? In the Royal Albert Hall? We're not too sure who came up with this bright idea, but they were obviously on to something – it's now in its 13th year, and attracts over 35,000 spectators over six days. The tournament marks the end of the ATP Champions Tour, a year-long international tour which pits former tennis legends against each other. To qualify, all competitors must have once been ranked number one in the world, been a singles finalist in a Grand Slam championship or been a singles player on a winning Davis Cup Team – so you know the quality of the matches will be high. It's not often you get to see your favourite tennis players all in one place, so book ahead.

📅 CHRISTMAS TREE LIGHTING CEREMONY   EARLY DEC

- 🛈 *Trafalgar Square, SW1Y*
- ☎ *www.london.gov.uk*
- ⊖ *Charing Cross*
- 💷 *FREE*

The Norwegians have chopped down a Christmas tree for us Brits ever since 1947, as a thank-you for our support in World War II. The right spruce is picked from the forests around Oslo months, even years, in advance, to make sure it's just right for Trafalgar Square. As usual, this year the 55-year-old tree will stretch up to 25 metres tall and be decorated with 500 white lights in the Norwegian tradition. Go along to watch the Lord Mayor of Westminster switch on the lights and listen to the choir of St Martin-in-the-Fields sing carols. You can join in if you like, for free.

📅 TASTE OF CHRISTMAS   EARLY DEC

- 🛈 *ExCeL Exhibition Centre, One Western Gateway, Royal Victoria Dock, E16 1XL*
- ☎ *Tel: 020 7069 5000; www.tasteofchristmas.com*
- ⊖ *Custom House DLR*
- 💷 *Price tbc*

Launched by Gordon Ramsay in 2008, this foodie exhibition allows visitors to sample and buy delicious seasonal foods, as well as watch talks, cook-offs and other special events.

TRAFALGAR SQUARE CHRISTMAS CAROLS   EARLY DEC

- *Trafalgar Square, SW1Y*
- *Trafalgar.square@london.gov.uk; www.london.gov.uk/trafalgarsquare*
- *Charing Cross*
- *FREE*
- *5pm–9pm*

Every year, carol singing groups take to Trafalgar Square to raise money for their charity of choice. You can start up your own group and book yourselves a free one-hour place, or just turn up to enjoy the music. Either way, it's a great way to get yourself into the festive mood.

ONE NEW CHANGE   DEC

- *Cheapside, EC4M 9AB*
- *Tel: 020 7260 2700; www.onenewchange.com, www.cityoflondon.gov.uk*
- *St Paul's*
- *FREE*

A new shopping mall opposite St Paul's Cathedral opens its doors to the public. It will have 20,00 square metres of shopping space (*see* p.118).

SPITALFIELDS WINTER FESTIVAL   1 WEEK IN DEC

- *Various venues*
- *Tel: 020 7377 0287; www.spitalfieldsfestival.org.uk*
- *Liverpool St, Aldgate and Aldgate East*
- *Various, depending on venue*

This seasonal, family-friendly festival celebrates winter with a series of outdoor events, concerts and talks around the Spitalfield area.

CHRISTMAS CAROLS AT HAMPTON COURT   LATE DEC

- *Hampton Court Palace, East Molesey, Surrey, KT8 9AU*
- *Tel: 087 0751 5175; www.hrp.or.uk/HamptonCourtPalace*
- *Hampton Court BR*
- *£3.50–£7*

Get into the Christmas spirit by singing traditional and contemporary carol songs in this beautiful setting. Each singer is given their own songbook to sing from and songs are accompanied by a full silver band.

EATING

In this city it's possible to try cuisine from countries you've never even heard of, but not quite as simple finding a restaurant you can be confident you'll enjoy – unless you've been there before. That's why the eateries below have been tested or recommended from several sources to ensure they're as fantastic as their menu. And, while most of the restaurants and cafes have been included for their quality of food, some may have been included more for their ambience or decor.

KEY TO PRICES

£   under £10 for a main
££   between £10 and £20 for a main
£££   over £20 for a main

▼ CENTRAL

ABENO

- 🛈 47 Museum Street, WC1A 1LY
- ✆ Tel: 020 7405 3211; www.abeno.co.uk
- ◉ Tottenham Court Road
- ⊕ £–££

Think of Japanese food and most people think of sushi, sashimi and noodles. But have you tried okonomiyaki? A sort of Japanese pancake, it's made with batter, egg, a ton of cabbage and whatever meat, fish or vegetables you fancy. Then comes the killer ingredient: okonomiyaki sauce – a gloopy, fish-based condiment. Abeno specializes in Osaka-style okonomiyaki, so the ingredients are mixed together first before being prepared on a hot plate in front of you – which you then eat off. Traditional pictures, daruma (wooden dolls) and the ubiquitous maneki neko (lucky beckoning cat) decorate the restaurant, which is filled with Japanese and Londoners sitting side by side at its eight tables.

ARCHIPELAGO

- 🛈 110 Whitfield Street, W1T 5ED
- ✆ Tel: 020 7383 3346; www.archipelago-restaurant.co.uk
- ◉ Warren Street
- ⊕ ££–£££

Crocodile, wildebeest, zebra and peacock: no, it's not London Zoo, it's Archipelago's menu. Expect chocolate-covered scorpions, cactus leaves, crunchy locusts and crickets in the love bug salad. Vegetarians need not despair – there's plenty for everyone on their extensive menu, which is presented as a ribbon-wrapped scroll. The decor is as eclectic as the dishes. The restaurant resembles a Moroccan market, vintage shop and bizarre bazaar all crammed into one. There is a wide choice of wines and cocktails, and adventurous types may want to look out for drinks with liquorice or 24-carat gold flakes, or try absinthe with a snake in the bottle.

CAMELLIA TEA ROOMS

❶ *Unit 2.12 Kingly Court, Carnaby Street, W1B 5PW*
⊕ *Tel: 020 7734 9939*
◉ *Oxford Circus*
❹ *£*

Unless you bother to visit the upper floors of Kingly Court, you wouldn't really know this delightful tea room is here, but that adds to its charm. Above bustling shoppers, you can relax on the balcony sipping Chinese pu'er tea, which, rather like a good wine, is best drunk after decades of ageing. There are over 75 teas available – from liquorice, antiviral and lover's tea (with passion flower, jasmine and damiana) to tea that relieves gout.

DANS LE NOIR?

❶ *30–1 Clerkenwell Green, EC1R 0DU*
⊕ *Tel: 020 7253 1100; www.danslenoir.com*
◉ *Farringdon*
❹ *££–£££*

This quirky restaurant is ideal for a 'true' blind date, as you dine in darkness and are served by blind or partially sighted waiters. There's no menu, but all dietary requirements are catered for – so if you're a diabetic vegan allergic to peanuts, you needn't worry. The modern European cuisine aims to tantalize your taste buds using spices, flower petals and a combination of sweet, sour, bitter and salty ingredients. When it's time for the bill, call out your waiter's name and hope they come to your rescue. (*N.B. Seating times are 7pm or 9pm, and the earlier option can feel rushed.*)

EV

❶ *The Arches, 97–9 Isabella Street, SE1 8DA*
⊕ *Tel: 020 7620 6191; www.tasrestaurant.com*
◉ *Southwark*
❹ *£–££*

Hidden under old railway arches away from the traffic on Southwark Road, this spacious Turkish restaurant bar is a handy place to know about. The menu is more varied than most Turkish restaurants; a more unusual option being squid stuffed with almonds, sultanas and rice, flavoured with mint and cinnamon and served with tomato sauce. Ev is part of a chain of nine.

FLANEUR

- *41 Farringdon Road, EC1M 3JB*
- *Tel: 020 7404 4422; www.flaneur.com*
- *Farringdon*
- *£–££*

Flaneur restaurant, food hall and cafe is a fan of the 'slow food' movement, so the philosophy here is to eat at leisure. Come before work or for a morning meeting and treat yourself to their breakfasts: French toast with banana and pecans, or pan-fried manouri cheese with pistachios and Greek honey. The rest of the dishes are a mix of European cuisines, which change daily according to what's in season; but as a rough guide, in the restaurant you might try their Catalan fish stew, with salmon, mussels and prawns; or white truffle tagliatelle with Jerusalem artichokes, parsley and pecorino. The food hall, with its floor-to-ceiling shelves, bakery and charcuterie, will tempt you with its tarts, cheeses and cuts of cold meat.

KENZA

- *10 Devonshire Square, EC2M 4YP*
- *Tel: 020 7929 5533; www.kenza-restaurant.com*
- *Liverpool Street*
- *££*

Everything about Kenza is sexy: sensual music and scattered rose petals guide you through corridors flickering with candlelight, which will seduce you deep into this Moroccan and Lebanese restaurant and lounge bar. Here you can combine eating out with a show; while you feast on mezze dishes of parcels of deep-fried pumpkin, walnuts and pomegranate, and mains of minced lamb or skewers of tender chicken, feast your eyes on the restaurant's exotic belly dancers. Occasional henna tattooists, tarot readers and drummers provide further entertainment.

L'ATELIER DE JOEL ROBUCHON

- *13–15 West Street, WC2H 9NE*
- *Tel: 020 7010 8600; www.joel-robuchon.com*
- *Leicester Square, Covent Garden*
- *£££*

Known for his multi-Michelin-starred status, chef Joel Robuchon now has eight restaurants in some of the most glamorous cities in the world. London's offering is no exception, with its sleek red-and-black decor and buzzing atmosphere. Its three floors each have their own ambience and purpose (casual dining, fine dining and bar). The seats by the open kitchen on the ground floor come highly recommended, as not only will your mouth moisten with the smells of the dishes the chefs are preparing in front of you, but you'll be entertained by their graceful moves. The chef's tasting menu, at £80 a head, doesn't come cheap, and the small portions may leave you feeling short-changed. Still, it's worth a visit for its smoked salmon, aniseed and Avruga egg tart, lamb cutlets with buttery mashed potato and, for dessert, macaroons with salted butter.

LEVANT

- ❶ Jason Court, 76 Wigmore Street, W1U 2SJ
- ✆ Tel: 020 7224 1111; www.levant.co.uk
- ◉ Bond Street
- ❶ ££

If you found this Lebanese restaurant, hidden down a candle-lit stairway on an alley off St Christopher's Place, without this guide, then you'd think it's a stroke of serendipity. The 'feast menu', with mezze such as pan-fried halloumi with chilli-spiced jam, sautéed tiger prawns and lamb skewers, is intended to be shared, which makes Levant ideal for groups. Parties will also enjoy the nightly belly dancing and Arabic music played at weekends. Snake charmers, fire eaters, tarot readers, henna tattooists and traditional Middle Eastern percussionists provide further entertainment – if you book them.

MOTHER MASH

- ❶ 26 Ganton Street, Soho, W1F 7QZ
- ✆ Tel: 020 7494 9644; www.mothermash.co.uk
- ◉ Oxford Circus
- ❶ £

Conveniently located for a big night out, this sausage and mash restaurant is a great place to line your stomach. Placing your order is easy: first choose your mash (variations include cheese, garlic and mustard), then your sausage (such as beef and Guinness, veg and herb) or pie, then smother it all in a gravy of your choice – the farmer's gravy, made from onion, red wine and smoked bacon, is popular. Classic puds are just as heavy and wholeheartedly British; try the gooey treacle pudding.

MRS MARENGO'S

- ❶ 53 Lexington Street, Soho, W1F 9AS
- ✆ Tel: 020 7287 2544
- ◉ Oxford Circus
- ❶ £

With its plain white walls, this 13-seat cake shop isn't much to look at, but that doesn't stop it from being in demand. It shares the same chef and owner as the popular vegetarian restaurant, Mildred's, four doors down (no. 45), which explains why Marengo's also has a vegetarian and vegan menu, with wheat-free and gluten-free options. If the lunchtime queues get too much, you could sit on one of the four seats outside, or get your order to go. Expect soups, pasta, organic salads and plump gyoza dumplings, but save room for dessert – it's the cupcakes that draw you here, with their generous swirls of butter icing.

PESCATORI

- ❶ 57 Charlotte Street, W1T 4PD
- ⊕ Tel: 020 7580 3289; www.pescatori.co.uk
- ◉ Goodge Street
- ❶ ££

A group of Italian families have been running Pescatori – which means 'fisherman' in Italian – since 1956. Their success is no secret: for the past 20 years the same buyer has selected their produce from Billingsgate fish market every morning, so you know it's as fresh as it gets. The menu takes inspiration from all over Italy – try the cacciucco, a Tuscan fish stew traditionally made with five different fish. More adventurous types might try squid ink risotto with carnaroli rice, scallops and mascarpone – the rice soaks up the ink so you won't end up with a fetching black, gummy smile. In summer you can dine out on the terrace.

PORTERS

- ❶ 17 Henrietta Street, Covent Garden, WC2E 8QH
- ⊕ Tel: 020 7836 6466; www.porters.uk.com
- ◉ Covent Garden
- ❶ ££

Since 1979, Porters has been serving a healthy dose of Brit humour alongside traditional English grub in a brasserie/cafe setting. Steak, Guinness and mushroom pie; shepherd's pie; and minced lamb with red wine, veggies and a dollop of creamy mashed potato will all draw you in. It also serves hefty portions of school dinner-style classic puds, such as sticky toffee pudding, spotted dick with custard and old-fashioned sherry trifle, just like Nan makes at Christmas.

RADHA KRISHNA TEMPLE

- ❶ 10 Soho Street, W1D 3DL
- ⊕ Tel: 020 7437 3662; www.iskcon-london.org
- ◉ Tottenham Court Road
- ❶ FREE

Head here for a free vegetarian feast on a Sunday afternoon. The temple has two floors and can seat over 300 people, some of whom simply sit on the floor. Dishes include deep-fried vegetables, pakora, salad and a selection of veggie curries. Donations welcomed.

RENDEZVOUS

- ❶ 48 Leicester Square, Leicester Square, WC2H 7LT
- ⊕ Tel: 020 7925 1082; www.rendezvousleicestersquare.co.uk
- ◉ Leicester Square
- ❶ £

Obviously, we're not suggesting you rendezvous in Rendezvous when temperatures are dipping to minus five, but in warmer months chill out over a cone of ice cream or cup of low-fat, low-sugar frozen yoghurt. There are 58 flavours to choose from – we liked the pomegranate and the strawberry cheesecake. The only downside is the chilly staff, and the prices – a couple of scoops cost as much as a main meal. So you won't be the first to lick your bowl to get your money's worth.

ROAST

- *The Floral Hall, Stoney Street, SE1 1TL*
- *Tel: 020 7940 1300; www.roast-restaurant.com*
- *London Bridge*
- *££–£££*

According to its founder, 'Roast celebrates this country's finest ingredients and uses them to help place Britain's food heritage onto the world map.' This is no empty philosophy – the menu lists their suppliers so you know exactly where your dish originated. Come on a Monday, and all the dishes are prepared with native breeds; Sundays are for quintessential British roasts, cooked in a spit oven; and every day is dessert day: try the quince, pear and sultana crumble with custard, or glazed rice pudding with Earl Grey prunes. English wine is on offer, too, from the Tenterden vineyard in Kent. The setting is just as classical as the cuisine: floor-to-ceiling windows not only let in sunlight, they give diners a view of St Paul's as well.

RULES

- *35 Maiden Lane, Covent Garden, WC2E 7LB*
- *Tel: 020 7836 5314; www.rules.co.uk*
- *Covent Garden*
- *£££*

Walking through the door to Rules is like walking back in time. Little has changed since it was established in 1798. Men in dapper tweed jackets hang their hats on a hat stand made from antlers and sit by a roaring fire, or at tables covered in crisp white cloths, under a stained glass ceiling. The only thing missing from the days of old is sweet smoke from expensive cigars. From the menu, splash out on pheasant, wild duck or game pie served with savoy cabbage – the game is sourced from the Lartington Estate in the High Pennines.

SARASTRO

- *126 Drury Lane, WC2B 5SU*
- *Tel: 020 7836 0101; www.sarastro-restaurant.com*
- *Covent Garden*
- *£–££*

Once inside this ornate restaurant, you'll feel like you're on the set of *Moulin Rouge*, with its hanging gold drapes and Renaissance paintings decorating the ceiling.

Reserve in advance to bag one of the theatre-style balconies – otherwise you'll be crammed on tables so close together, you might as well be sharing a communal table. You'll be served a three-course set menu of grilled duck breast or salmon in a champagne sauce, with an enormous fruit platter per couple to finish. But the food isn't Sarastro's biggest draw: dubbed 'the show after the show', diners are treated to entertainment throughout dinner by professional opera singers.

SKETCH

- ❶ 9 Conduit Street, Soho, W1S 2XG
- ✆ Tel: 020 7659 4500; www.sketch.uk.com
- ◉ Oxford Circus
- ❹ £££

A model/doorman greets you as you enter Sketch, which feels rather like stepping into *Alice in Wonderland*. Wacky art is dotted throughout the five main rooms in this restaurant bar, which was once Christian Dior's headquarters. Look out for chairs that blend into the wall, a vertical strip light that shows the word 'love' out of the corner of your eye when you walk away and paint that's been poured down the staircase and left to harden. If you're here to dine, there's The Gallery, a contemporary restaurant for 100. Here, a two-course meal might include roast deer with mango, pear and parsnip cream, followed by Malabar – bubble gum ice cream with orange blossom marshmallow. For a more formal dinner, book The Lecture Room, with its padded leather walls and Michelin-star chef Pierre Gagnaire. But be warned, such glamour doesn't come cheap.

SOUK

- ❶ 1a Short's Gardens, WC2H 9AT
- ✆ Tel: 020 7240 1796; www.soukrestaurant.net
- ◉ Covent Garden
- ❹ ££

You'll be led through this labyrinthine grotto into a dimly lit cavern adorned with sumptuous fabric, cushions and thick rugs. Heavy copper lanterns cast a soft glow over your meal, making Souk an ideal venue for a romantic dinner. Parties are also welcome, and will no doubt enjoy the belly dancer who shimmies between the rooms in a glittering, barely-there costume. The north African cuisine is an experience, too, and reasonably priced. Choose a set menu or individual dishes to share, such as the tangy orange, feta and olive salad, a tagine for your main or the chicken pastilla – flaky filo pastry filled with almonds, egg and Moroccan spices, with a hint of rose water.

ST MORITZ

- ❶ 161 Wardour Street, W1F 8WJ
- ✆ Tel: 020 7734 3324; www.stmoritz-restaurant.co.uk
- ◉ Piccadilly Circus
- ❹ ££

This Swiss fondue restaurant is unashamedly cheesy – excuse the pun – as it makes no attempt to stray from the alpine decor Heidi was so fond of. Fondue options vary, though most come with simple crusty bread, vegetables or strips of beef to dip into Gruyère, Vacherin and Emmental cheese. A selection of Swiss wine is also on the menu. And for dessert? Why, there's chocolate fondue, of course.

UMU

- 14–16 Bruton Place, W1J 6LX
- Tel: 020 7499 8881; www.umurestaurant.com
- Bond Street
- ££–£££

The Japanese love their ice cream, and give the Italians a run for their money here, with flavours such as black bean, white miso, pumpkin and tofu. If Michelin-starred restaurants are your thing, head here to try the *kaiseki* (tasting menu). Sample dishes include ginger juice foie gras, grade-six Wagyu roast beef, rape blossom Wagyu sushi and chestnut cake. Need a drink to wash it all down? Then choose from one of 70 different types of sake.

THE VINCENT ROOMS

- Westminster Kingsway College, 76 Vincent Square, SW1P 2PD
- Tel: 020 7802 8391; www.thevincentrooms.com
- Victoria
- ££

If you've always dreamed of fine dining but simply can't afford it, try The Vincent Rooms, whose chefs are also students enrolled at Westminster Kingsway College. There are two rooms; an informal brasserie and the Escoffier room, where you can enjoy a three-course meal with canapés in an elegant setting. Start with a warm duck liver salad, served with tart berries; for your main, try the roasted wood pigeon, served with pigeon and black pudding sausage and parsnip purée. Who knows, maybe your chef will be the next Ainsley Harriott or Jamie Oliver – both of whom are alumni.

VITA ORGANIC

- 74 Wardour Street, Soho, W1F 0TE
- Tel: 020 7734 8986; www.vitaorganic.co.uk
- Leicester Square, Piccadilly Circus
- £

The wooden, earthy interior of this little restaurant on a corner in Soho sets the scene for its cuisine: choose one, two or three scoops of hearty, nutritionally balanced dishes, such as grain-free yellow squash laksa. And as you fill up on steaming bowls of spicy chickpea Malaysian curry, you can feel smug with the knowledge that your meal is low fat, low GI and free from artificial nasties.

10 BEST CHEAP EATS

Cheap food doesn't have to mean bad food, even in London. Plenty of eateries serve good-quality food for under a tenner and below are some favourites.

★ 1 JACKETS, SOUTH

- ⓘ *140 Clapham High Street, Clapham, SW4 7UH*
- ✆ *Tel: 020 7622 5027*
- ⊖ *Clapham Common*
- ⓔ *£*

Jackets is an ideal joint for after the pub or following Bonfire Night fireworks on the common. Garish plastic tables with benches bolted to the floor seat 32.

★ 2 BEATROOT, CENTRAL

- ⓘ *92 Berwick Street, Soho, W1F 0QD*
- ✆ *Tel: 020 7437 8591; www.beatroot.org.uk*
- ⊖ *Oxford Circus*
- ⓔ *£*

This compact vegetarian place is popular with Soho-ites, especially at lunchtime. The food is served in small, medium or large containers, and you can mix dishes together – a slice of lasagne, a spoonful of potato salad and a few faux sausage rolls should keep you going till dinner.

★ 3 RAINFOREST, EAST

- ⓘ *Old Spitalfields Market, 105a Commercial Street, E1 6EW*
- ✆ *Tel: 07985 235 219; www.rainforestcreations.co.uk*
- ⊖ *Liverpool Street*
- ⓔ *£*

You could easily miss this stall in the centre of Spitalfields market for the huddle of people around it. But jostle to the front and you'll be met with bright purple cabbage, red quinoa and raw falafels. You can pick ingredients to add to a 'rainforest box' or stuff a roti, which has so much flavour you could eat it plain.

★ 4 KURZ & LANG, EAST

- ⓘ *1 St John Street, Smithfield, EC1M 4AA*
- ✆ *Tel: 020 7253 6623; www.kurzandlang.com*
- ⊖ *Farringdon*
- ⓔ *£*

On Fridays, this cheap 'n' cheerful caff doesn't bother closing – so you can pig out on bratwurst dripping with mustard and ketchup all through the night. Popular wurst include the beef rindswurst; käsewurst, made with pork, beef and cheese; or 'currywurst', which, funnily enough, is served with a mild madras curry sauce. All the produce comes from a small family-run farm in Germany.

★ 5 MANDALAY, WEST

- ⓘ *444 Edgware Road, W2 1EG*
- ✆ *Tel: 020 7258 3696; www.mandalayway.com*
- ⊖ *Edgware Road*
- ⓔ *£*

Since 1994, the Ally family have been cooking traditional Burmese cuisine, blending that of India, China, Laos and Thailand. Try the green papaya salad, prepared with raw (not sweet) papaya, tamarind, ginger and fish sauce, or the coconut and chicken noodles – their most popular dish.

★ 6 POLANKA, WEST

- 258 King Street, W6 0SP
- Tel: 020 8741 8268;
  www.polanka-rest.com
- Ravenscourt Park
- £

The surrounding Polish community come here in droves for its Polish newspapers, TV and traditional fare. Polanka serves warming winter food that's hearty, heavy and salty. Apart from a mannequin in national costume and a boar skin on one wall, the decor is as relaxed as the service. It's unlicensed, so it's BYO.

★ 7 CHA CHA MOON, CENTRAL

- 15–21 Ganton Street, Soho, W1F 9BN
- Tel: 020 7297 9800;
  www.chachamoon.com
- Oxford Circus
- £

Cha Cha Moon manages to be both cheap and stylish, with its low lighting, bamboo and open-view kitchen. This place is great for a quick bite to eat – once seated at a communal table you'll be served quickly and expected to eat quickly. The extensive menu includes northern and western Chinese fare, as well as dishes from Hong Kong, Taiwan and Singapore.

★ 8 LALIBELA, NORTH

- 137 Fortess Road, Kentish Town, NW5 2HR
- Tel: 020 7284 0600
- Tufnell Park
- £

Even though this Ethiopian restaurant is a bit of a trek to get to, it's worth it. The wooden masks, old photographs of Emperor Haile Selassie and national costumes decorating its six rooms tell you Ethiopia's story, and the cuisine is as traditional as the decor. Food is served on low tables – you sit on low, carved wooden chairs (which are actually rather uncomfortable). Expect the dishes to be served on a large piece of *injera* (a sour, flat pancake) which you rip into pieces to scoop up your food. At the end of your meal you'll be treated to an authentic coffee ceremony.

★ 9 M. MANZE, SOUTH

- 105 High Street, Peckham, SE15 5RS
- Tel: 020 7277 6181;
  www.manze.co.uk
- Peckham Rye BR
- £

This family-run pie shop has been serving local classics, such as handmade minced beef pies and jellied eels, since 1902 – the current owner still uses the same recipes his grandfather did.

★ 10 VIET-ANH CAFE, NORTH

- 41 Parkway, Camden, NW1 7PN
- Tel: 020 7284 4082
- Camden Town
- £

You'll be served in about five minutes once you've crammed into one of the small tables in this lively Vietnamese joint. This warm, cosy cafe/restaurant is great for a small group of friends, as you can share a mix of dishes. At lunchtime, expect a media crowd; if it's too packed, there are a couple of seats outside or get it to go.

▼ NORTH

THE BLUE LEGUME

- *101 Stoke Newington Church Street, N16 0UD*
- *Tel: 020 7923 1303*
- *Angel, then bus 73, 476*
- *£*

This bohemian cafe/bistro is decorated with mosaics, a 1.5-metre wooden puppet and a golden sun on the ceiling. There are two rooms – the one at the front has a European flavour, the other is an airy conservatory at the back. It's renowned for its weekend brunches – try the waffles or the eggs benedict. They also serve salads, tarts, pasta and quiches, as well as more substantial meals and cakes, but when all 50 seats are taken, the food can be a bit hit or miss.

CAFE GALLIPOLI

- *102 Upper Street, N1 1QN*
- *Tel: 020 7359 0630; www.cafegallipoli.com*
- *Angel, Highbury & Islington*
- *£*

The first of a trio of Gallipolis along Upper Street (there's also Gallipoli Bazaar at 107 and Gallipoli Again at 120), all of which are perennially popular. On the pavement, a dozen diners can sit on luxurious velvet and carved wooden chairs, wafting sweet smoke from hookah pipes. Inside, framed pictures crowd the walls, which are dimly lit by lanterns. Gallipoli is ideal for a date earlier in the evening, with its intimate, low tables made from gold trays. Later on, friendly staff ensures a lively atmosphere, and Turkish/Lebanese mezze, such as stuffed vine leaves and chicken tagine with saffron and ginger, are ideal for groups.

CANDID CAFE

- *3 Torrens Street, EC1V 1NQ*
- *Tel: 020 7837 4237; www.candidarts.com*
- *Angel*
- *£–££*

Considering its location directly behind Angel tube station, it's baffling that more people don't know about Candid. Follow the sign up a grotty stairwell, and you'll arrive in this cosy cafe. There's a friendly feel to this place; most visitors are regulars who come to read a book on the comfy sofas, host informal meetings or combine their trip with a visit to the art market downstairs. There's no wifi, and laptops are discouraged to maintain its laid-back ambience. Hot meals include mixed vegetables in coconut sauce and organic chicken in a soya and honey sauce.

COFFEE CAKE

- *28 Broadway Parade, Crouch End, N8 9DB*
- *Tel: 020 8342 8989*
- *Hornsey BR, then bus 41, 91, W5, W7*
- *£*

This family-run cafe is hugely popular with locals for its selection of continental pastries, quiches, salads and smoothies, as well as its friendly and welcoming manager. The quinoa with pan-fried aubergine or pearl barley with mushrooms, almonds and yoghurt are popular, as are the cafe's unusual desserts – chocolate and courgette tart, chocolate cake with beetroot or pear and ginger. With its exposed brick walls, white tables and all-glass front, Coffee Cake is light and spacious – an ideal location to finish off your latest novel.

CUBA LIBRE

- *72 Upper Street, Islington Green, N1 0NY*
- *Tel: 020 7354 9998; www.cubalibrelondon.co.uk*
- *Angel, Highbury & Islington*
- *£–££*

This lively Cuban restaurant is known for its painted walls showing women hanging out their laundry from a balcony, and papier-mâché models of Che Guevara. Typical dishes include fried plantain gratin, melange of pork, Spanish sausage and shredded beef served with black beans and rice. There is a bar at the back if you just fancy some tapas and drinks. Don't leave without trying a cocktail, particularly their classic mojitos or the Havana Daydreaming (made from vodka, Malibu, banana liqueur, cream and orange juice).

FIG & OLIVE

- *151 Upper Street, Islington, N1 1RA*
- *Tel: 020 7354 2605; www.figolive.co.uk*
- *Angel, Highbury & Islington*
- *£*

For an evening out, this late-night cafe makes a sweet alternative to a bar, as it's usually open till midnight. Diners can sit on mismatched antique chairs next to a gilt mirror near the window, or on tables more suited to sit-down meals. There's also a long communal table in the sunny conservatory at the back. Mains are mostly meat-based, such as wild boar with apple sausages, which can be matched with wine from Italy, France, South Africa and Chile. Vegetarian options include aubergine with sautéed mushrooms or Mediterranean vegetables with halloumi. Dieters beware – few can resist the window's tempting cake display; try the lemon tart decorated with swirls of dark chocolate, which crack at the touch of a spoon.

THE GATE

- *11 Albion Road, Newington Green, N16 9PS*
- *Tel: 020 7923 9227; www.the-gate-n16.com*
- *Angel, then bus 73, 476*
- *£–££*

The Gate, on the corner of Newington Green, is whatever you want it to be. For those looking for a cafe, there's a laid-back vibe and free papers (alas, no wifi). But if you're looking for a restaurant, the extensive menu with seafood, vegetarian options, a massive Sunday lunch with lashings of gravy and a bias towards Turkish dishes will suit a mixed group. It's licensed, too, so until 11pm every night you can sit at a stool at the bar with a bottled beer in your hand, or at the window overlooking the green.

GEM

- *265 Upper Street, Islington, N1 2UQ*
- *Tel: 020 7359 0405; www.gemrestaurant.org.uk*
- *Highbury & Islington*
- *£*

When you're craving something a bit different, why not try Kurdish – the *beyti* (minced lamb seasoned with garlic and onion) comes recommended. The service here is excellent; you'll receive complimentary stuffed flatbread and generous traditional desserts (ice cream with *irmik* – a sweet almond-tasting dish made from fine semolina wheat), and the mains are under £10. There's a second branch, Gem & I, in Clapham.

KHOAI CAFÉ

- *6 Topsfield Parade, Middle Lane, Crouch End, N8 8PR*
- *Tel: 020 8341 2120*
- *Hornsey BR, then bus 41, 91, W5, W7*
- *£*

All of the staff is Vietnamese, and this shows in the quality of the cuisine. To start, try the summer rolls – prawns, crab and bean sprouts mixed with chopped mint, fresh basil and cucumber, with a squeeze of lime, all wrapped in soft rice vermicelli. Mains include noodle soup, fish dishes and stir-fries. The decor is understated, but the pictures of Vietnam are a nice touch.

LE MERCURY

- *140a Upper Street, Islington, N1 1QY*
- *Tel: 020 7354 4088; www.lemercury.co.uk*
- *Angel, Highbury & Islington*
- *£–££*

From street level, this looks like a rather cramped, expensive French bistro. But there are actually three floors to Le Mercury, with a total capacity for 110.

If you choose from the set menu, it's easy to eat here on a budget, but you may need to fill up on the complementary bread. The menu is mostly fish and meat – to start, try the mussels marinated in white wine, shallots, garlic and lemon; for your main, the sea bass, with its crispy skin, minted pesto and new potatoes, is recommended. Save room for dessert – the roasted rhubarb with basil ice cream is an unusual option.

LITTLE BAY

- ❶ *228 Belsize Road, NW6 4BT*
- ⊕ *Tel: 020 7372 4699; www.littlebay.co.uk*
- ❸ *Kilburn*
- ❹ *£*

Those in the know have been drawn to this branch of Little Bay since it opened in 1992. Red walls, tapestry seating, Renaissance paintings on the tables and candles dripping wax down wine bottles create a romantic atmosphere, which doesn't come with the price tag you'd expect. The three main rooms seat 200 in total, but call ahead to reserve one of the few intimate tables high in the ceiling above the rest of the diners, in the style of a theatre balcony. There are also a few tables with curtains for privacy. The mussels and crab are popular dishes on its limited modern European menu.

LOUIS

- ❶ *32 Heath Street, NW3 6TE*
- ⊕ *Tel: 020 7435 9908*
- ❸ *Hampstead*
- ❹ *£*

This cafe, established in 1963, feels more like a French tea room than a Hungarian patisserie, which is how it describes itself. Old-school trollies piled high with pastries are wheeled over to your table so you can 'ooh' and 'ahh' before selecting the one you want. Needless to say, this traditional cafe still has bona fide china cups, carpet and wooden panelling on the walls.

O'S THAI CAFE

- ❶ *10 Topsfield Parade, Crouch End, N8 8JN*
- ⊕ *Tel: 020 8348 6898; www.osthaicafe.com*
- ❸ *Hornsey BR, then bus 41, 91, W5, W7*
- ❹ *£*

This Thai restaurant is popular with locals because it's lively, noisy and reasonably priced. The staff is young, friendly and keen to serve you quickly – though this may make you feel rushed. The dishes are what you'd expect: variations of king prawn/chicken/pork/beef or tofu curry with vegetables, lime and basil leaves, all served with mounds of rice. There's also the ubiquitous spicy tom yam soup with lime, lemongrass and galangal, and pad Thai noodles, scattered with ground peanuts, spices and bean sprouts.

ST JAMES

- 4 Topsfield Parade, Middle Lane, Crouch End, N8 8PR
- Tel: 020 8348 8348; www.stjamesn8.co.uk
- Hornsey BR, then bus 41, 91, W5, W7
- £

Decked out in midnight-blue velvet and fairy lights resembling stars, the cocktail lounge in St James's is sleek sophistication and strip club in equal parts. The dining room, however, has completely different decor: plain cream walls, smooth wooden floors and floor-to-ceiling mirrors. The menu features modern twists on traditional British and French dishes, such as roasted venison wrapped in pancetta, served with potato gnocchi, egg-yellow chanterelles and spinach, in a redcurrant sauce. Classic desserts include treacle sponge and apple crumble. The bar is, again, totally different, though still as smooth as the other rooms, with neon lights and mirrors. There's also a patio that seats 12.

THAT PLACE ON THE CORNER

- 1–3 Green Lanes, Newington Green, N16 9BS
- Tel: 020 7704 0079; www.thatplaceonthecorner.com
- Angel, then bus 73, 476
- £

The owners have clearly hit on a landmine: this cafe isn't just child-friendly; it's designed entirely with little people in mind. There's ample space for pushchairs near the door, a safe, fun and inspiring children's play area towards the back and high chairs aplenty. What's more, if your children start screaming, you'll be met with sympathetic smiles rather than frowns from the other diners here. The cafe also runs ballet, French and cookery classes, as well as baby yoga, music for toddlers, face-painting and craft activities. Pasta, sandwiches and boiled egg and soldiers are on the menu.

ZIGNI HOUSE

- 330 Essex Road, Islington N1 3PB
- Tel: 020 7226 7418; www.zignihouse.com
- Highbury & Islington
- £–££

Run by a former Eritrean refugee, Tsige Haile, this east African restaurant is as authentic and homely as one you might find in Asmara. From the outside it looks shabby, but inside, the dining area is decorated with African artefacts and animal hides. As in Tsige's native country, the food is served without cutlery, as it's meant to be eaten with your hands. The cuisine is spicy and meaty – expect hearty casseroles served with *injera* (a spongy crêpe-like bread made with teff flour, wheat or corn); its sour flavour doesn't suit every palate, but you could wash it down with Asmara, a light beer made from organic hops. Service can be slow, so if you're in a hurry, go for the all-you-can-eat buffet.

▼ SOUTH

BEAUBERRY HOUSE

- ❶ *Gallery Road, West Dulwich, SE21 7AB*
- ⊕ *Tel: 020 8299 9788; www.beauberryhouse.co.uk*
- ❷ *North Dulwich BR*
- ❸ *£££*

Even if you're used to being spoiled, you'll still be impressed with the setting of this beautiful Georgian mansion, built in 1785 and set in extensive grounds. The menu takes inspiration from east Asia, with dishes such as tuna tartar, salmon caviar and shiso (a kind of Japanese basil) to start, followed by grilled aubergine with miso and black sesame in a tart, citrus ponzu sauce. The desserts also blend ingredients you might not think to marry, such as white chocolate and passion fruit brûlée. Leave your choice of wine to the sommelier, with his impressive CV. Whether you sit in the elegant dining room or on the terrace, Beauberry House is entirely suitable if you're popping the question tonight.

BISCUIT CERAMIC CAFE

- ❶ *3–4 Nelson Road, Greenwich, SE10 9JB*
- ⊕ *Tel: 020 8853 8588; www.biscuit-biscuit.com*
- ❷ *Cutty Sark DLR*
- ❸ *£*

This place is great for kids' parties – or hen parties, for that matter – as you get to design your own crockery. Once you've picked a ceramic cup, plate, teapot or vase, you paint whatever pattern you like before it's glazed and put in the kiln (starts at £10). A private party room, which seats 20, is available. The menu offers dips, crudités and unlimited toast to nibble on while you're hard at work.

BLUE MOUNTAIN

- ❶ *18 North Cross Road, East Dulwich, SE22 9EU*
- ⊕ *Tel: 020 8299 6953; www.bluemo.co.uk*
- ❷ *East Dulwich BR, then bus 40*
- ❸ *£–££*

The outside of this Caribbean restaurant/cafe will draw you in: broken pottery, mirror and whole china plates create a colourful mosaic embedded in the cafe's patio. The Jamaican influence is reflected in the menu: curried goat, fried plantain or steamed fish in creole sauce are favourites; and the coffee beans come from Nicaragua. Poetry readings and live music feature most nights.

BOULANGERIE PATISSERIE

- ❶ *22 The Pavement, SW4 0HY*
- ⊕ *Tel: 020 7498 2636*
- ❷ *Clapham Common*
- ❸ *£*

This cafe shares the same owner as nearby Gastro (*see* opposite), which explains the eclairs, macaroons and communal table. But instead of a menu listing wine, there are 22 types of tea to choose from – try the cherry blossom.

BREADS ETCETERA

- ❶ *127 Clapham High Street, SW4 7SS*
- ⊕ *Tel: 020 7720 3601; www.breadsetcetera.com*
- ✆ *Clapham Common*
- ❹ *£–££*

On a weekend morning, this cosy restaurant deli smells of toast as diners make their own. As well as sourdough breads and toasted open sandwiches, you can pick up free-range bacon, eggs, sausages and butter for a home-cooked breakfast. All the ingredients are sourced locally.

BUENOS AIRES

- ❶ *17 Royal Parade, Blackheath, SE3 0TL*
- ⊕ *Tel: 020 8318 5333; www.buenosairesltd.com*
- ✆ *Blackheath BR*
- ❹ *£–£££*

The waiters in this classic Argentinean restaurant, all smartly dressed in black, give you a hint of the menu's prices. The menu is meaty, with a wide selection of free-range Argentinean steaks and homemade chorizos, which you can match with a limited edition bottle of Laborum 2005, a spicy red. The framed photos on the wall were taken by the manager, Reinaldo Vargas, a former paparazzo.

CACTUS PIT

- ❶ *10–11 Royal Parade, Blackheath, SE3 0TL*
- ⊕ *Tel: 020 8852 0883; www.cactuspit.net*
- ✆ *Blackheath BR*
- ❹ *£–££*

With its bright orange walls adorned with Mexican hats, mirrors and pictures of cacti painted in garish colours, this Mexican restaurant is great for hen nights, stag dos or kids' parties. All the usuals are here: enchiladas, chimichangas, burritos and fajitas, plus burgers and Texan T-bone steak. After you've sunk a few Cactus Bangers (tequila, Grand Marnier and orange juice), have a boogie on the dance floor downstairs. There's a hotel upstairs if it all gets too much.

ECO

- ❶ *162 Clapham High Street, SW4 7UG*
- ⊕ *Tel: 020 7978 1108; www.ecorestaurants.com*
- ✆ *Clapham Common*
- ❹ *£*

This place does such good pizza, the second, third and fourth times you go you'll want exactly what you ordered the first time. Dare to experiment and you'll find each pizza is as delicious as your last. Try the Amore, with red onions, black olives, goat's cheese, roasted red peppers and tender slices of aubergine, but bare in mind the olives aren't pitted and the knives are so blunt you may well leave with arthritic forefingers. For smokers, there are nine seats outside.

ESCA

- 160 Clapham High Street, SW4 7UG
- Tel: 020 7622 2288; www.escauk.com
- Clapham Common
- £

The 20 or so patisseries in the window will draw you in to this cosy, laid-back deli. Once inside, you'll drool over goodies such as truffles, olives and crystallized orange peel stacked on floor-to-ceiling shelves – staff reel a ladder on wheels across the shelves if you can't reach the item you're after. For a treat, buy a bespoke hamper for £15. Light mains, such as seafood salad or pumpkin, almond and pomegranate rice, are also available – just take a seat at one of the two communal tables at the back, or enjoy polenta cake and coffee at the few tables on the pavement.

GASTRO

- 63–7 Venn Street, SW4 0BD
- Tel: 020 7627 0222
- Clapham Common
- ££

As soon as you enter this authentic French bistro, you'll be greeted with calls of 'bonjour' and 'serveece!' from French staff. Portions are reasonable; popular dishes include the mussels and escargot, or you can choose your crab from the aquarium at the back. Meat dishes include rabbit with turnip purée, roasted guinea fowl for Sunday lunch or 28-day-aged roast beef for two. Antique wine cabinets and steamy stained glass windows create a musky atmosphere.

THE GOAT

- 66a Battersea Rise, SW11 1EQ
- Tel: 020 7350 0349; www.thegoatpub.com
- Clapham Junction BR
- £

If there are at least six of you, why not host your own roast? The staff does all the hard work, leaving you with the fun bit – they cook it, you carve it, then scoff it. The Goat does a mean Sunday roast, too, and for vegetarians, there's the option of roasted carrot and parsnip sausages. It's not just the cuisine that makes The Goat popular – black exposed piping, red tassled lampshades and crystal chandeliers make this gastropub right on trend.

LA PAMPA GRILL

- ❶ 60 Battersea Rise, SW11 1EG
- ✆ Tel: 020 7924 4774
- ⊖ Clapham Junction BR
- ❻ £–££

Celebrity chef John Torode gave this Argentinean restaurant the thumbs up for its steaks, and he knows a thing or two about beef. Sit at butcher's-block tables and sharpen your knives in preparation for rib-eye steak or roasted breast of duck. Go hungry, and go with fellow carnivores. If you can't get in here, there's another, livelier branch round the corner, on Northcote Road.

LA RUEDA

- ❶ 66–8 Clapham High Street, SW4 7UL
- ✆ Tel: 020 7627 2173; www.larueda-restaurant.co.uk
- ⊖ Clapham North
- ❻ ££

Jaunty music welcomes you into this rustic Spanish restaurant. For your main, choose a meat, rice or fish dish, such as grilled monkfish with garlic and chillies. There's also an extensive tapas selection – the Spanish tuna patties and Iberian chorizo slices are popular. To wash it all down, pick one of the 40 Spanish wines on the menu; Marques de Caceres Crianza (from Rioja), a full-bodied, fragrant red, is the most popular. There are Italian, Chilean and French wine options, too. Look up and you'll see where all the used bottles go: wine bottles, wooden wheels and mosaic tiles cover the arched ceiling. On weekend nights, there's dancing till 2am, and a Latin band on Sundays.

LE CHANDELIER

- ❶ 161 Lordship Lane, East Dulwich, SE22 8HX
- ✆ Tel: 020 8299 3344; www.lechandelier.co.uk
- ⊖ East Dulwich BR, then bus 40
- ❻ £

Housed in a former antique shop, this stylish cafe is characterized by its mismatched chandeliers, all of which are for sale. Seating is available for 70, either outside, overlooking the busy road, on the ground floor or up a spiral staircase in the Moroccan-themed attic. Young couples with their pushchairs come here for a light afternoon bite – try the aubergine and garlic soup, or if you're hungry, guinea fowl with winter vegetables and a wild mushroom sauce.

LE CHARDON

- ❶ 65 Lordship Lane, East Dulwich, SE22 8EP
- ✆ Tel: 020 8299 1921; www.lechardon.co.uk
- ⊖ East Dulwich BR, then bus 40
- ❻ £–££

As you may expect from an upmarket French restaurant, the few vegetarian options are uninspiring and clichéd. The fish and meat dishes, however, are what get people talking. Start with a whole Devon crab, served in its shell; for your main, try the honey-glazed duck with a tart blackcurrant sauce. There's a second branch in Clapham.

MONTPELIERS

- 35 Montpelier Vale, Blackheath, SE3 0TJ
- Tel: 020 8852 5258
- Blackheath BR
- ££

Montpeliers is a quaint cafe with a cream bookshelf, an old-fashioned gold till and jars of sweets for the kids (or you). There's seating outside or in the small room at the back – unfortunately on uncomfortable metal chairs. Serves panini, sandwiches and salads, as well as milkshakes, ice cream and homemade tarts.

OSTERIA ANTICA BOLOGNA

- 23 Northcote Road, SW11 1NG
- Tel: 020 7978 4771; www.osteria.co.uk
- Clapham Junction BR
- £

This popular Italian restaurant opened 22 years ago, and still serves authentic Italian cuisine cooked by a chef from Genoa. The chef uses seasonal, local ingredients to make dishes such as homemade chestnut spaghetti with Italian sausage ragout and Taleggio cheese. There are seats for 75 in the dimly lit main room and down the adjacent corridor; it's small enough to create an intimate atmosphere.

THE PANTRY

- 342 Old York Road, Wandsworth, SW18 1SS
- Tel: 020 8871 0713; www.thepantrylondon.com
- Wandsworth Town BR
- £–££

This cafe/deli serves a range of posh sandwiches, hot meals (such as smoked salmon tartine), pastries (such as plum and frangipani tart) and bread, which is baked daily and free from chemicals, preservatives and additives. It even does organic baby food – which tells you a little about its clientele. It's not so cheap, but it is welcoming – friendly staff invite you to sit at the communal table, which seats 10.

10 PLACES FOR AFTERNOON TEA

From top hotels to quaint tea rooms – below you'll find a selection of places offering cucumber sandwiches, scones and cream and a lovely pot of tea...

★ 1 THE LANESBOROUGH, CENTRAL

- ❶ Hyde Park Corner, SW1X 7TA
- ☎ Tel: 020 7259 5599; www.lanesborough.com
- ⊖ Hyde Park Corner
- ❸ ££

In 2008, The Lanesborough was awarded the 'top London afternoon tea award' for the second time by the UK Tea Council – and they know a thing or two about afternoon tea. Besides, what place could be better to nibble on dainty sandwiches than next door to the Queen herself?

★ 2 ATHENAEUM HOTEL, CENTRAL

- ❶ 116 Piccadilly, W1J 7BJ
- ☎ Tel: 020 7499 3464; www.athenaeumhotel.com
- ⊖ Green Park
- ❸ ££

Sadly, a recent refurb has seen the gloriously pink and girly lounge morph into one fit for a business function room. However, the Athenaeum still serves delicious Ladurée macaroons and you get second helpings of tea, sandwiches – and if you can fit more in – tea cakes and crumpets!

★ 3 VOLUPTÉ, CENTRAL

- ❶ 9 Norwich Street, EC4A 1EJ
- ☎ Tel: 020 7831 1622; www.volupte-lounge.com
- ⊖ Chancery Lane
- ❸ ££

If you care for a little afternoon tease with your afternoon tea, come here to watch glamorous burlesque dancers twizzling their tassles, just be sure you don't choke on your scone.

★ 4 THE GORING, CENTRAL

- ❶ Beeston Place, Grosvenor Gardens, SW1W 0JW
- ☎ Tel: 020 7396 9000; www.thegoring.com
- ⊖ Victoria
- ❸ ££

Take a sip of tea from a porcelain cup and nibble at cucumber sandwiches. Sit on the terrace, which overlooks the manicured gardens.

★ 5 THE CHESTERFIELD MAYFAIR, CENTRAL

- ❶ 35 Charles Street, W1J 5EB
- ☎ Tel: 020 7491 2622; www.chesterfieldmayfair.com
- ⊖ Green Park
- ❸ £–££

Here you can relax in a beautiful conservatory overlooking the fountains in the English garden. Choose the chocolate lovers afternoon tea option and splurge on rich hot chocolate, chocolate scones and chocolate pastries.

★ 6 THE TEA ROOMS, NORTH

- 155 Stoke Newington Church Street, N16 0UH
- Tel: 020 7923 1870
- Angel, then bus 73, 476
- £

Why choose this delightful art deco cafe? Well, for about £10 you can sample homemade cakes and scones, and tea made with proper tea leaves, served in retro teapots.

★ 7 THE RITZ HOTEL, CENTRAL

- 150 Piccadilly, W1J 9BR
- Tel: 020 7493 8181; www.theritzlondon.com
- Green Park
- ££

Delicate salmon sandwiches, slices of cake and scones served with Devonshire clotted cream are served in the stunning Palm Court. A pianist plays under chandeliers, a domed ceiling and marble columns, making this one of the finest rooms to partake in afternoon tea. The hotel also caters for coeliacs (order in advance).

★ 8 CLARIDGE'S, CENTRAL

- Brook Street, Mayfair, W1K 4HR
- Tel: 020 7629 8860; www.claridges.co.uk
- Bond Street
- ££

If you're celebrating a special occasion, Claridge's offers an array of themed afternoon teas – think heart-shaped macaroons for Valentine's Day, and hot cross buns at Easter. It also serves floral afternoon tea in spring and lawn tennis afternoon tea in early summer. The exclusive Royal white-silver needle tea, which is picked at dawn on just two days of the year, is a must-try. Live pianists, violinists and harpists perform daily.

★ 9 THE DORCHESTER, CENTRAL

- 53 Park Lane, W1K 1QA
- Tel: 020 7629 8888; www.thedorchester.com
- Hyde Park Corner
- ££

What could be more British than Marmite afternoon tea? If that takes your fancy, then to The Dorchester you shall go. Here, their recipe for scones hasn't changed for over 50 years, although they keep their afternoon tea experience up to date with themed events, such as tea accompanied by a fashion show. Past designers include Escada, Matthew Williamson, Sonia Rykiel and Diane von Furstenberg.

★ 10 AQUASIA, WEST

- Wyndham Grand London, Chelsea Harbour, SW10 0XG
- Tel: 020 7823 3000; www.wyndhamgrandlondon.co.uk
- Fulham Broadway
- £

Don a polo shirt and smart slacks, or a tea dress and pearls for an alfresco afternoon tea overlooking the exclusive Chelsea Harbour marina. In summer, sip a cool glass of champagne as you view marina yachts from a wooden decking terrace.

▼ EAST

BOGAYO

- 320 Old Street, EC1V 9DR
- Tel: 020 7012 1226; www.bogayo.com
- Old Street
- £–££

The menu serves fish and chips and pesto penne, as if the chef can't decide. But Bogayo is largely a traditional Moroccan restaurant in decor and cuisine – mains include a fish dish with artichoke hearts, mushrooms and saffron rice. Tea is served in ornate golden teapots; just make sure you don't splutter when the belly dancer starts dropping her hips on a Friday and Saturday night. If you need to cool down, leave your Moroccan tent and smoke a hookah pipe outside on the terrace.

CAMPANIA GASTRONOMIA

- 95 Columbia Road, Bethnal Green, E2 7RG
- Tel: 020 7613 0015; www.campaniagastronomia.com
- Old Street, then bus 8, 26, 48, 55, 388
- £

This compact Italian restaurant seats just 25, so it soon fills up. The single seats near the window suit lone diners; groups should get here early to bag the deli's only communal table. The menu changes daily, but you can expect homemade pizza, cheeseboards with grapes and a platter of Italian meats. From the deli, choose marinated aubergine, sun-dried tomatoes and fresh buffalo mozzarella. The decor is as authentic as the menu: with its wooden floorboards, blackboards and hunks of meat hanging from the ceiling, crack open a bottle from Naples and you could be in southern Italy.

COOKE JELLIED EELS

- 9 Broadway Market, London Fields, E8 4PH
- Tel: 020 7254 6458
- London Fields
- £

This pie 'n' mash shop has been selling jellied eels since it was established in 1862, and it's been on the same premises since 1900. With its original tiling, traditional sign and canteen-style benches, it's not just the food that still has an old-school feel.

E PELLICCI

- 332 Bethnal Green Road, Bethnal Green, E2 0AG
- Tel: 020 7739 4873
- Bethnal Green
- £

Looking for a proper cockney caff? Then you've found it, mate – this East End taxi-driver hangout couldn't be more authentic, with its greasy fry-ups, black pudding, chip butties and steak pies. Yet, while the cuisine – sorry, food – is as far from fine dining as you can get, the interior isn't as down at heel as some of the surrounding takeaways. Fifties plastic ketchup bottles adorn the (cramped) tables, but you won't see a grease-spattered extractor fan here; instead, wooden panelling and decorative tiling dating from 1900 cover the walls.

LAXEIRO

- 93 Columbia Road, Bethnal Green, E2 7RG
- Tel: 020 7729 1147; www.laxeiro.co.uk
- Old Street, then bus 8, 26, 48, 55, 388
- £–££

This family-run Spanish restaurant has been at its current location, at one end of Columbia Road, for about 20 years. It's cosy, warm, lively and busy – if you find that the tables are too crammed inside, there may be an empty table on the pavement. The speciality is its seafood paella, with oversized, succulent prawns, the rice the colour of saffron. The decor is as authentic as the food, with terracotta walls, wine bottles on the ceiling and the scent of lemons in the air.

LE TAJ

- 96 Brick Lane, E1 6RU
- Tel: 020 7247 0733; www.letaj.co.uk
- Aldgate East
- £–££

This stylish, busy restaurant has two menus, one Indian and one Bangla, both of which have a few unusual options, such as *sat kora* – a chicken curry with a citrus flavour – and *tawg murgh* – a stir-fry made with chicken, peppers and onions, which is served on a *tava* (a flat cooking utensil which gives the dish more flavour). Attention to detail shows in the presentation of the dishes, which aren't too oily. Le Taj offers good value for money, and the 'bring your own' option reduces your bill further; the restaurant provides discount vouchers from a nearby off-licence, too, as an added bonus.

LMNT

- 316 Queensbridge Road, Hackney, E8 3NH
- Tel: 020 7249 6727; www.lmnt.co.uk
- Dalston Kingsland BR, London Fields BR
- £

This restaurant, with its Cleopatra statues, faux gold tombs and Egyptian sphinx fireplaces, would fit in well with the decadent restaurants of the West End – and yet it's in Hackney. Despite its over-the-top decor and the classical opera that plays, LMNT still has East End prices. The menu throws up a few surprises. To start, try the roast wood pigeon with cauliflower purée and mushroom jus; for your main, the confit of duck, served with potato rosti, pak choi and a sweet plum sauce will hit the spot. Book ahead if you want to sit in one of the restaurant's five theatre balconies.

LOTUS FLOATING RESTAURANT

- 38 Limeharbour, Inner Millwall Dock, E14 9RH
- Tel: 020 7515 6445; www.lotusfloating.co.uk
- Crossharbour DLR
- £–££

This two-tier floating restaurant serves cuisine from three of the most famous provinces of China. Try a spicy dish from Sichuan, such as Szechuan hot and sour soup; steamed dumplings stuffed with pork, prawns or chives from Guangdong; or, if there's a few of you, a whole roasted duck, cooked Beijing-style. Feeling adventurous? Then ditch your British reserve and go for chicken claws in black bean sauce (they extract the fingernails first), or jellyfish flavoured with sesame.

PLATEAU

- 4th floor, Canada Place, Docklands, E14 5ER
- Tel: 020 7715 7100; www.plateaurestaurant.co.uk
- Canary Wharf
- ££

Even though it's only on the fourth floor, diners can enjoy panoramic views of Dockland skyscrapers and the sculptures of Canada Square Park through the all-glass walls of this bar and grill. The decor, with its glass ceiling, cool grey carpet and white marble tables, is as futuristic as its surrounds. As for the menu, while there are no surprises, it does satisfy, with mains such as pork-belly confit and prawns in a charcoal oil emulsion. The tarot reader on Thursday evenings provides an interesting interlude.

SAF

- 152–4 Curtain Road, Shoreditch, EC2A 3AT
- Tel: 020 7613 0007; www.safrestaurant.co.uk
- Old Street
- £–££

This restaurant serves Asian-inspired, organic, vegan food, and it's all served raw. Well, some of the dishes are cooked – but rarely above 48°C, so the flavour and nutrients of each ingredient are preserved. Flavour bursts from each dish, many of which contain 'nut cheese', which is made from nut milk. Try the betel leaves to start and your taste buds won't know what to think of its combination of fried shallots, creamy coconut, slightly tart pomelo and pomegranate and salty soy sauce. There are no typical mains on the menu, but the Thai green curry, flavoured with lychee, gives you a clue about what to expect. Book ahead if you want to sit at the chef's table, where you can watch your meal being prepared.

SHISH

- 313–19 Old Street, EC1V 9LE
- Tel: 020 7749 0990; www.shish.com
- Old Street
- £–££

On the ground floor, this light and spacious restaurant and lounge bar on the corner of Old Street serves kebab and couscous dishes in front of an open kitchen. Downstairs, in the lounge bar, belly-dancing classes for beginners are held on the last Sunday of every month. The class is followed by a show by the shimmying BellyBliss Allstars, who mix their Eastern moves with Western hip hop and sword balancing. There are also branches in Bayswater and Willesden Green.

TAY DO

- 65 Kingsland Road, E2 8AG
- Tel: 020 7729 722
- Dalston Kingsland BR, then bus 26, 55, 67, 149, 242, 243; Old Street
- £

Tay Do stands out from its competitors along this stretch of Kingsland Road, for its authentic Vietnamese cuisine at low prices. It's always a good sign when you see Vietnamese eating in a Vietnamese restaurant, and here they're queuing with locals out the door and down the street. So take your own bottle of booze and head here for roast duck soba noodles with pak choi, caramelized catfish, spicy soft-shell crab and won ton soup, which will be brought to your table almost before you've had the chance to take off your coat. It's not perfect: while the buzzing crowds create a lively atmosphere, you might feel rushed, the staff has a habit of forgetting your order and the decor is more greasy spoon than fancy restaurant. Still, you'll leave feeling full and with change from a tenner.

TREACLE

- 110–12 Columbia Road, E2 7RG
- Tel: 020 7729 5657; www.treacleworld.com
- Old Street, then bus 8, 26, 48, 55, 388
- £

A typically English tea room, Treacle sells endless mugs of tea to accompany a selection of jazzy iced fairy cakes. It's also a shop, so you can buy china tea sets and other kitchen paraphernalia.

▼ WEST

BEACH BLANKET BABYLON

- 🕦 45 Ledbury Road, W11 2AA
- ✆ Tel: 020 7229 2907; www.beachblanket.co.uk
- ⊖ Notting Hill Gate
- 💷 ££–£££

Swinging bridges, spiral staircases and brick tunnels guide you under arches and through elaborate grottoes to your candle-lit table in this Georgian mansion, which seats about 160 over three floors. The cuisine can be patchy but, as long as don't compare the dishes to Michelin-starred ones, you'll enjoy your meal. There's also a branch in Shoreditch.

BIBENDUM

- 🕦 Michelin House, 81 Fulham Road, SW3 6RD
- ✆ Tel: 020 7581 5817; www.bibendum.co.uk
- ⊖ South Kensington
- 💷 ££–£££

Bibendum has been serving French–British cuisine in Michelin House since Sir Terence Conran took over the Michelin Tyre headquarters 23 years ago, turning it from a garage into a fine dining restaurant for 100. Many of the original art nouveau fixtures still exist, most notably three large stained glass windows featuring the Michelin man. Dishes include escargots, steak au poivre and roast pheasant with game crêpinette. For a meal lighter on the waistline, but not on the wallet, visit the more informal Oyster Bar downstairs.

BUONA SERA AT THE JAM

- 🕦 289a Kings Road, SW3 5EW
- ✆ Tel: 020 7352 8827
- ⊖ Sloane Square, South Kensington
- 💷 £

It's the seating that makes this place special; get there early if you want the novelty of climbing a ladder to your table. Steak, salad and pasta are on the menu – the seafood spaghetti is popular.

CAFE GLOSS

- 🕦 34 Kensington Church Street, W8 4HA
- ✆ Tel: 020 7938 4781
- ⊖ High Street Kensington
- 💷 £

This is a delightful place to read the papers over a slice of gooey fudge cake. There's just one sofa plus seats for 30 in the back room. Don't forget to look up – the ceiling is ornately painted, as the cafe was once an antique shop.

EXPLORE: FOODIE ROADS

Not sure which restaurant to pick? Head to one of the streets below, all of which have a great selection of eateries that cater for most budgets.

▶ Upper Street N1, north, Angel, Highbury & Islington

▶ Stoke Newington Church Street N16, north, Stoke Newington BR

▶ Old York Road SW18, south, Wandsworth Town BR

▶ Clapham High Street SW4, south, Clapham Common

▶ Northcote Road SW11, south, Clapham Junction BR

▶ Brick Lane E1, east, Aldgate East

▶ Chiswick High Road W4, west, Chiswick Park

▶ King's Road SW6, west, Sloane Square

▶ St James's Street W1, central, Bond Street

▶ Charlotte Street W1T, central, Goodge Street

THE HUMMINGBIRD BAKERY

- ❶ 47 Old Brompton Road, South Kensington, SW7 3JP
- ⊕ Tel: 020 7584 0055; www.hummingbirdbakery.com
- ◉ South Kensington
- ❶ £

It's a shame there are so few seats, as it would make a lovely place to while away an afternoon. Still, the snazzy cupcakes, each with a good inch of icing swirled on top, keep the customers coming, even if they have to eat their cake while standing. There are also branches on Portobello Road and Old Brompton Road.

JACOB'S

- ❶ 20 Gloucester Road, SW7 4RB
- ⊕ Tel: 020 7581 9292
- ◉ Gloucester Road
- ❶ £

There's a homely, welcoming and relaxed feel to this Armenian restaurant. While the owner is Armenian, the manager is Iranian, which is reflected in the decor: both *samovar* (old Iranian teapots) and pictures of Armenian churches adorn the walls. The cuisine, too, is a blend of cultures – expect Armenian beef casserole, kebabs and lamb wrapped in cabbage (an old Iranian family recipe).

NAPKET

- ❶ 342 Kings Road, Chelsea, SW3 5UR
- ✆ Tel: 020 7352 9832; www.napket.com
- ◉ Sloane Square
- ❸ £–££

It looks like a glamorous jewellery shop from the outside, but it's actually a casual cafe/restaurant, painted black, with fresh roses and iPods on the tables. A selection of light bites or, in their words, 'snob food', is available, such as panini and salads made with pomegranate, figs and Gorgonzola. There are three other London branches in Mayfair, Piccadilly and the City.

OTTOLENGHI

- ❶ 63 Ledbury Road, W11 2AD
- ✆ Tel: 020 7727 1121; www.ottolenghi.co.uk
- ◉ Westbourne Park, Notting Hill Gate
- ❸ £–££

The first of four branches, all of which are popular for their mouth-watering pastries, savoury tarts, soups and salads, as well as for their rich hot chocolate. This family-friendly mediterranean restaurant also serves a selection of pasta dishes, though its worth trying the roasted lamb with pistachio, orange blossom and mint instead. There's a deli area, too, so you can buy mediterranean staples to recreate your favourite dishes at home.

PARADISE BY WAY OF KENSAL GREEN

- ❶ 19 Kilburn Lane, W10 4AE
- ✆ Tel: 020 8969 0098; www.theparadise.co.uk
- ◉ Kensal Green, Ladbroke Grove
- ❸ ££

Exposed floorboards, floor-to-ceiling bookshelves and stag heads mounted on the wall characterize this elegant, high-end gastropub. The spacious dining room, with its faux gilt French furniture, is glamorous and feminine – perfect for a girly afternoon trying the knickerbocker glory, crème brûlée and sticky toffee pudding. Typical mains include skate with capers and spinach, and lamb with mixed beans and lavender essence – they also do a good Sunday lunch, which is popular with locals. On a warm night, take a seat in the courtyard garden, or on the roof terrace.

FOODIE TIP

Make like John and Yoko and stay in bed all day. Call **Brunch Bed** (07527 049 327; www.brunchbed.com), which does exactly what it says on the tin – they'll bring your brunch to your bed. They'll deliver croissants, muffins, omelettes, sandwiches and juice. Delivery is to west London only.

10 BEST INDIAN RESTAURANTS

Whatever your budget, you're bound to be satisfied by these Indian, Pakistani and Bangladeshi restaurants, whether you want a quick curry after work or to linger over a buffet.

★ 1 BELASH, NORTH

- ❶ 53 Topsfield Parade, Tottenham Lane, Crouch End, N8 8PT
- ☏ Tel: 020 8340 9513
- ❷ Hornsey BR, bus 41, 91, W5
- ❸ £

This Indian restaurant stands out for its wide selection of tasty, not-too-oily dishes, such as the tandoori chicken, cooked in a clay oven, and *aloo gobi* (cauliflower and potato), which has a strong, smoky flavour. You'll find yourself finishing every dish, regardless of how full you are. Belash gives a nod to interior design: faux golden balconies overlook diners and its seats are separated by wooden screens, which ensure an element of privacy.

★ 2 CHUTNEYS, CENTRAL

- ❶ 124 Drummond Street, NW1 2PA
- ☏ Tel: 020 7388 0604
- ❷ Euston Square
- ❸ £

Chutneys offers great value for money, friendly waiters and a calm, relaxed feel. Both veggies and carnivores will be satisfied with their wide selection of 'roadside snacks' and south Indian vegetarian dishes. The lunchtime buffet is particularly popular; for under £10 you can eat as much curry, dhal, fragrant rice and salad as you want, as well as dessert – try the gulabjamun (sweet semolina balls in syrup).

★ 3 MIRCH MASALA, SOUTH

- ❶ 213 Upper Tooting Road, SW17 7TG
- ☏ Tel: 020 8767 8638; www.mirchmasalarestaurant.co.uk
- ❷ Tooting Bec
- ❸ £

This bright pink, chaotic Indian restaurant is always packed with locals. Still, you'll be seated and served quickly. If you're after an Indian with ambience, this isn't it, but it does offer a wide selection of meat and fish dishes, such as *bhindi gosht* (lamb with okra). Vegetarians should try the tomato-based *karahi*, made with Quorn. If you're dining on a budget, there's the added bonus of BYO.

★ 4 NOUVELLE SPICE, SOUTH

- ❶ 315 New Cross Road, SE14 6AS
- ☏ Tel: 020 8691 6644; www.nouvellespice.co.uk
- ❷ New Cross BR, New Cross Gate BR
- ❸ £

Every diner at this Indian restaurant will tell you the same things: excellent value, generous portions, consistently high-quality dishes and outstanding service. There's a wide selection of dishes, too, all of which are well-presented and not too spicy or oily – try the pumpkin masala with roasted sesame seeds, or the shatkora lamb, served in a rich citrus sauce. Added bonus: it's BYO, with no corkage fee.

★ 5 CLIFTON, EAST

- *1 Whitechapel Road, Tower Hamlets, E1 6TY*
- *Tel: 020 7377 5533; www.cliftonrestaurant.com*
- *Aldgate East*
- *£–££*

Like its sister restaurant, Shampan, which brought Indian, Bangladeshi and Pakistani cuisine to Brick Lane in the 1950s, Clifton is popular for its varied menu. The menu is divided into regional dishes – try the chicken kofta from south India, or Pakistani *palak gosh*, made with chicken, lamb and spinach. There are a few surprises, too, such as duck tikka, cooked over charcoal. Huge floor-to-ceiling windows drench this place in natural light, making the spacious restaurant bar (150 seats over two floors) seem bigger than it already is. An open kitchen, carved pine mural and the stainless-steel ventilation pipes which snake round the lights add style.

★ 6 TAYYABS, EAST

- *83–9 Fieldgate Street, E1 1JU*
- *Tel: 020 7247 6400; www.tayyabs.co.uk*
- *Whitechapel*
- *£*

This cheap Pakistani restaurant opened in 1974. Yet word didn't spread until just a few years ago, probably because of its out-of-the-way location. Still, this hasn't put off the lively hordes that visit for its fiery tandoori grills, spicy kebabs and soft, fluffy naan bread. The 'dry meat' curry, their hottest dish, might not sound so appealing, but its name comes from its preparation: the lamb is cooked until most of the thick onion and ginger sauce has been absorbed, leaving the lamb moist, but not swimming in sauce. The menu's focus on protein-laden dishes means fewer vegetarian options, although the thick, soupy *tarka dahl*, made with lentils, garlic, spices and tomato, is recommended. A refurbishment in 2005 brought the decor up to the same high standards as the food. It's BYO – with no corkage fee.

★ 7 BRILLIANT, WEST

- *72–6 Western Road, Southall, Middlesex, UB2 5DZ*
- *Tel: 020 8574 1928; www.brilliantrestaurant.com*
- *Hounslow West, then bus H32*
- *£–££*

This smart, family-run restaurant beats its nearby competition and rightly deserves its reputation for high-quality Punjabi cuisine (with a Kenyan twist). So, it's no wonder Gordon Ramsay chose Brilliant to learn how to use a clay oven for his *Cookalong* show. The service is attentive and the waiters have a sense of humour. Bollywood films and cricket on TV provide further entertainment. Portions are big, so order less than you think you need. Start with *aloo tikki*, a combination of chickpeas, tamarind, yoghurt and coriander; then plump for methi chicken, which has tender pieces of chicken in a rich, spicy sauce. Save room for some *kulfi*, handmade onsite. As a bonus, it's licensed, unlike others in the area.

★ 8 CHULA, WEST

- 116 King Street, W6 0QP
- Tel: 020 8748 1826;
  www.chularestaurant.co.uk
- Hammersmith
- £

World music creates a calm, relaxed vibe here – so relaxed, in fact, that there's an area at the back where you take your shoes off and sit cross-legged on cushions, at knee-high tables. The four booths offer intimate, romantic seating. But it's not just the decor that makes Chula popular, diners come here for its variety of well-presented Indian/Bangladeshi fusion dishes. The menu includes a few surprises: cress and pomegranate pastries served with sweet chilli sauce make a change from the usual poppadoms-and-chutney starter. For a main, the duck phoora (duck breast marinated in garlic and ginger, served with yoghurt) is an unusual choice – or try the badami chicken, cooked in thick almond gravy, with a side of lemon and cashew rice. Service is friendly, flirty and a little disorganized.

★ 9 THE QUILON RESTAURANT AND BAR, CENTRAL

- 41 Buckingham Gate, SW1E 6AF
- Tel: 020 7821 1899;
  www.thequilon.co.uk
- St James's Park
- £££

Both Quilon and Bombay Brasserie share the same owner (Taj Hotels), so it was only a matter of time before Quilon earned a Michelin

star, which it received in 2008. It specializes in innovative coastal Indian cuisine – so an emphasis on seafood, flavoured with coconut, tamarind and lemon is to be expected. Colourful chargrilled prawns flavoured with lime and chilli comes recommended, as does the cod roasted in banana leaf. If you haven't yet had your fill of coconut, try the bibinca for dessert – a flan made from coconut milk, with a hint of nutmeg.

★ 10 CINNAMON CLUB, CENTRAL

- The Old Westminster Library,
  30–2 Great Smith Street,
  SW1P 3BU
- Tel: 020 7222 2555;
  www.cinnamonclub.com
- St James's Park, Westminster
- ££–£££

Set in the Grade II-listed Old Westminster Library, original features, such as domed skylights and shelves of dusty books, lend a grand colonial feel to this otherwise contemporary Anglo– Indian restaurant. Downstairs is the Cinnamon Club bar, where you can sip a pre-dinner Bollywood passion martini or sake by the glass. Come at lunch and you may spot a politician you recognize trying regional dishes such as Rajasthani sangri beans, served with fenugreek and raisins, followed by innovative desserts, such as pear William poached with anise, pomegranate and mint jelly. Unusually, the Cinnamon Club also serves breakfast; rice pancakes with lentil broth, or spiced scrambled eggs are served by slow, yet polite, waiters.

SHOPPING & MARKETS

You go to Milan for shoes and Hong Kong for tailor-made suits. But where do you go if you want an antique bottle stopper, three-tier afternoon-tea cake stand or, should you want them, long johns? More unusual requests may take several days' worth of Tube relay – but in London, you will find them.

▼ CENTRAL

ALFIE'S ANTIQUE MARKET

- *13–25 Church Street, Marylebone, NW8 8DT*
- *Tel: 020 7723 6066; www.alfiesantiques.com*
- *Edgware Road, Marylebone*

Over 100 antique dealers are housed in this art deco building. Items on sale vary from coins and medals to old radios, teddy bears and perfume bottles. Among the more unusual dealers are Dodo, specializing in vintage posters, signs and bric-a-brac, and Tony Durante, which has a selection of wedding dresses from the 1920s. There's a restaurant on the top floor with a rooftop terrace.

BLACK TRUFFLE

- *52 Warren Street, W1T 5NJ*
- *Tel: 020 7388 4547, 020 7923 9450 (P & M School); www.blacktruffle.co.uk*
- *Warren Street*

Black Truffle, which has a second branch in London Fields, sells men's, women's and children's shoes, bags, gifts, jewellery and homeware. If you're looking for something different, this is the place to pick up a vegan bag, trilby hat or patterned raincoat. And kids will love their handmade children's shoes. To top it all off, if you have a strong desire to learn how to make a tutu (or corsets, hats, shoes or bags, for that matter), sign up to one of the courses at the Prescott & Mackay School of Fashion and Accessory Design, which is in the same building.

BOROUGH MARKET

- *Green Dragon Court (off Borough High Street), Southwark, SE1 1TL*
- *Tel: 020 7407 1002; www.boroughmarket.org.uk*
- *London Bridge*
- *Thur 11am–5pm; Fri 12pm–6pm; Sat 8am–5pm*

The 4.5-acre spot under the bridge next to Southwark Cathedral (see p.218) has been home to one of London's most popular open-air markets since it opened in 1999, although a market has been on or near this site since 1014. Over 10,000 tourists and locals visit each week – so go early if you want to avoid the stampede. Many of the stalls offer free samples (cheese, bread, brownies) and it's all so yummy you won't resist buying no matter how big your breakfast was.

BRUNSWICK SQUARE

- ❶ *The Brunswick Centre, Marchmont Street, WC1N 1AE*
- ⊕ *Tel: 020 7833 6066; www.brunswick.co.uk*
- ⊘ *Russell Square*
- ▢ *Sat 11am–5pm*

This modern shopping centre and Saturday market is tucked away in the central courtyard of an Eldorado-style apartment block, directly opposite Russell Square tube station. The shops are all chains, with the exception of Chocolat Chocolat (020 7833 4121), which sells enormous truffles as well as polka-dot teapots, vintage biscuit tins and pretty cake stands. Still, it's worth a visit for its Saturday market. There are about 20 stalls, selling items such as crêpes, homemade cakes, second-hand books and bohemian clothes.

BURLINGTON ARCADE

- ❶ *Mayfair, W1*
- ⊕ *Tel: 020 7493 1764; www.burlington-arcade.co.uk*
- ⊘ *Piccadilly Circus, Green Park*

Passing this covered shopping arcade, you'd never guess it has had such a dramatic history since it opened in 1819. It survived a fire in 1936, World War II bombs and a smash-and-grab robbery by thieves driving a Jaguar at high speed into the arcade. Thank goodness the mall has the Beadles to look after it. They guard the walkway, dressed in Edwardian coats and gold-plaited top hats, refusing entry to rif-raf. These days the arcade is still lined with elegant shops selling antiques, expensive jewellery, Church's shoes and Ladurée macaroons. *Insider info: no. 42 is said to be haunted by a poltergeist, known as Percy.*

CABBAGES AND FROCKS

- ❶ *St Marylebone Parish Church, Marylebone High Street, W1*
- ⊕ *Tel: 020 7794 1636; www.cabbagesandfrocks.co.uk*
- ⊘ *Baker Street*
- ▢ *Sat 11am–5pm*

Since 2006, 40 stalls have been selling a mix of organic produce, such as fine breads and the ubiquitous brownies, as well as crafts, trinkets and jewellery in the compact grounds of St Marylebone Parish Church. Look out for Marie Spector, who sells her semi-precious handcrafted jewellery here, as well as in the Tate Modern. The market specializes in nearly new designer women's clothes, so you might find half-price Jimmy Choos or worn-once Prada designs.

CLAIRE ARISTIDES JEWELLERY SCHOOL

- *Unit 2.11, Kingly Court, Carnaby Street, W1B 5PW*
- *Tel: 020 7434 2161; www.clairearistides.com*
- *Oxford Circus*
- *£125 daytime workshop; £20–60 evening classes*

This shop sells contemporary jewellery by Australian jewellery designer Claire Aristides (necklaces start at £60). It also runs jewellery-making workshops, where you can either bring in your own beads or stones or pick from a selection in the shop to make accessories.

CRAFT CENTRAL

- *33–5 St John's Square, EC1M 4DS*
- *Tel: 020 7251 0276; www.craftcentral.org.uk*
- *Farringdon*

Craft Central sells individual pieces of art from textiles, fashion and furniture to ceramic vases and jewellery. It also hosts regular art exhibitions and unusual events, such as 'How to Make a Fresco', and you can visit their working studios twice a year. There's a second, smaller branch on Clerkenwell Green.

DAUNT BOOKS

- *83–4 Marylebone High Street, W1U 4QW*
- *Tel: 020 7224 2295; www.dauntbooks.co.uk*
- *Baker Street, Bond Street*

Natural light from the conservatory ceiling sweeps through the oak galleries in this Edwardian bookshop, which dates from 1910. It specializes in travel guides and literature, so shelves are arranged by country – sometimes by region. Daunt mainly stocks new titles, but second-hand books can be found on the balconies. There are also branches in Belsize Park, Hampstead, Holland Park and Chelsea.

DOVER STREET MARKET

- *17–18 Dover Street, W1S 4LT*
- *Tel: 020 7518 0680; www.doverstreetmarket.com*
- *Green Park*

This six-storey building stocks independent, rare labels and up-and-coming designers. Look out for Silly Thing from Hong Kong, Supreme from New York and Dior Homme. The decor – concrete floors, exposed pipes and corrugated iron – is as eclectic as the clothing. There's a patisserie on the top floor.

EXMOUTH MARKET

- *Exmouth Market, Clerkenwell, EC1R 4QP*
- *Tel: 020 7837 1861; www.exmouth-market.com*
- *Angel, Farringdon*
- *Wed–Fri 11am–2.30pm*

Considering its location, just a five-minute walk from Angel or Farringdon, few people know of this hidden pedestrianized street, lined with independent shops selling records, furniture and handmade bags. At the far end, close to Mount Pleasant sorting office, there's a small artisan market that sells food and crafts.

FAMILY TREE

- 🛈 53 Exmouth Market, EC1R 4QL
- ⊕ Tel: 020 7278 1084; www.familytreeshop.co.uk
- ⊖ Angel, Farringdon

Taking inspiration from their Japanese background, the designers at Family Tree create lighting, furniture and jewellery. Items include hand-printed lamps made from *washi* (Japanese rice paper) and patterned owl cushions. The shop also sells products created by local designers and items collected from around the world.

FORTNUM & MASON

- 🛈 181 Piccadilly, W1A 1ER
- ⊕ Tel: 020 7734 8040; www.fortnumandmason.com
- ⊖ Piccadilly Circus, Green Park

If you're after ingredients for a quintessentially British picnic, then join the tourists to stock up on strawberry jam, smoked salmon and cheese crackers.

GAY'S THE WORD

- 🛈 66 Marchmont Street, WC1N 1AB
- ⊕ Tel: 020 7278 7654; www.gaystheword.co.uk
- ⊖ Russell Square

This compact independent bookshop sells books for the lesbian, gay and transgender market. Here you'll find a mix of new and second-hand fiction and non-fiction, such as plays, academic books on gender studies and books on coming out. It also sells DVDs and has information on the local gay community.

GRAYS

- 🛈 58 Davies Street, W1K 5LP; 1–7 Davies Mews, W1K 5AB
- ⊕ Tel: 020 7629 7034; www.graysantiques.com
- ⊖ Bond Street
- ▦ Mon–Fri 10am–6pm

This antique market is housed in two locations within the same Grade II-listed building, in the former offices of a toilet manufacturer of all places. Doormen open the door as you enter the market, where you'll find 200 dealers selling jewellery, vintage clothes and rare, signed and antique books. You can also browse artefacts from around the globe, such as a tortoiseshell and gold lacquer comb-and-pin set dating from the Japanese Meiji era (1868–1912). Continuing with the Oriental theme, a stream running from Hampstead to the Thames passes through the basement of Gray's Mews; it's full of plump goldfish.

EXPLORE: BELGRAVIA

- Elizabeth Street, Belgravia, SW1W
- www.inbelgravia.com
- Sloane Square, Victoria

Head to Elizabeth Street, home of the 'bespoke' cliché, if you want tailor-made goods. For those of you with money to burn, you can design your own jewellery, perfume, clothes and hats (*see* **Philip Treacy**, p.120). You can also buy custom-made sweets, although chocoholics will already know about **The Chocolate Society** at no. 36 (020 8743 1325; www.chocolate.co.uk).

HOPE AND GREENWOOD

- *1 Russell Street, Covent Garden, WC2B 5JD*
- *Tel: 020 7240 3314; www.hopeandgreenwood.co.uk*
- *Covent Garden*

If you have a craving for boiled sweets, cola cubes, Refreshers or Drumsticks, then head for H & G. Or perhaps you'd prefer some truffles? They have those, too, but not in your normal flavours – try the Earl Grey and lemon.

IRREGULAR CHOICE

- *39 Carnaby Street, Soho, W1F 7DT*
- *Tel: 020 7494 4811; www.irregularchoice.co.uk*
- *Oxford Circus*

If you want a pair of heels that will get people talking (whether they like them or not), choose from the Japanese-inspired split-toe designs, boots which look like they've been made from kids' pyjamas or shoes with gremlins printed on them.

JAMES SMITH & SONS (UMBRELLAS) LTD

- *53 New Oxford Street, WC1A 1BL*
- *Tel: 020 7836 4731; www.james-smith.co.uk*
- *Tottenham Court Road, Holborn*

James Smith & Sons was established in 1830 and looks like it hasn't had a refurb since. This is no bad thing. With its wooden floorboards and black-and-white photographs showing each stage of the umbrella-making process, this shop oozes character and charm. The staff, too, seem to be from another era, with their public-school accents, impeccable manners and service and knowledge of their craft. The shop specializes in umbrellas and walking sticks and nothing else.

MAGMA

- *117–19 Clerkenwell Road, Clerkenwell, EC1R 5BY*
- *Tel: 020 7242 9503; www.magmabooks.com*
- *Farringdon*

There's a strong emphasis on design at Magma, which sells style magazines, comics and some European children's books. You'll also find books devoted to cartoons, graffiti, architecture and film that you might not find elsewhere, all housed in a suitably trendy interior. There's another branch in Covent Garden.

THE OLD CURIOSITY SHOP

- 📍 13–14 Portsmouth Street, WC2A 2ES
- 📞 Tel: 020 7405 9891; www.curiosityuk.com
- Ⓔ Holborn

Built in 1567, this quaint little shop is so old and warped with time, it looks like it's about to fall down. But that simply adds to its charm, as do its winding staircases and wooden floorboards. Daita Kimura creates most of the shop's unisex footwear by hand in the workshop downstairs. The footwear ranges from £100 to £400. Take a look at the great display items – there's the Big Foot for Smelly Foot, with a wide toe with a cork in it that you can pull out to cool down your feet, and Hog Toe Cat, with a square toe and fur footprints.

PHONICA

- 📍 51 Poland Street, Soho, W1F 7LZ
- 📞 Tel: 020 7025 6070; www.phonicarecords.com
- Ⓔ Oxford Circus

There are lots of record shops in Soho, but this one has the most character. Near the window is a rundown leather sofa, retro chairs and two transparent swing chairs you can curl up in. It has records from every genre imaginable. Pick a record and listen to it on one of the eight available record players.

PIMLICO ROAD MARKET

- 📍 Orange Square (on the corner of Pimlico Road and Ebury Street), Westminster, SW1W 8LP
- 📞 Tel: 020 7833 0338 (London Farmers' Markets); www.lfm.org.uk
- Ⓔ Sloane Square
- ▦ Sat 9am–1pm

Since 2002, there's been a large farmer's market held in Orange Square, a leafy courtyard close to Sloane Square.

EXPLORE: MARYLEBONE

Ⓔ Baker Street, Bond Street, Marylebone

Upmarket Marylebone is best known for its high street, which is lined with smart cafes and shops. Church Street, off Lisson Grove, is quieter and has a number of antique shops, such as **Andrew Nebbett Antiques** (020 7723 2303; www.andrewnebbett.com).

PLAYLOUNGE

- 𝑖 *19 Beak Street, W1F 9RP*
- ⊕ *Tel: 020 7287 7073; www.playlounge.co.uk*
- ◉ *Oxford Circus, Piccadilly Circus*

This shop fuses art and design with toys, so it's a great place for presents. Here you'll find action figures, gadgets, comics, T-shirts and Astro Boy books.

ROYAL MILE WHISKIES

- 𝑖 *3 Bloomsbury Street, WC1B 3QE*
- ⊕ *Tel: 020 7436 4763; www.royalmilewhiskies.com*
- ◉ *Tottenham Court Road*

This specialist whisky shop sells 800 different types of whisky. The most popular is the Old Pulteney from Wick, with hints of apple, vanilla, oak, chocolate and battenberg cake. You can sample some of the whiskies on sale in the shop; but if you're serious about tasting or want to learn more about the drink, sign up to their evening tasting events. The shop also sells a range of rum and cigars.

STANFORDS

- 𝑖 *12–14 Long Acre, Covent Garden, WC2E 9LP*
- ⊕ *Tel: 020 7836 1321; www.stanfords.co.uk*
- ◉ *Covent Garden, Leicester Square*

If you're planning your next holiday, then this is the place to come. As well as travel guides and phrase books, it's got maps, globes and posters to inspire you.

STROMBOLI'S CIRCUS

- 𝑖 *Unit 1.5, Kingly Court, Carnaby Street, W1B 5PW*
- ⊕ *Tel: 020 7734 1978; www.circusvintage.com*
- ◉ *Oxford Circus*

Formerly known as Twinkled, this vintage shop sells a range of clothes, accessories, wallpaper and curtains from the 1950s, 1960s and 1970s. It also has a selection of 1950s-style telephones – you can order the colour you want.

TAYLOR OF OLD BOND STREET

- 𝑖 *74 Jermyn Street, St James's, SW1Y 6NP*
- ⊕ *Tel: 020 7930 5544; www.tayloroldbondst.co.uk*
- ◉ *Green Park, Piccadilly Circus*

Jeremiah Taylor, the great-grandfather of Taylor's current chairman, founded this shop in 1854, and there's still an old boys' club feel to the place. It specializes in men's grooming products, particularly shaving brushes, and sells traditional leather manicure sets, tortoiseshell combs and even cuticle manicure oil made from avocados. *Insider info: Bill Clinton once turned up with a police entourage and bodyguard, and Johnny Depp and Bruce Willis are regular clients.*

THE TEA HOUSE

- 15a Neal Street, Covent Garden, WC2H 9PU
- Tel: 020 7240 7539
- Covent Garden

Stacked with ornamental teapots, ornate teacups and saucers and packets of tea from all around the world, the window of The Tea House invites you to try and buy all sorts of flavours. It sells approximately 131 types of tea, varying from gunpowder green pearls and white monkey to the treasured Formosa oolong silvertip from Taiwan. Choose to buy some marzipan tea and you'll feel positively boring.

WEARDOWNEY GET-UP BOUTIQUE

- 9 Ashbridge Street, NW8 8DH
- Tel: 020 7725 9694; www.weardowney.com
- Marylebone

Housed in a converted pub, this boutique is owned by two former models. It sells a variety of modern handmade knits – anything from woolly boas, pashminas and dresses to pocket scarves – and hosts knitting classes for adults and kid's knitting parties (£125 for a course of six two-hour classes). All the yarn is sourced from the UK and is hand-dyed.

THE WINE LIBRARY

- 43 Trinity Square, EC3N 4DJ
- Tel: 020 7481 0415; www.winelibrary.co.uk
- Tower Hill

This independent wine merchant sells over 400 different types of wine. It also organizes informal blind tastings, where you get to try eight types of wine without knowing what they are, as well as tutored tastings, which are accompanied by an informative talk. Both events can be tailored to your budget.

EXPLORE: KINGLY COURT

- Carnaby Street, W1B 5PW
- Tel: 020 7333 8118; www.carnaby.co.uk
- Oxford Circus

Tucked away off Carnaby Street are 32 independent shops over three floors, all of which overlook the main courtyard. Considering it's so close to London's shopping Mecca, Oxford Street, it's refreshing to see so many individual shops, such as **Fur Coat No Knickers** (07814 002 295, www.furcoatnoknickers.co.uk, vintage clothes), **Lazy Oaf** (020 7287 2060, www.lazyoaf.com, printed T-shirts) and **All the Fun of the Fair** (020 7287 2303, www.allthefunofthefair.biz, haberdashery). Look out for handmade beaded jewellery, bird cages and novelty fairy cakes, too.

▼ NORTH

ALEXANDRA PALACE MARKET

- 🛈 Alexandra Palace, Muswell Hill, N10 3TG
- ✆ Tel: 020 8302 9010; www.weareccfm.com
- ☻ Finsbury Park, then bus W3, W7; Wood Green, then bus W3; Turnpike Lane
- ▦ Sun 10am–3pm

In 2005, 30 to 50 food stalls popped up in the grounds of Alexandra Palace. It's since won awards, and up to 2,000 people flock to the market every Sunday. As well as fruit from farms in Kent, local pork sausages, olives and handicrafts, stalls sell freshly prepared food (crêpes and toasted sandwiches, mainly), so you can stop for lunch. The market is occasionally held at Campsbourne School (Nightingale Lane, Haringey, N8 7AF) – check the website for details.

ARIA

- 🛈 Barnsbury Hall, Barnsbury Street, Islington, N1 1PN
- ✆ Tel: 020 7704 6222; www.ariashop.co.uk
- ☻ Highbury & Islington, Angel

This shop displays contemporary design products on wooden crates in the airy attic of Barnsbury Hall. Items range from Danish watches, pop-art Marmite jars and gnome tables by Philippe Starck to hammocks and doormats with ants crawling on them (not real ones, obviously). It also has an array of kitchen utensils you won't know what to do with. Need a break from shopping? The visit the small cafe on the ground floor.

CAMDEN PASSAGE MARKET

- 🛈 Camden Passage, Islington, N1 8EF
- ✆ Tel: 020 7359 0190; www.camdenpassageislington.co.uk
- ☻ Angel
- ▦ Wed 7am; Sat 7am antiques market; Thur 7am; Sun 7am general market

There's a number of permanent antique shops on this lane (see opposite), but on Wednesdays and Saturdays, there's a quaint outdoor market selling antique bric-a-brac – some of it's a bit tatty, but most of it's worth hunting through.

EXPLORE: MUSWELL HILL

- ☻ Bus 43, 102, 134, 234, 299

As it's not close to a tube station, few people bother making the trip to Muswell Hill, unless they live there or go with the hope of spotting a celebrity with a home in the area. But the village has enough to keep you occupied for an afternoon: cafes, restaurants, a cinema and independent clothes boutiques that particularly cater to yummy mummy types. There's a good view of London, too.

EXPLORE: ISLINGTON

◉ *Angel, Highbury & Islington*

The main thoroughfare, Upper Street, is a mix of boutiques and chains – among the trendy bars you'll find shops selling bespoke contemporary furniture (**David Scotcher**, 020 7354 4111), jewellery (**Dinny Hall**, 020 7704 1543; www.dinnyhall.co.uk) and clothes and gifts (**Oliver Bonas**, 020 7424 5305; www.oliverbonas.com). Close to Angel, just off the main road near the Tesco, is a paved alley called **Camden Passage** (020 7359 0190; www.camdenpassageislington.co.uk). Over 200 traders operate from the passage, many of whom sell antiques. Look out for the **African Waistcoat Company** (020 7704 9698; www.africanwaistcoatcompany.com).

COBBLED YARD

❶ *1 Bouverie Road (off Stoke Newington Church Street), N16 0AH*
⊕ *Tel: 020 8809 5286; www.cobbled-yard2.co.uk*
◉ *Angel, then bus 73, 476*

This antique-furniture showroom is housed in old stables with exposed beams and a cobbled yard outside. It specializes in pine and retro furniture, particularly coffee tables and lamps. You may well come across some more unusual items, however, such as a fairground carousel motorcycle or the contents of an old railway carriage. A second, larger showroom is opposite, which, in the 1950s, was a Jewish ballroom known as Bouverie Hall.

CROCODILE ANTIQUES

❶ *120–2 Muswell Hill Broadway, Muswell Hill, N10 3RU*
⊕ *Tel: 020 8444 0273; www.crocodileantiques.com*
◉ *Highgate, then bus 43, 134; East Finchley*

This gift shop has an array of handmade jewellery, cards, kids' toys, mirrors and lighting. Joined to the shop is an outdoor garden cafe with heaters, fairy lights and wooden garden furniture, and its wall is painted with a cartoon crocodile mural. On Tuesday mornings in summer, the garden hosts free singing and storytelling for children, and the kids can take home a balloon sculpture.

FLASHBACK

❶ *144 Crouch Hill, Crouch End, N8 9DX*
⊕ *Tel: 020 8342 9633 (Crouch End), 020 7354 9356 (Essex Road); www.flashback.co.uk*
◉ *Finsbury Park, then bus W7*

Following the success of its flagship shop on Essex Road, Islington, this second branch of Flashback opened in 2006. It sells vinyls and CDs of all kinds of music except classical. It exchanges vinyls, too, so whatever your vinyls sell for, you'll get 40 per cent back in cash, or 60 per cent in vouchers.

EXPLORE: HIGHGATE

⊘ Highgate

Best known for its cemetery (see p.206), Highgate village also has a few shops worth browsing – thrifty types will especially like the local charity shop, where you might pick up a designer cast-off.

MOTHER EARTH

ⓘ 5 Albion Parade, Albion Road, Stoke Newington, N16 9LD
☎ Tel: 020 7275 9099; www.motherearth-health.com
⊖ Angel, then bus 73, 476

This organic deli is expensive, but handy if you're in the area, because as well as selling herbal remedies, veggie sausages and oat cakes, it also does healthy fast food to take away – choose from fat Spanish omelettes, spinach tortillas and salad pots. There are two other branches: one near Newington Green and one close to Highbury & Islington tube station.

PARLIAMENT HILL MARKET

ⓘ William Ellis School, Highgate Road, NW5 1RN
☎ Tel: 020 7833 0338 (London Farmers' Markets); www.lfm.org.uk
⊖ Tufnell Park, Kentish Town
▦ Sat 10am–2pm

You're never far from a farmer's market in London; this one is held on Saturdays. Look out for the homemade pies and biodynamic honey.

PAUL A. YOUNG FINE CHOCOLATES

ⓘ 33 Camden Passage, Islington, N1 8EA
☎ Tel: 020 7424 5750; www.paulayoung.co.uk
⊖ Angel

All the chocolates are handmade on the premises – they're so fresh they must be eaten within five days. But you know the truffles you buy won't last that long once you're hit by the smell of bitter chocolate. It's hard to choose which ones to buy – Marmite, kalamansi or geranium? Flavours change weekly, sometimes daily. On Mother's Day, expect rose-flavoured treats; during winter, rhubarb is popular.

VIVIEN OF HOLLOWAY

ⓘ 4 The Arches, 49 Kentish Town Road, Camden, NW1 8NX
☎ Tel: 020 7284 2074; www.vivienofholloway.com
⊖ Camden Town

This shop, housed under an old railway arch, makes and sells a fantastic range of good-quality retro fashion. The limited-edition selection includes polka dot 1950s halter-neck dresses with nipped-in waists, big belts and petticoats, as well as men's rockabilly T-shirts – the rockers Led Zeppelin are fans. Girls, while you shop, your man can look at the retro motorcycles in the shop downstairs.

W. MARTYN

- 135 Muswell Hill Broadway, Muswell Hill, N10 3RS
- Tel: 020 8883 5642; www.wmartyn.co.uk
- Highgate, then bus 43, 134

Specializing in tea and coffee, this shop looks like it hasn't changed much since it was established in 1897 as there is still the original tiling in the entrance hallway and a 1930s coffee roaster in the window. It also sells dried fruit, mixed nuts, English jam and chutney.

THE WELL WALK POTTERY

- 49 Willow Road, Hampstead, NW3 1TS
- Tel: 020 7435 1046
- Hampstead

Christopher Magarshack has been creating and painting earthernware ceramics and pottery since 1957. His work is for sale in this family-run shop, on the corner of Gayton Road – five minutes' walk from Hampstead High Street. He also holds one-hour classes in which you can learn how to create stained glass and how to throw a pot (plates are more difficult, apparently). Call for prices.

WEMBLEY MARKET

- Wembley Stadium, Wembley, HA9 0DW
- Tel: 018 9563 2221; www.wembleymarket.co.uk
- Wembley Park
- Sun 9am–4pm

This enormous market, held in the car park of Wembley Stadium, has been going for 30 years. It now has over 500 stalls selling fresh produce, handicrafts and hot meals.

EXPLORE: STOKE NEWINGTON

- Angel, then bus 73, 476; Stoke Newington BR

A few years ago, Stoke Newington was up and coming, and creative types moved in; now its hip status is well and truly established. It does have a Nando's, but the rest of Stoke Newington Church Street is lined with vintage shops – **Ribbons & Taylor** (no. 157; 020 7254 4735; www.ribbonsandtaylor.co.uk), second-hand bookshops – **Ocean Books** (no. 127; 020 7502 6319) – and trendy kids' clothes boutiques – **Olive Loves Alfie** (no. 84; 020 7241 4212; www.olivelovesalfie.co.uk).

CAMDEN MARKET

What most people think of as Camden Market is actually four markets in one – Camden Lock Market, Stables Market, Inverness Street and Camden Market – all of which are rammed at the weekend. Over 500,000 visit each week to browse stalls selling leather coats and photos of London as well as those well-meaning traders who insist on washing your hands with salt. (*N.B. Opening times are approximate.*)

★ CAMDEN LOCK MARKET

❶ *(Off Chalk Farm Road), 4–6 Haven Street, Camden, NW1 8XJ*
☎ *Tel: 020 7485 5511; www.camdenlockmarket.com, www.camdenlock.net*
❖ *Camden Town, Chalk Farm*

Since it opened in 1973 around a canal lock, this market has gained a reputation for its independent stalls selling vintage jewellery, bohemian fashion and music that's hard to find elsewhere. Look out for **Robot** (020 7267 1271; www.iloverobotshop.com), which sells Lego-inspired jewellery and Scrabble tile T-shirts, and **House of Guadalupe** (www.houseofguadalupe.co.uk), for its colourful Mexican folk art.

★ STABLES MARKET

❶ *(Off Chalk Farm Road), Chalk Farm Road, Camden, NW1 8AH*
☎ *Tel: 020 7485 5511; www.stablesmarket.com*
❖ *Camden Town, Chalk Farm*

You'll find Stables Market halfway between Camden and Chalk Farm stations, parallel to Chalk Farm Road. The market gets its name from the horse hospital, which was built on the site in 1828 (the horses worked on the nearby railway). Look out for **Cyberdog** (www.shop.cyberdog.net) among the 450 shops – you can't really miss it, as it sells rave gear that looks like it's been designed by a child for an alien. If you're hungry, choose world cuisine from one of 50 food stalls; the quality can be hit or miss, but it's cheap enough.

★ CAMDEN MARKET/INVERNESS STREET MARKET

❶ *Camden High Street, NW1 8AH*
☎ *Tel: 020 7467 5787; www.camdenmarkets.org*
❖ *Camden Town, Chalk Farm*

Over 200 stalls selling slogan T-shirts, tartan Doc Martins and tutus line the narrow alleyways of this market, located just off Camden High Street. The quality of items varies; there are a few gems, but most traders sell bog-standard market junk teenagers convince themselves they need. Still, it's worth a hunt, especially if you're after a fancy-dress outfit. The smaller Inverness Street Market is directly opposite. Traditionally a fruit and veg market, some of the stalls now sell bags, clothes and 'leather' shoes.

▼ SOUTH

THE BOOKSHOP ON THE HEATH

- ❶ 74 Tranquil Vale, Blackheath, SE3 0BW
- ⊕ Tel: 020 8852 4786; www.bookshopontheheath.co.uk
- ◎ Blackheath BR

For the past 65 years, this dusty little bookshop has been selling rare and out-of-print books, comics and annuals, which is why the *Independent* voted it number five in the UK's top 100 bookshops in 2008. It specializes in fine first editions and has a range of books, maps and posters dedicated to London.

THE CHEESE BLOCK

- ❶ 69 Lordship Lane, East Dulwich, SE22 8EP
- ⊕ Tel: 020 8299 3636
- ◎ East Dulwich BR, then bus 40, 176, 185

This well-stocked deli feels like it's from another era. As well as cheese – Colston Basett blue stilton is a best-seller – fill your eco-friendly bag with handmade fudge, fresh olives and a selection of meat, jam and chutney.

EAST DULWICH DELI

- ❶ 15–17 Lordship Lane, East Dulwich, SE22 8EW
- ⊕ Tel: 020 8693 2525
- ◎ East Dulwich BR, then bus 40, 176, 185

Stepping into this deli is like going back in time – it looks like corner shops did a century ago. One of the two main rooms has floor-to-ceiling shelves stocked with hamper-style delicacies, such as hot mango sauce, cheese biscuits and olive oil. There is a cheese counter in another room and a room with a selection of wine.

ED

- ❶ 41 North Cross Road, East Dulwich, SE22 9ET
- ⊕ Tel: 020 8299 6938; www.dulwichtrader.com
- ◎ East Dulwich BR, then bus 40, 176, 185

After nearly two decades of trading, Ed is still going strong. Come here for retro homeware, books, cards and men's and women's clothes.

EXPLORE: EAST DULWICH

- ◎ East Dulwich BR, then bus 40, 176, 185

East Dulwich has one main road, Lordship Lane, lined with shops and eateries. It's popular with families picking up eco-friendly deals and arty one-offs.

ED WAREHOUSE INDOOR MARKET

- 🌑 *1 Zenoria Street, East Dulwich, SE22 8HP*
- ⊕ *Tel: 020 8693 3033; www.edwarehouse.co.uk*
- ◎ *East Dulwich BR*
- ▦ *Tues–Thur 10.30am–5.30pm; Fri & Sat 10am–6pm; Sun 11am–5pm*

There are about 25 stalls in this indoor market, including five tucked away in the upper gallery. It's a local, home-grown affair, with independent stalls selling natural soaps, handmade winter woollies and cheese. There's also a cafe, a small photographer's studio at the back and space to exhibit the work of local artists.

FRANKLINS FARM SHOP

- 🌑 *155 Lordship Lane, East Dulwich, SE22 8HX*
- ⊕ *Tel: 020 8693 3992; www.franklinsrestaurant.com*
- ◎ *East Dulwich BR, then bus 40, 176, 185*

While not all of Franklins' produce is organic, much is locally sourced, mostly from Kent and Sussex. If you ask, the manager will tell you exactly which farm your ingredients came from. Stock up on bramble jam, Neal's Yard yoghurt and fruit from Faversham in Kent, or, if you're feeling lazy, pop across the road to Franklins bar and restaurant (no. 157) for freshly prepared dishes – all its ingredients come from the same suppliers as the farm shop.

GREENWICH MARKET

- 🌑 *Greenwich, SE10 9HZ*
- ⊕ *Tel: 020 8293 3110, 07851 018 007; www.greenwichmarket.net*
- ◎ *Cutty Sark DLR*
- ▦ *Wed 11am–6pm food, homeware; Thur 10am–5.30pm food, antiques, crafts*
  Fri 10am–5.30pm food, crafts, antiques; Sat–Sun 10am–5.30pm food, crafts

This is the place to find a melted Becks bottle that's been turned into a clock, a handmade charm bracelet, or a hand-crafted mirror from Richard Pell Creative Metalwork (020 8693 5740; www.richardpell.com). The market is at its busiest on Saturdays and Sundays, when it sells mostly arts and crafts, although there a few food stalls near the main entrance – the brownie cheesecake slices from The Real Baking Company (020 8293 4646) are out of this world.

EXPLORE: DEPTFORD

- ◎ Deptford Market, Deptford High Street, Lewisham, SE8 3PQ
- ◎ Deptford Bridge

Despite its reputation as gritty/grimy, Deptford is heading for Shoreditch-cool status. It hasn't forgotten its roots – there's still a buzzy *EastEnders*-style market on the high street (Wed, Fri, Sat 9am–5pm) – but it now has a burgeoning art scene (see p.131).

EXPLORE: BLACKHEATH

◉ *Blackheath BR*

You can walk to this peaceful village in about 20 minutes from Greenwich. There's a wild, windy common with a church in the middle, a farmer's market at the train station (Sundays 10am–2pm) and a circuit of independent shops, cafes and restaurants.

HAND MADE FOOD

❶ *40 Tranquil Vale, Blackheath, SE3 0BD*
⊕ *Tel: 020 8297 9966; www.handmadefood.com*
◉ *Blackheath BR*

HMF is one of the most ethical delis around – downstairs it sells only organic, seasonal and local produce in biodegradable packaging to take away, such as game pie with Cumberland sauce; upstairs there is space for 16 to eat in at 3 large communal tables. The first floor is also an art gallery, Osokool, which displays abstract paintings, prints and sketches that change every three months.

KARAVAN

❶ *167 Lordship Lane, East Dulwich, SE22 8HX*
⊕ *Tel: 020 8299 2524; www.karavaneco.co.uk*
◉ *East Dulwich BR, then bus 40, 176, 185*

Karavan opened 17 years ago, long before eco-shopping went mainstream. Come here for recycled wool blankets, towels and locally sourced home products.

MY BACK PAGES

❶ *8–10 Station Road, Balham, SW12 9SG*
⊕ *Tel: 020 8675 9346*
◉ *Balham*

If you're waiting for a train, pop into this second-hand bookshop, named after a Bob Dylan song. The shop has some new books, but mostly stocks used books, which cover fiction as well as history, politics, psychology and the classics.

NAUTICALIA

❶ *25 Nelson Road, Greenwich, SE10 9JB*
⊕ *Tel: 020 8858 1066; www.nauticalia.com*
◉ *Cutty Sark DLR, Greenwich BR*

This shop bills itself as 'the first shop in the world'. No, it's not the oldest; but at 00°00.4'W, it's four seconds' west of the prime meridian line (a few yards away). In keeping with the history of Greenwich, it has a nautical theme, and sells an array of maps, globes, compasses and model boats.

EXPLORE: CLAPHAM

○ *Clapham Common, Clapham North*

Most of the shops in this area stretch along the high street from the common towards Clapham North tube station. The side streets are also worth dipping into, especially The Pavement, which has a few gift shops and small cafes, and Clapham Common North Side.

NORTH CROSS ROAD MARKET

- ❶ *North cross Road, East Dulwich, SE22 9EV*
- ⊕ *www.southwark.gov.uk*
- ◉ *East Dulwich BR*
- ▥ *Mon–Sat 10am–4pm*

Historically, there's been a market in some form on this site for decades. In recent years, though, it's become gentrified. Stalls now line one side of the street from Lordship Lane to Crystal Palace Road. Browsers can sample bread, organic cheese and Somerset fudge, pick up handmade crafts or buy furniture.

THE NORTH CROSS VINTAGE STORE

- ❶ *31 North Cross Road, SE22 0HZ*
- ⊕ *Tel: 07984 419 373*
- ◉ *East Dulwich BR, then bus 40, 176, 185*

You might miss this one-off vintage store, as its entrance is tucked away on a side street off the main drag. Enter the gate and you'll find yourself in a small courtyard dotted with garden furniture, then a large garage-style room full of vintage items such as old-fashioned bread tins and wobbly cake stands.

PLACES AND SPACES

- ❶ *30 Old Town, Clapham, SW4 0LB*
- ⊕ *Tel: 020 7498 0998; www.placesandspaces.com, www.droog.com*
- ◉ *Clapham Common*

This one-off design shop is a great place to find a talking point for your home; it stocks lace parasols, a lampshade made from antlers or a plant in a swing. Most of their items are designed by droog, fjordfiesta, kyouei and Vittorio Bonacina.

SISTERS & DAUGHTERS

- ❶ *18 Tranquil Vale, Blackheath, SE3 0AX*
- ⊕ *Tel: 020 8852 8507*
- ◉ *Blackheath BR*

This shop has gifts for all ages – everything from kids' toys and raincoats to silky women's nighties, abstract canvases and decorative stationery.

WHIPPET

- *71 Bedford Hill, Balham, SW12 9HA*
- *Tel: 020 8772 9781*
- *Balham*

If you're an impulse buyer who's strapped for cash, then this is one shop you should avoid. Despite its compact size, Whippet manages to cram in a range of miscellaneous items (key rings, magnets, cushions) onto its shelves, which no doubt you'll convince yourself you really need, as well as homeware created by Scandinavian designers. It's a great little shop for unique gifts and cards.

WILLIAM ROSE

- *126 Lordship Lane, East Dulwich, SE22 8HD*
- *Tel: 020 8693 9191; www.williamrosebutchers.com*
- *East Dulwich BR, then bus 40, 176, 185*

On a Saturday morning, the 30-strong queue outside this family-owned butchers speaks for itself. Come here if you're looking for free-range pigeon, pheasant, teal or woodcock, as well as organic hare, rabbit or game.

WIMBLEDON PARK MARKET

- *Wimbledon Park First School, Havana Road, Wimbledon, SW19 8EJ*
- *Tel: 020 7833 0338; www.lfm.org.uk*
- *Wimbledon, then bus 156*
- Sat 9am–1pm

Since 2000, there's been a farmer's market serving the local community in Wimbledon in the school playground.

ZEITGEIST

- *17 The Pavement, Clapham Common, SW4 0HY*
- *Tel: 020 7622 5000*
- *Clapham Common*

Zeitgeist has a wide selection of silver jewellery with and without semi-precious gems. It also sells cards and gadgets that make great presents, as well as homeware, such as vases and Buddha heads.

EXPLORE: WANDSWORTH

- *Clapham Junction BR, Wandsworth Town BR*

Battersea Rise and Northcote Road, close to Wandsworth Common, both have a strip of non-chain shops, bars and restaurants popular with locals. Old York Road also has some unique shops and pubs; it's closer to the river, near Wandsworth Town train station.

▼ EAST

@WORK

- 📍 156 Brick Lane, E1 6RU
- ☎ Tel: 020 7377 0597; www.atworkgallery.co.uk
- 🚇 Aldgate East

Watch British and international artisans at work in this shop, which stocks an eclectic mix of jewellery; you might find semi-precious jewels set in silver, fairy-cake stud earrings, a fabric poodle brooch or a recycled bottle cap necklace. It also runs workshops, so you can design your own silver or beaded jewellery. There's another branch in Pimlico (020 7821 9723).

ABSOLUTE VINTAGE

- 📍 15 Hanbury Street, Spitalfields, E1 6QR
- ☎ Tel: 020 7247 3883; www.absolutevintage.co.uk
- 🚇 Aldgate East

Housed in an old Truman Brewery warehouse are bags, belts, jewellery and hats for men and women from the 1930s right up to the 1980s, as well as a selection of prom dresses. But the footwear is its biggest draw; staff estimate they have well over a thousand pairs of vintage shoes in their collection.

ATLANTIS ART MATERIALS

- 📍 7–9 Plumber's Row, E1 1EQ
- ☎ Tel: 020 7377 8855; www.atlantisart.co.uk
- 🚇 Aldgate East

If you can't find the item you're after in this massive art warehouse, then it probably doesn't exist, as it is Britain's biggest collection of oil, acrylic and watercolour paints, canvases, brushes and paper.

BEYOND RETRO

- 📍 110–12 Cheshire Street, E2 6EJ
- ☎ Tel: 020 7613 3636; www.beyondretro.com
- 🚇 Whitechapel

Whether you're after a dapper 1950s trouser suit, an original tea dress or a 1980s rock T-shirt, you'll find it in Beyond Retro. At any time it displays 15,000 items collected from around the world, with a further 500 items added each day. There's a second branch in Soho.

BILLINGSGATE MARKET

- 📍 Trafalgar Way, E14 5ST
- ☎ Tel: 020 7987 1118; www.cityoflondon.gov.uk
- 🚇 Canary Wharf
- ▪ Tues–Sat 5am–8.30am

It's worth getting up at the crack of dawn to meet the cockneys selling fish at this largely wholesale market, which dates from 1699. Whether you buy some fish or not, the banter from the 50 stall-traders is fun to listen to.

BRICK LANE MARKET

- *Brick Lane, Tower Hamlets, E1*
- *Tel: 020 7364 1717; www.towerhamlets.gov.uk*
- *Aldgate East*
- *Sun 8am–3pm*

There's been a market on this site since medieval times, when stallholders would sell fresh produce to the workers in the nearby brick-making fields. These days, every Sunday sees Brick Lane and its surrounding streets lined with people selling second-hand clothes, records, books and general bric-a-brac; items are often displayed on a simple rug on the ground.

BROADWAY MARKET

- *Broadway Market, Hackney, E8 4PH*
- *www.broadwaymarket.co.uk*
- *London Fields BR*
- *Sat 9am–5pm*

There's been a street market on this spot in Hackney since the 1800s, and it still retains its village-like charm. Friendly locals buy and sell paintings, ceramics, furniture and fresh produce at reasonable prices. Next Saturday, escape Oxford Street and try Broadway Market.

CERISE

- *94 Columbia Road, E2 7QB*
- *Tel: 020 8245 4656; www.ceriseuk.com*
- *Old Street, then bus 8, 26, 48, 55, 388*

With silver rings selling for up to £1,500, you could say Cerise is a bit on the pricey side. Still, ladies of leisure will enjoy browsing their contemporary jewellery designs, scarves and leather handbags covered in peacock feathers.

COLUMBIA ROAD FLOWER MARKET

- *Columbia Road, Hackney, Tower Hamlets, E2 7RG*
- *www.columbiaroad.info*
- *Old Street, then bus 8, 26, 48, 55, 388*
- *Sun 7am–2.30pm*

The name is a bit of a misnomer – while over 50 market stalls sell mostly flowers, the road also has cafes, vintage boutiques and retro tearooms that have sprung up on either side of it. It's also misleading to think of the market as an early Sunday morning destination – there's enough to keep your interest till about 2.30pm.

COMFORT STATION

- 🅞 *22 Cheshire Street, E2 6EH*
- ⊕ *Tel: 020 7033 9099; www.comfortstation.co.uk*
- ◉ *Aldgate East, Whitechapel*

Comfort Station blends the past with the future by converting battered vintage suitcases into shelves displaying contemporary silver jewellery. A piano, sliced in half, displays scarves, crockery and handbags.

DUKE OF UKE

- 🅞 *22 Hanbury Street, E1 6QR*
- ⊕ *Tel: 020 7247 7924; www.dukeofuke.co.uk*
- ◉ *Aldgate East*

D of U stocks new and second-hand musical instruments, such as mandolins, horns and harmonicas. And if you've always wanted to learn the ukulele or banjo, you can sign up for lessons here, or enrol on one of their 10-week courses. There's also a recording and rehearsal studio, and the shop squeezes in an audience of 50 when it hosts occasional free live music on-site.

EASTSIDE BOOKS

- 🅞 *166 Brick Lane, E1 6RU*
- ⊕ *Tel: 020 7247 0216; www.eastsidebooks.co.uk*
- ◉ *Aldgate East*

If you're local, and want to learn more about your roots, this independent bookshop is a good place to start, as it specializes in literature on East London and the history of the capital. It stocks a number of small publishers which are not found elsewhere. It also hosts book signings, poetry readings, writing classes, a reading club, storytelling sessions for children and monthly talks by authors.

EVOLUTION

- 🅞 *59–61 Roman Road, Bethnal Green, E2 0QN*
- ⊕ *Tel: 020 8981 7219; www.evolutiongifts.co.uk*
- ◉ *Bow Road, Bethnal Green*

A Buddhist charity, The Windhorse Trust, owns this gift and homeware shop. Most of their goods are bought directly from suppliers in developing countries – the charity pledges to check the producer's wages and that working conditions are fair, and promises to pay a fair price. Plus, some of their profits get pumped back into the communities that made the products – so you can shop for trinkets, puzzles and board games with a clear conscience.

FABRICATIONS

- 🅞 *7 Broadway Market, Hackney, E8 4PH*
- ⊕ *Tel: 020 7275 8043; www.fabrications1.co.uk*
- ◉ *London Fields BR*

Fabrications opened in 2000 before Broadway Market became the arty destination it is today. The shop and downstairs studio focuses on eco-design, and many products are created from recycled fabrics – cushions made from woven strips of men's shirts and ties are popular. Creative types can sign up to craft classes to make jewellery or rugs from fabric scraps; or join a knitting workshop, where you can knit using strips of plastic bags instead of wool.

FAR

- ❶ 124 Columbia Road, E2 7RG
- ⊕ Tel: 07931 151 663; www.farglobal.co.uk
- ◉ Old Street, then bus 8, 26, 48, 55, 388

Come here for one-off pieces of furniture from Rajasthan and Kerala. They're all individually hand-painted, so they're expensive – but with an eye-catching turquoise cabinet from India, guests won't notice your wobbly Ikea shelves.

I KNIT LONDON

- ❶ 106 Lower Marsh, Waterloo, SE1 7AB
- ⊕ Tel: 020 7261 1338; www.iknit.org.uk
- ◉ Waterloo
- ❹ £10 per hour; £65 for three two-hour classes

You'll find I Knit London on a trendy street tucked behind Waterloo station. It describes itself as a 'club, shop and sanctuary' for knitters, so as well as choosing from its selection of wool, patterns and Japanese silk, you can also join the club – so you can opt to take one its knitting classes, if you enjoy a good yarn. The classes are held during the day and at night, when you can take advantage of the shop's in-house bar. And all abilities are catered for, so you can learn how to knit backwards, use a spinning wheel or how to crochet a pair of pants.

MACBLACK

- ❶ 47 Broadway Market, London Fields, E8 4PH
- ⊕ Tel: 020 8376 5205; www.macblack.com
- ◉ London Fields BR

Whether your style is minimalist, Laura Ashley or retro, you're bound to spot something you like in MacBlack, which stocks original Victorian and Edwardian furniture, 1970s lamps and a range of contemporary glass and ceramics.

THE MENU

- ❶ 45 Brushfield Street, E1 6AA
- ⊕ Tel: 020 7539 9269; www.shopmenu.co.uk
- ◉ Liverpool Street

This boutique sells smart casual men's clothes, such as jeans and jumpers from designers Nicole Farhi and Michiko Koshino. Because of its location, it tries to cater for city boys as well as arty types in their 20s and 30s.

MILAGROS

- *61 Columbia Road, E2 7RG*
- *Tel: 020 7613 0876; www.milagros.co.uk*
- *Old Street, then bus 8, 26, 48, 55, 388*

All the products in Milagros are handmade by artisans in local workshops using traditional techniques. The end result is an East End shop full of contemporary designs more colourful than a Dulux paint chart. You can buy ceramic tiles in 21 colours, plus woven laundry baskets, hand-blown shot glasses or bold print bags.

NOM

- *102a Columbia Road, E2 7HP*
- *Tel: 020 7729 5509; www.nomliving.com*
- *Old Street, then bus 8, 26, 48, 55, 388*

Run by a Vietnamese manager, Nom has been working with Vietnamese artisans for over 17 years to bring lacquerware, baskets and ceramic products to London's East End. Look out for the stylish recycled glass bottles outside.

OLD SPITALFIELDS MARKET

- *105a Commercial Street, E1 6EW*
- *Tel: 020 7247 8556; www.visitspitalfields.com*
- *Liverpool Street*
- *Mon–Fri, Sun: miscellaneous; Wed, Fri, Sun: food; Fri: clothes, accessories; Thur: antiques; 1st and 3rd Wed of every month: records and books*

Since 1682, traders have been shouting their wares at Spitalfields. Yet this market feels less frenzied than others because of its neat rows of undercover stalls. Here you'll pick up giant world maps, herbal remedies and the type of clothes you thought you'd find only in Bangkok. Sunday is the busiest day.

ONE NEW CHANGE

- *Cheapside, EC4M 9AB*
- *Tel: 020 7260 2700; www.onenewchange.com, www.cityoflondon.gov.uk*
- *St Paul's*

One New Change is a new £500 million shopping complex which is set to open in December 2010, in competition with Bluewater and Westfield. The mall's shops and offices cover a 52,000-square metre space next to St Paul's Cathedral along Cheapside, with three floors dedicated to 70 local boutiques, upmarket shops and high-street chain, restaurants, plus a public viewing deck on the roof.

RUSSELL CALLOW

- *7 Sunbury Workshops, Swanfield Street, Shoreditch, E2 7LF*
- *Tel: 07958 561 691; www.londontimepiece.co.uk*
- *Old Street*

Russell Callow carefully restores all the clocks in his clock shop personally, by hand. He sells period clocks dating back to the 1700s, and industrial clocks sourced from the former Eastern Bloc. Call before visiting.

SQUINT

- 178 Shoreditch High Street, E1 6HU
- Tel: 020 7739 9275; www.squintlimited.com
- Old Street

Lisa Whatmough, a former sculptor and painter, has been revamping antique chaise longues, mirrors and lampshades to suit boho, hippy types since 2005. Her bold, flamboyant patchwork designs won't be to everyone's tastes, but put one in your home and they *will* be a talking point. Each piece is unique.

SUNDAY (UP) MARKET

- Old Truman Brewery, Ely's Yard, 91 Brick Lane, E1 6QL
- Tel: 020 7770 6028; www.sundayupmarket.co.uk
- Aldgate East, Liverpool Street
- Sun 10am–5.30pm

There's an eclectic mix of traders at this covered Sunday market, selling photography, handmade jewellery, vintage clothes, records and textiles. If you're hungry, there are food stalls as well. Try the paella at Spanish Caravan (07709 599 065) or Caribbean curries from Majay Tout (07919 141 218), washed down with a mug of Ethiopian coffee at Red Tent Ethiopian (07882 320 510).

TATTY DEVINE

- 236 Brick Lane, E2 7EB
- Tel: 020 7739 9191; www.tattydevine.com
- Aldgate East

Wearing an item of jewellery from Tatty's feels more like you're wearing a piece of art inspired by the 1980s. Here you might pick up some plastic lightening bolt earrings, Gilbert and George-inspired cufflinks, a miniature 3-D glasses badge made from enamel or a necklace made from 70 Perspex bones.

VINTAGE HEAVEN

- 82 Columbia Road, Bethnal Green, E2 7QB
- Tel: 01277 215 968; www.vintageheaven.co.uk
- Old Street, then bus 8, 26, 48, 55, 388

Browse through flower-power biscuit tins, dainty teapots and porcelain teacups at Vintage Heaven, stopping for a cream tea (or 1970s-style quiche) in Cake Hole, the small 1960s cafe at the rear of the shop. Items displayed in the cafe are also for sale.

▼ WEST

CATH KIDSTON

- ❶ 322 King's Road, SW3 5UH
- ⊕ Tel: 020 7351 7335; www.cathkidston.co.uk
- ◉ Sloane Square, then bus 11, 21, 49; South Kensington

Cath Kidston is unashamedly old-fashioned, and is known for its floral patterns and English country-cottage style. Expect floral hankies, Mary Poppins-style umbrellas, decorative ironing-board covers and radios from a bygone era. It also has a range of kids' clothes and accessories, fabrics and wallpaper.

JAPANESE GALLERY

- ❶ 66d Kensington Church Street, W8 4BY
- ⊕ Tel: 020 7229 2934; www.japanesegallery.co.uk
- ◉ High Street Kensington

This shop has a large collection of antique and modern Japanese art, 90 per cent of which is original. Here you'll find scenes of the red *torii* gate rising from the sea off Miyajima island, fierce kabuki actors and genteel geisha, as well as a small selection of Japanese paraphernalia, such as folded fans and kimonos. There's a second branch in Islington, on Camden Passage (*see* p.104).

LA CAVE À FROMAGE

- ❶ 24–5 Cromwell Place, Kensington, SW7 2LD
- ⊕ Tel: 0845 108 822; www.la-cave.co.uk
- ◉ South Kensington

About 70 per cent of the cheese here comes from France, and all of it is traceable back to the farmer who produced it. Inside, black-and-white photos of cheese hang next to shelves of red wine – a suitable backdrop for the informal tasting events held each month for up to 20 people. Try the pungent Boulette d'Avene or perhaps the Fourme Maury, a creamy cheese riddled with blue veins. Bouton doc is popular in spring because it's so light – great for salads.

PHILIP TREACY

- ❶ 69 Elizabeth Street, SW1W 9PJ
- ⊕ Tel: 020 7730 3992; www.philiptreacy.co.uk
- ◉ Sloane Square

Philip Treacy learned to sew when he was five, and went on to train at the Royal College of Art, specializing in millinery. Since opening this flagship shop in 1994, he's designed hats for Alexander McQueen and for the wedding of the Prince of Wales and Camilla Parker Bowles. It takes up to 10 weeks to design a made-to-order hat – prices start from £500. Otherwise you can pick a hat from Treacy's collection – outrageous statement hats for women or trilby hats covered in bright graffiti or canary yellow flat caps for men.

PORTOBELLO ROAD MARKET

- *Portobello Road, Notting Hill, W10*
- *Tel: 020 7229 8354; www.portobelloroad.co.uk*
- *Ladbroke Grove, Notting Hill Gate*
- *Mon, Wed, Fri, Sat 8am–6.30pm & Thur 8am–1pm miscellaneous; Sat 5.30am–5pm antiques*

Despite its location, this market remains pretty chain-free and the 2,000 stalls selling antiques, food, fashion and second-hand items that line the street on Saturdays have kept their charm. The road runs off Notting Hill Gate and continues on to Ladbroke Grove. Many of the streets off the main thoroughfare are also well worth exploring, particularly Westbourne Grove.

OXFAM BOUTIQUE

- *245 Westbourne Grove, W11 2SE*
- *Tel: 020 7229 5000; www.oxfam.org.uk*
- *Notting Hill Gate*

You won't find dodgy cardigans here; instead, London College of Fashion students revamp the second-hand clothes into original designs. Laura Queening is a fashion graduate and an advocate of the shop's eco-friendly ethos – she takes old leather jackets and turns them into belts and bags. The shop also sells clothes created by People Tree, an Internet company which specializes in organic, sustainable and Fairtrade clothes. Even the shop interior is designed to reduce waste; the floor is made from reclaimed wood. There are two other Oxfam boutiques, one in Chiswick and the other off King's Road in Chelsea.

WESTFIELD

- *Ariel Way, W12 7SL*
- *Tel: 020 3371 2300; www.westfield.com*
- *Wood Lane, White City*

While Westfield is Europe's biggest city mall, there are few surprises. Even before you get here you know what to expect: River Island, Mango, Burton, Topman, Nando's and Starbucks. There's also a strip of luxury designer shops, such as Dior, Tiffany & Co. and Sienna Miller and her sister's boutique, Twenty8Twelve, in an area known as The Village. If shopping all just gets too much, you can hop on a bar stool at Searcys Champagne Bar.

GALLERIES

London has some of the best art galleries in the world, and many of them are free. Yet while you may make the effort to visit the big ones such as the Tate Modern and the Saatchi Gallery, few people bother with the independent galleries tucked off the high streets. But some of London's most interesting artwork can be found in these smaller galleries; they're worth more than a passing browse. On a rainy day, why don't you pick an area, arm yourself with the *London Almanac 2010* and make a day of it?

▼ CENTRAL

BARBICAN ART GALLERY

- ❶ *Barbican Centre, Silk Street, EC2Y 8DS*
- ⊕ *Tel: 020 7638 4141; www.barbican.org.uk*
- ⊜ *Barbican*
- ❹ *FREE; special exhibitions extra*

The Barbican Centre, which opened in 1982, is the biggest multi-arts venue in Europe. It has two theatres, three cinemas, three halls and three restaurants. It is also home to the Barbican Art Gallery, which hosts three changing exhibitions a year, focusing on architecture, design, fashion and photography created by international artists from the 20th and 21st centuries. There's also a second, smaller gallery, The Curve, which is a continuous space that wraps round the back of the Concert Hall. This gallery's three changing exhibitions show commissions by international and contemporary artists. Past exhibitions have included the artists Huang Yong Ping and Rafael Lozano-Hemmer. The main gallery is open till 10pm every Thursday; the Curve is open till 10pm on every first Thursday of the month.

CONTEMPORARY APPLIED ARTS

- ❶ *2 Percy Street, W1T 1DD*
- ⊕ *Tel: 020 7436 2344; www.caa.org.uk*
- ⊜ *Tottenham Court Road, Goodge Street*
- ❹ *FREE*

Established in 1948, the CAA moved to its current location 17 years ago. It has two floors; the ground floor holds temporary exhibitions and the first-floor space displays a range of jewellery, furniture, textiles and glasswork for sale. It also hosts free drop-in sessions, such as paper-making classes and demonstrations by textile artists and furniture makers.

THE COURTAULD INSTITUTE OF ART

- Somerset House, the Strand, WC2R 1LA
- Tel: 020 7848 2526 (gallery), 020 7845 4600 (Somerset House); www.courtauld.ac.uk, www.somersethouse.org.uk
- Temple, Covent Garden
- £5; free admission to house

For the sake of £5 you can escape the crowds of the National Gallery and come here instead, where you can wander the halls of the institute in relative peace. The collection of 7,000 drawings and 20,000 prints was founded in 1932, and includes a selection of medieval paintings, gothic Italian paintings, Renaissance pieces and 18th-century portraits. The gallery is particularly known for its impressionist and post-impressionist paintings on the first floor – well-known artists on display include Monet, Cézanne, Renoir and Matisse. As well as paintings, the gallery displays sculpture, ceramics and glass objects.

DALI UNIVERSE

- County Hall Gallery Ltd, County Hall, Riverside Building, SE1 7PB
- Tel: 0870 744 7485; www.thedaliuniverse.com
- Westminster, Waterloo
- £14

Since 2000, this two-storey gallery has been home to over 500 pieces of art. On the ground floor, there is a permanent exhibition dedicated to the Spanish artist, Salvador Dalí. A black corridor with neon blue lights guides you past images of the artist, a timeline and a series of his quotes into a room of sketches and bronze figures. Here you'll see Dalí's 1977 sculpture of a melting clock dripping off a tree trunk, *The Profile of Time*, and his 1937 Mae West lips sofa. A second room at the back has more of Dalí's work, such as *The Minotaur* (1988) – a bronze of a woman's body with the head of a beast, with a lobster crawling out of her stomach and drawers coming out of her chest and right ankle. Some of the artwork is for sale, if you have a spare £22,000 or so. Downstairs is a space for temporary exhibitions which change once a year.

THE DAVID ROBERTS ART FOUNDATION

- 111 Great Titchfield Street, W1W 6RY
- Tel: 020 7637 0868; www.davidrobertsartfoundation.com
- Great Portland Street, Warren Street, Goodge Street
- FREE

Since 2007, this gallery has exhibited a diverse collection of contemporary art in various media by recent graduates, emerging artists and internationally recognized artists. The gallery has two exhibition spaces across two floors, both of which are dedicated to solo and group exhibitions, which change six to seven times a year. Previous shows have included the work of the 2001 Turner Prize-winner, Martin Creed, and Danish artists Nina Beier and Marie Lund. A second gallery is due to open in Camden this autumn.

THE HAYWARD

- Southbank Centre, Belvedere Road, SE1 8XX
- Tel: 0871 663 2501; www.southbankcentre.co.uk
- Waterloo, Embankment
- £7

The South Bank Centre dates back to the 1951 Festival of Britain and is the UK's largest arts space, occupying a 21-acre site on the South Bank. Inside is the Royal Festival Hall, which seats 2,500; the Queen Elizabeth Hall, which seats 900; the Purcell Room, with seats for 350; You'll find the Saison Poetry Library, the Arts Council Collection and The Hayward art gallery here too. Since it opened in 1968, The Hayward has had no permanent collection; its temporary collection changes three to five times a year. The gallery has exhibition spaces across two floors. In 2009, the gallery showed the work of: Yayoi Kusama, the Japanese artist known for her garish polka dots; Mark Wallinger, the artist who won the 2007 Turner Prize for dressing up as a bear; and Ujino, who combines household appliances with DJ mixing decks to create musical sculpture.

ICA

- Nash House, The Mall, SW1Y 5AH
- Tel: 020 7930 0493 (switchboard), 020 7930 6393 (24-hour information); www.ica.org.uk
- Charing Cross, Piccadilly Circus
- FREE

Since 1947, the Institute of Contemporary Arts has brought modern art, theatre and film to The Mall. The venue has two cinemas and a theatre (see p.151), as well as two galleries, a bookshop, bar and cafe. Through a variety of media, exhibitions in the galleries have explored themes as diverse as prostitution, the parallel of life and art, destruction and eroticism. They host about five exhibitions a year. The galleries are open till 9pm on Thursdays.

LESLEY CRAZE GALLERY

- 33–35a Clerkenwell Green, EC1R 0DU
- Tel: 020 7608 0393; www.lesleycrazegallery.co.uk
- Farringdon
- FREE

This gallery showcases jewellery, metalwork and textiles created by new, young artists – particularly recent graduates from Central St Martin's School of Art – as well as some established international artists. The designers work with mixed media and use a range of techniques, such as etching metalwork, screen printing and weaving to create unique pieces of art. Items on display include bold necklaces made from plastic beads and cotton, designed by Karola Torkos, a Royal College of Art graduate; metal vases made from recycled food containers by Claire Malet, who then lines them with 24-carat gold leaf; and Victoria Richards' hand-painted silk ties. The gallery hosts four exhibitions a year.

NATIONAL GALLERY

- *Trafalgar Square, WC2N 5DN*
- *Tel: 020 7747 2885; www.nationalgallery.org.uk*
- *Charing Cross, Leicester Square*
- *FREE; special exhibitions extra*

Unlike most European national galleries, this collection didn't develop from a royal archive. Instead, the Government bought a private collection of 38 pictures from a banker in 1824. Another 186 years on, and that collection has grown to 2,300, and includes Vincent Van Gogh's *Sunflowers*, *Bathers at Asnières* by Georges Seurat and *The Virgin and Child Enthroned with Narrative Scenes*, by Margarito of Arezzo, which is thought to be the gallery's oldest piece (it dates from the 1260s). Today, up to 5 million people visit the gallery every year. As well as the permanent collection on the second level, the gallery hosts three temporary exhibitions every year.

NATIONAL GEOGRAPHIC

- *83–97 Regent Street, W1B 4EW*
- *Tel: 020 7025 6960; www.natgeolondonstore.co.uk*
- *Piccadilly Circus*
- *FREE*

It's no longer enough for an art gallery to be just that. These days they also have to have a library, shop, cafe, restaurant and now, it seems, a chamber for extreme weather conditions. At National Geographic you can don all-weather travel gear before testing your kit against -15°C temperatures and extreme winds in a room designed for just that, then check out displays of photography, sculpture and paintings in the gallery on the ground floor. There is also an Africa studio, showcasing handmade artefacts, where you can support African artisan communities by buying original handmade jewellery or camel-hide bags.

NATIONAL PORTRAIT GALLERY

- *2 St Martin's Place, Westminster, WC2H 0HE*
- *Tel: 020 7306 0055; www.npg.org.uk*
- *Charing Cross, Leicester Square*
- *FREE*

The portrait gallery's collection began in 1856, and it has now grown to 120,000 paintings, sculptures and miniatures – about 60 per cent is on public display at any one time. The collection is displayed over three of the gallery's six floors; for more contemporary portraits, visit the Lerner Galleries on the ground floor, which house a temporary collection as well as some pictures from the permanent contemporary collection. The first floor galleries shows older portraits. The Tudor Galleries on the second floor is a highlight – look out for King Henry VII's portrait; completed in 1505; it is the oldest in the collection. *Insider info: the criteria for selecting artwork is been based on the status of the sitter rather than the quality of the work.*

THE PHOTOGRAPHERS' GALLERY

- *16–18 Ramillies Street, W1F 7LW*
- *Tel: 0845 262 1618; www.photonet.org.uk*
- *Oxford Circus*
- *FREE*

The gallery's £15.5 million development project, completed in 2008, saw it move from Great Newport Street to its current location behind Oxford Street. Now, there are three floors open to the public: the main gallery and second gallery, a cafe and bookshop, and a space where you can buy prints. As well as exhibitions by emerging and established photographers, the gallery holds events such as films, talks and educational programmes.

THE ROSALINDE AND ARTHUR GILBERT GALLERIES

- *Victoria & Albert Museum, Cromwell Road, SW7 2RL*
- *Tel: 020 7942 2468 (gallery), 020 7942 2000 (V&A);*
  www.gilbert-collection.org.uk, www.vam.ac.uk
- *South Kensington*
- *FREE*

This collection reopened in the V&A last June, following its move from Somerset House. Regular themed exhibitions give the public a glimpse of what used to be a private collection of Italian mosaics, snuff boxes, portraits and decorative vases and urns. Over 400 artefacts are on display.

ROYAL ACADEMY OF ARTS

- *Burlington House, Piccadilly, W1J 0BD*
- *Tel: 020 7300 8000; www.royalacademy.org.uk*
- *Piccadilly Circus, Green Park*
- *FREE permanent collection; £8–12 temporary collections*

Since its foundation by George III in 1768, the academy has developed its collection of art made from all media throughout the ages. The 11 main galleries host most of the temporary exhibitions, as do the three smaller Sackler galleries. Exhibitions change three or four times a year. The John Madejski Fine Rooms house the gallery's permanent collection. Highlights include *A Closer Grand Canyon* by David Hockney, etchings by J.M.W. Turner and *The Leaping Horse* by John Constable. The academy has an annual summer exhibition (*see* p.34).

SERPENTINE GALLERY

- *Kensington Gardens, W2 3XA*
- *Tel: 020 7402 6075; www.serpentinegallery.org*
- *Lancaster Gate, South Kensington*
- *FREE*

The Serpentine puts on changing exhibitions of contemporary art created from a range of mixed media. It also has a lively events programme, which in the past has included clay-modelling classes, electronic music jam sessions, film screenings and book launches. Outside, the Serpentine Pavilion is redesigned by a different architect each summer.

TATE BRITAIN

- **❶** *Millbank, Pimlico, SW1P 4RG*
- **⊕** *Tel: 020 7887 8888; www.tate.org.uk/britain*
- **◉** *Pimlico*
- **❻** *FREE; special exhibitions extra*

As Britain's national gallery, Tate Britain shows art so famous it's a cliché: portraits by William Hogarth, landscapes by John Constable and illustrations for Dante's *Divine Comedy* by William Blake, are among the highlights. The gallery exhibits work from 1500 to the present day, in a chronological order. More recent work includes Henry Moore, Francis Bacon and the Young British Artists (YBAs) of the 1990s. The gallery stays open till 10pm on the first Friday of every month.

TATE MODERN

- **❶** *Bankside, SE1 9TG*
- **⊕** *Tel: 020 7887 8888; www.tate.org.uk/modern*
- **◉** *Southwark, Mansion House*
- **❻** *FREE; special exhibitions extra*

You can't miss this enormous former power station on the South Bank, which became the Tate Modern in 2000. The gallery is home to a national collection of contemporary art from around the world. The artwork is spread across three floors, two of which host the gallery's permanent collection – the third is dedicated to temporary exhibitions, which change three times a year. The 3,400-square metre Turbine Hall, now a cavernous entrance hall, is used to display large pieces of art, such as Carsten Höller's *Test Site* (five spiral slides visitors could slide down) and Doris Salcedo's *Shibboleth*, better known as 'the big crack in the floor'. About 4.8 million visitors visit each year, which led to the gallery winning the Guinness World Record for the most visited art gallery in 2002.

THE WALLACE COLLECTION

- **❶** *Hertford House, Manchester Square, W1U 3BN*
- **⊕** *Tel: 0207 563 9500; www.wallacecollection.org*
- **◉** *Bond Street*
- **❻** *FREE*

This elegant three-storey town house is home to a former private collection dating back to 1760. The house opened as a museum in 1900, and displays over 5,500 pieces of 18th- and 19th-century art, such as ornate porcelain snuff boxes, bronzes and ceramics, although the majority of the collection is made up of swords and armour from around the world. Highlights from the paintings on display include a self-portrait by Rembrandt, *The Swing* by Jean-Honoré Fragonard and *The Laughing Cavalier* by Frans Hals.

▼ NORTH

CANDID ARTS TRUST

- *3 Torrens Street, Islington, EC1V 1NQ*
- *Tel: 020 7837 4237; www.candidarts.com*
- *Angel*
- *FREE*

Two Victorian warehouses make the perfect location for this exhibition space, which is housed over three floors. The basement, ground floor and first floor all host regular contemporary art exhibitions, most of which show work by recent art and design graduates. The buildings are also home to 20 artists' studios and a cosy cafe (*see* p.74). The gallery is used for painting, drawing and singing classes and sculpture workshops as well.

THE CRYPT GALLERY

- *St Pancras Church, Euston Road, NW1 2BA*
- *Tel: 020 7388 1461; www.cryptgallery.org.uk*
- *Euston*
- *FREE*

Exposed-brick archways, dark tunnels and hidden vaults are more suited to the set of a horror film than the venue for a contemporary art gallery. But a series of stone steps leads you down into this dimly lit crypt beneath St Pancras Church, which was built in 1822. The exhibition space has about 14 rooms which are home to 557 graves and, since 2002, regular art exhibitions as well – come here if you want to see neon sculptures or installation videos set in eerie caverns.

ESTORICK COLLECTION

- *39a Canonbury Square, N1 2AN*
- *Tel: 020 7704 9522; www.estorickcollection.com*
- *Highbury & Islington*
- *£5*

This selection of modern Italian art is housed in a suitably elegant Grade II-listed Georgian house, overlooking Canonbury Square. The gallery is particularly known for its futurist paintings and sculptures created in the early 20th century. Most of the artwork, which includes portraits by Amedeo Modigliani, were once the personal collection of an American sociologist and writer, Eric Estorick. The gallery opened to the public in 1998; it now has a library with 2,000 books on 20th-century Italian art, as well as a cafe in the gallery's landscaped garden.

FRAMEWORKS

- *17 Park Road, Crouch End, N8 8TE*
- *Tel: 020 8348 3834; www.frameworkscrouchend.co.uk*
- *Crouch Hill*
- *FREE*

Established in 1984, Frameworks exhibits the work of urban artists, particularly that of Stuart J.H. Free, who is known for his gritty portrayal of London's run-down, neglected buildings. Free wanders the city's streets taking photos, which he then draws onto paper before painting. His work includes paintings of the Walthamstow dog-track sign, Hornsey baths and laundry, the Phoenix Theatre in East Finchley and the old umbrella shop James Smiths & Sons (see p.100) on New Oxford Street. The gallery may not be much to look at, but the artwork is.

GRAHAM FINE ART

- 56 Crouch End Hill, N8 8AA
- Tel: 020 8341 2526; www.grahamfineart.com
- Crouch Hill
- FREE

Since 2003, this single-room art gallery has exhibited original work of 40 local and international artists. Paintings include signed work by Rolf Harris – who makes an occasional appearance when visiting his daughter who lives round the corner – and Gleb Goloubetski, a Soviet Union artist known for painting with a palette knife loaded with rich oils.

KINGS PLACE

- 90 York Way, N1 9AG
- Tel: 020 7841 4860 (general enquiries), 020 7520 1490 (box office); www.kingsplace.co.uk
- King's Cross
- FREE

Behind St Pancras station is this modern arts venue, which hosts classical concerts, jazz performances and workshops (see p.176). It also has two main galleries: Kings Place Gallery, which hosts temporary exhibitions by new and established international artists; and Pangolin London, which is dedicated to sculpture. Kings Place has a third, smaller exhibition space, the Guardian Gallery (020 3353 2000), which hosts changing exhibitions related to journalism. Here, you can see archive material from the *Guardian* and the *Observer*. Some of the images on display date back to the 1860s, so many are black and white or discoloured. The centre also has a restaurant overlooking the canal.

PROJECT SPACE 176

- 176 Prince of Wales Road, Chalk Farm, NW5 3PT
- Tel: 020 7428 8940; www.projectspace176.com
- Chalk Farm
- FREE

Since 2007, this gallery, housed in a former Methodist chapel, has hosted three annual exhibitions – one solo and two group shows, of up to 30 artists. The temporary exhibitions show the work of young, emerging experimental artists who display their latest work in the chapel gallery's eight rooms.

PROUD

- *Horse Hospital, Stables Market, Chalk Farm Road, Camden, NW1 8AH*
- *Tel: 020 7482 3867; www.proudcamden.com*
- *Chalk Farm*
- *FREE*

Housed in 200-year-old, Grade-II-listed former stables, you can still see many original features. Three rooms make up the 930-square-metre exhibition space: the South Gallery, Stables and the Main Gallery. Around 350,000 people visit Proud annually for their changing contemporary music photography exhibitions and permanent 'best of Proud' print sales area.

ROCK ARCHIVE

- *110 Islington High Street, Camden Passage, N1 8EG*
- *Tel: 020 7704 0598; www.rockarchive.com*
- *Angel*
- *FREE*

For all you rockers out there, this small gallery/shop is the place to come for iconic rock 'n' roll photography. Rock Archive is part of a chain of seven around the world, all of which portray fine-art prints taken by emerging and well-established photographers.

SARTORIAL CONTEMPORARY ART

- *26 Argyle Square, WC1H 8AP*
- *Tel: 020 7278 0866; www.sartorialart.com*
- *King's Cross*
- *FREE*

Apart from a white door surrounded by graffiti, there's nothing to set this art gallery apart from its neighbouring houses. The artist-run gallery, which was founded in 2002 in Kensington, moved to the suburban streets opposite King's Cross station in 2008. The space hosts a different contemporary art exhibition each month, with an emphasis on emerging artists.

SESAME ART GALLERY

- *354 Upper Street, Islington, N1 0PD*
- *Tel: 020 7226 3300; www.sesameart.com*
- *Angel*
- *FREE*

Since it opened in 2003, Sesame has encouraged new talent. And, unusually, the gallery aims to discover and promote emerging artists from around the globe, rather than just local ones. Sesame is a small, one-room gallery that shows mostly paintings; exhibitions change every two months. A handful of artists, such as Matthew Small, hosted exhibitions at Sesame early in their career and have now gone on to become well-established names.

▼ SOUTH

ALBION

- 8 Hester Road, Battersea, SW11 4AX
- Tel: 020 7801 2480
- Queenstown Road BR, Battersea Park BR
- FREE

Looming over the Thames is this modern aluminium-and-glass curved building. Since the gallery opened in 2004, its four galleries – some of which have ceilings as high as 7 metres – have shown temporary exhibitions by international artists who explore social and cultural issues. Past exhibitions have focused on the work of the Brazilian Campana Brothers, known for using found objects to design furniture, such as *Banquete Chair*, made from children's soft toys. More artwork is on display on the gallery's riverside terrace. The artwork is for sale.

ART IN PERPETUITY TRUST (APT)

- Harold Wharf, 6 Creekside (off Creek Road), Deptford, SE8 4SA
- Tel: 020 8694 8344; www.aptstudios.org
- Deptford BR, then bus 53, 177, 188, 199, 47
- FREE

Tucked off the main road is this little-known art gallery, housed in an old warehouse with a modern steel extension at the front. The gallery shows mostly paintings and sculptures in its two main rooms. Apt runs open studio events as well, so you can see artists at work in their studios. While you're in the area, you can visit Cor Blimey Arts (020 8691 1201; www.corblimeyarts.com), Creekside Artists (www.creeksideartists.co.uk), Art Hub (020 8691 5140; www.arthub.org.uk) and Cockpit Arts (020 8692 4463; www.cockpitarts.com) – all of which are on the same road. (*N.B. Cockpit Arts is open only by appointment and only during open studio events, held three times a year.*)

GX GALLERY

- 43 Denmark Hill, Peckham, SE5 8SR
- Tel: 020 7703 8396; www.gxgallery.com
- Oval, then bus 36, 436; Denmark Hill BR
- FREE

Don't be mistaken into thinking this is a framing studio with a few select pieces of art on display. Step inside and the room opens up into a light, airy space at the back, with Italian marble flooring and glass stairs down to the basement. There's a leaning towards artists who favour impressionism and figurative painting over abstract. There's also a mix of landscape paintings, installations and found objects, such as the £1 *Electric Metre* by London-based Spanish artist Carlos Cortes. Downstairs, several features from the site's former Wilson's bakery, which closed in 1890, are highlighted, including two ovens that stretch under the road and an old pulley system.

HOUSE

- 70 Camberwell Church Street, Camberwell, SE5 8QZ
- Tel: 020 7358 4475; www.house-gallery.co.uk
- Oval, then bus 36, 436; Denmark Hill BR
- FREE

From the street, this looks just like a homely cafe, with people tapping at their laptops (free wifi) over cups of tea. In the basement, though, there's a room dedicated to emerging contemporary artists. Exhibitions change at least once a month, and show mostly experimental photography and paintings.

PECKHAM SPACE

- Peckham Square, Peckham, SE15 8RS
- Tel: 020 7514 2299; www.peckhamspace.com
- Peckham Rye BR
- FREE

Since it opened in 2008, Peckham Space has commissioned four local artists a year. It aims to create original work that will benefit the local community and invites the public to get involved with its installations, films and photography. Past projects have included an artist-led discussion on play in public spaces and a walking tour for children, which saw them rediscover their local urban area.

SOUTH LONDON GALLERY

- 65 Peckham Road, SE5 8UH
- Tel: 020 7703 6120; www.southlondongallery.org
- Peckham Rye BR, then bus 12
- FREE; special events extra

This gallery dates back to 1868, but opened to the public at its current location in 1891. Each year, the gallery exhibits four or five temporary modern art exhibitions across one floor. Past exhibitions have showcased the work of Tracey Emin and Gilbert and George. The gallery's £1.6 million building project will be completed this spring, which will double the size of the gallery and add an education studio, a studio for resident artists and a cafe.

STARK GALLERY

- 386 Lee High Road, Lee Green, SE12 8RW
- Tel: 020 8318 4040; www.starkgallery.com
- Lewisham DLR then bus 178, 261, 321
- FREE

There are three galleries at Stark, all of which show temporary exhibitions of mixed media, such as a ceramics, bronze and textiles, as well as jewellery, sculpture and prints. The focus is on original British design and craft, and most of the artists are local and unknown. The gallery also holds poetry evenings, creative writing classes and children's art classes.

▼ EAST

491 GALLERY

- ❶ *491 Grove Green Road, Leytonstone, E11 4AA*
- ⊕ *www.491gallery.com*
- ⊜ *Leytonstone*
- ❷ *FREE gallery and workshops; donations welcomed*

Housed in a former derelict factory and drug den, 491 Gallery hosts mixed-media exhibitions across its two floors. Fortnightly exhibitions are held in the main room downstairs, although the artists also display their work in the hallways, on doors and up the stairs. The art can be anything from installations and murals to live performance and photography. The gallery also has art, textile and music studios, and a cinema and a dark room. It also hosts various workshops from digital imagery to fist fighting.

THE FLEAPIT

- ❶ *49 Columbia Road, Hackney, Tower Hamlets, E2 7RG*
- ⊕ *Tel: 020 7033 9986; www.thefleapit.com*
- ⊜ *Old Street, then bus 8, 26, 48, 55, 388*
- ❷ *FREE*

Housed in a former warehouse, The Fleapit is now a cafe/bar on a corner of Columbia Road, with a gallery at the back. Also known as the Freedom Gallery, the space hosts wall-art exhibitions, which change every two to four weeks, and workshops run by emerging contemporary artists. The space is also used for music events and independent film screenings on a projector.

SMUDGE GALLERY

- ❶ *117 Commercial Street, E1 6BG*
- ⊕ *Tel: 020 7247 9004; www.spitalfieldsartmarket.co.uk*
- ⊜ *Liverpool Street; Algate East*
- ❷ *FREE*

Smudge specializes in photographs and prints of urban scenes. For under £100, you might find an original stencil of the sun setting over the South Bank on canvas, or an image of some gritty high-rise flats to go over your mantelpiece.

START SPACE

- ❶ *150 Columbia Road, E2 7RG*
- ⊕ *Tel: 020 7729 0522; www.st-art.biz*
- ⊜ *Old Street, then bus 8, 26, 48, 55, 388*
- ❷ *FREE*

This small gallery and shop exhibits only original work by well-known British and international artists who are often in the middle of their career, such as Corinne Charton. All exhibitions are temporary and change every six to eight weeks.

WHITECHAPEL ART GALLERY

- 77–82 Whitechapel High Street, E1 7QX
- Tel: 020 7522 7888; www.whitechapel.org
- Aldgate East
- FREE

Since 1901, this art gallery has given east-enders a chance to see contemporary art for free. Following a £13 million expansion, which added the adjoining Passmore Edwards Library to the gallery's existing exhibition space, Whitechapel reopened in April a whopping 78 per cent bigger than it was before. It now has a permanent gallery and research room, galleries dedicated to new commissions, a study and a creative studio. It also works with local groups through a community outreach programme. Notable past exhibitions include Picasso's masterpiece, *Guernica* (1939); the first major UK show of the American abstract expressionist, Jackson Pollock, in 1958; and in 1970 and 1971, the first shows of David Hockney and Gilbert and George. This winter, the gallery will present photography from south Asia from the 1840s to the present day.

WHITE CUBE

- 48 Hoxton Square, N1 6PB
- Tel: 020 7930 5373; www.whitecube.com
- Old Street
- FREE

White Cube opened this gallery on Hoxton Square in 2000, in a former light industry building dating from the 1920s. The gallery's exhibition space covers two floors and attracts up to 110,000 visitors annually. The gallery shows temporary exhibitions by new and established artists, which change every six to eight weeks. Past exhibitions have shown Darren Almond's series of eerie full moon photographs as well as Marcus Harvey's *White Riot*, a portrait of Margaret Thatcher – made up of sex toys. A second White Cube gallery is close to St James's tube station.

EXPLORE: VYNER STREET

- Vyner Street, E2
- Bethnal Green

Like its more established neighbours, Shoreditch and Hackney, Bethnal Green is gaining a reputation as an East End art hub. Head to Vyner Street and you'll see why. Look out for **Ibid Projects** (no. 21; 020 8983 4355; www.ibidprojects.com), which exhibits video installations, animation and sketches, and **Vyner Street Gallery** (no. 23; 07970 484 316; www.vynerstreetgallery.co.uk), a modern space next door. There is also **Fred** (no. 45; 020 8981 2987; www.fred-london.com), which shares its location with **One in the Other** (no. 45; 020 8983 6240; www.oneintheother.com), and **Wilkinson** (nos. 50–8; 020 8980 2662; www.wilkinsongallery.com) further down.

▼ WEST

FLOW

- ❶ 1–5 Needham Road, W11 2RP
- ⊕ Tel: 020 7243 0782; www.flowgallery.co.uk
- ⊖ Notting Hill Gate
- ❹ FREE; £30 workshops

This bright and airy art gallery has a permanent collection, showcasing a range of media such as metal, wood, ceramics, glass, jewellery and textiles, as well as six temporary exhibitions each year.

MINT

- ❶ 2 North Terrace, SW3 2BA
- ⊕ Tel: 020 7225 2288; www.mintshop.co.uk
- ⊖ South Kensington
- ❹ FREE

This interior design gallery/shop displays a range of one-off ceramics, glass, textiles and furniture, half of which is created by independent artists. Items on display might range from porcelain piggy banks to handmade wobbly vases.

PM GALLERY

- ❶ Pitzhanger Manor, Walpole Park, Mattock Lane, Ealing, W5 5EQ
- ⊕ Tel: 020 8567 1227; www.ealing.gov.uk
- ⊖ Ealing Broadway
- ❹ FREE

The three rooms within this gallery host exhibitions from professional artists, displaying media from sculpture and film to photography and installation. It also organizes occasional late-night openings and talks by the curator.

SAATCHI GALLERY

- ❶ Duke of York's HQ, King's Road, Chelsea, SW3 4SQ
- ⊕ Tel: 020 7811 3070; www.saatchi-gallery.co.uk
- ⊖ Sloane Square
- ❹ FREE

Throughout its 20-year history, the Saatchi Gallery has aimed to exhibit modern art by young artists or internationally recognized artists whose work is largely unknown to the British audience. Past exhibitions have shown the work of Andy Warhol and Jeff Koons in the 1980s, and Lucian Freud, Cindy Sherman and Damien Hirst in the 1990s. After it moved from County Hall, this collection of contemporary art reopened to the public in 2008 in its current home, which was once an orphanage and old army barracks. The gallery has 15 rooms across 4 floors and exhibitions change every 3 months.

MUSEUMS

There are so many museums in London, many of which you've probably not even heard of. And the best thing about them is that most are free. So, the next weekend that's a complete washout, instead of hiding under your duvet, make the most of what's on your doorstep.

(N.B. Prices are for the cheapest adult ticket available.)

▼ CENTRAL

BANK OF ENGLAND MUSEUM

- ❶ *Bartholomew Lane (off Threadneedle Street), EC2R 8AH*
- ✆ *Tel: 020 7601 5545; www.bankofengland.co.uk*
- ⊖ *Bank*
- ❹ *FREE*

Ever dreamed of getting your hands on a two-stone solid bar of gold? Then visit the Bank of England Museum, which is joined to the Bank of England. You can also learn about the bank's history and its currency since its foundation in 1694. Five permanent galleries lead you through the museum's 1,000-square-metre space, which showcases a chronological interactive display. As well as having the largest collection of Bank of England banknotes in the world, the museum displays engraved silverwork, rare coins and original artwork by note designers. The museum also runs events, from testing your handwriting using authentic quills and designing your own banknote to learning about how to stop forgery.

BRITISH MUSEUM

- ❶ *Great Russell Street, WC1B 3DG*
- ✆ *Tel: 020 7323 8000; www.britishmuseum.org*
- ⊖ *Russell Square, Holborn*
- ❹ *FREE*

Visitors to the British Museum have the physician, Sir Hans Sloane (1660–1753), to thank, as it was the preservation of his personal collection of 71,000 artefacts which led to its creation. The museum opened to the public six years after Sloane's death, and has grown and grown ever since – today its collection boasts 7 million objects and the museum receives 5 million visitors a year. There are 10 departments, which cover each continent as well as conservation, treasures, coins, medals, prints and drawings.

THE BRITISH POSTAL MUSEUM AND ARCHIVE

- *Freeling House, Phoenix Place, WC1X 0DL*
- *Tel: 020 7239 2570; www.postalheritage.org.uk*
- *Farringdon, Russell Square*
- *FREE*

Historians and stamp collectors may be interested in this museum, which is only open for monthly events and open days. The free archive tours explore old Royal Mail records, uniforms and stamp collections. It also has research facilities.

CARTOON MUSEUM

- *35 Little Russell Street, WC1A 2HH*
- *Tel: 020 7580 8155; www.cartoonmuseum.org*
- *Russell Square*
- *£5.50*

From *Beano* and *Rupert* comic strips to World War Two cartoons of Winston Churchill and caricatures of George W. Bush and Tony Blair, you're bound to find a cartoon in this museum that tickles your fancy. As well as the 1,500 cartoons and comics displayed across the museum's two floors, the museum library (reference only) has over 5,000 books and 6,000 comics, including old *Punch* magazines. Since the museum opened in 2006, it has run exhibitions on cartoonist Carl Giles (1916–95) and some remarkably funny local schoolchildren. The museum runs regular cartoon and animation workshops for kids.

CENTRE FOR THE MAGIC ARTS

- *12 Stephenson Way, Euston, NW1 2HD*
- *Tel: 020 7387 2222; www.themagiccircle.co.uk*
- *Euston Square*
- *£32, includes show*

This museum opened its doors to the public in 1998 and, since then, visitors have enjoyed its collection of magic tricks, Europe's largest collection of magic books, a model of Houdini's Chinese water torture cell and a magician's straitjacket. The entry price includes a magic stage show, snacks and a tour. As well as seeing valuable turn-of-the-century posters advertising old magic shows, you'll also see the costume of Chung Ling Soo, the magician famous for catching bullets in his hand (he died when the last one hit him in the chest). The tour takes about three hours. The museum is usually open by appointment only.

CHURCHILL MUSEUM AND THE CABINET WAR ROOMS

- *Clive Steps, King Charles Street, SW1A 2AQ*
- *Tel: 020 7930 6961; cwr.iwm.org.uk*
- *Westminster, St James's Park*
- *£12.95*

With its period furniture, some of which is original, you can try to imagine what it must have been like when Winston Churchill and his ministers gathered in the underground Cabinet Room to discuss their strategy at the start of World War II. You can picture the prime minister broadcasting a speech to the world over the BBC microphones; or pouring over atlases in the Map Room, then talking in code to the US president in the Transatlantic Telephone Room late at night. Once you've explored the Cabinet War Rooms, you can find out more about Churchill in the adjacent museum. By touching buttons on a 15-metre timeline, visitors can explore his childhood and career through soundtracks, photographs and film. A tour of the premises takes about 90 minutes.

HUNTERIAN MUSEUM

- 🛈 *Royal College of Surgeons of England, 35–43 Lincoln's Inn Fields, WC2A 3PE*
- ☏ *Tel: 020 7869 6560; www.rcseng.ac.uk*
- ⊖ *Holborn, Chancery Lane*
- 💰 *FREE*

If you have a burning desire to examine pickled organs, then this museum, housed in the Royal College of Surgeons, has floor-to-ceiling shelves stacked with jars full of them. Of the 3,500 specimens on display, there are seven ears, 26 penises, 17 feet and 15 spleens – that's not to mention a tapir's anus, giraffe's eyelid and rectum of a bishop. The collection originally belonged to the 18th-century surgeon, anatomist and dentist John Hunter, and opened to the public on its current site in 1813. More specimens have since been added, such as a denture belonging to Winston Churchill, a twisted spine and the skeleton of the 'Irish giant', Charles Byrne. One of the highlights is the section on the intricacies of keyhole surgery, where a hands-on display gives you the chance to practise surgery for yourself, watching your movements on a TV monitor.

LONDON TRANSPORT MUSEUM

- 🛈 *Covent Garden Piazza, WC2E 7BB*
- ☏ *Tel: 020 7379 6344; www.ltmuseum.co.uk*
- ⊖ *Covent Garden*
- 💰 *£10*

This museum looks at public transport in London from 1800, from the point of view of both passengers and staff. There are 375,000 items on display, which include Victorian trams, old double-decker buses, vintage uniforms and 5,000 posters. There are also drawings and photographs on display. *Insider info: there are currently 270 tube stations, and the first underground rail line was the Metropolitan, which opened in 1863.*

NATURAL HISTORY MUSEUM

- 🛈 *Cromwell Road, SW7 5BD*
- ☏ *Tel: 020 7942 5000; www.nhm.ac.uk*
- ⊖ *South Kensington, Gloucester Road*
- 💰 *FREE*

Here are some figures for you: about 3.8 million people visit the museum annually, to see its 28 million insects, 27 million animals, 9 million fossils, 6 million algae and plants, 500,000 rocks and minerals and 3,200 meteorites. Impressed? You should be, as this museum covers 95,000 square metres, making it the second largest museum in London after the British Museum. Just a quarter is open to the public, though, as the rest is occupied by curators carrying out research. And yet there's still plenty of room in its 30 galleries to house a t-rex skeleton, a blue whale skeleton and, in the central hall, a 1,300-year-old giant sequoia tree. Make time to visit the eight-storey Darwin Centre, which opened last September. Costing £78 million, it's the most significant expansion to the museum since it opened to the public in 1881. Highlights include Inside the Cocoon, where you can see researchers at work, and the David Attenborough Studio, where visitors can interact with museum scientists. This year, a new art and illustration gallery is planned.

POLLOCKS TOY MUSEUM

- ❶ 1 Scala Street, W1T 2HL
- ⊕ Tel: 020 7636 3452; www.pollockstoymuseum.com
- ⊖ Goodge Street
- ❷ £5

Housed in two connected properties, there are six rooms, linked by narrow hallways, which are packed with old board games, mechanical toys, dolls' houses, puppets and, yes, the odd creepy clown. There's also a toy shop.

ROYAL ACADEMY OF MUSIC

- ❶ Marylebone Road, NW1 5HT
- ⊕ Tel: 020 7873 7373; www.ram.ac.uk
- ⊖ Regent's Park, Baker Street
- ❷ FREE

Budding musicians will be interested in the academy's museum collection of musical memorabilia, original manuscripts and instruments, all of which are kept in working order.

SCIENCE MUSEUM

- ❶ Exhibition Road, South Kensington, SW7 2DD
- ⊕ Tel: 0870 870 4868; www.sciencemuseum.org.uk, www.danacentre.org.uk
- ⊖ South Kensington
- ❷ FREE; £6.25 temporary exhibitions

It would take days, or weeks, to explore all 300,000 objects in this museum's 25 galleries. The exhibits are spread over seven floors and cover topics as diverse as health and medicine, time and space, flight and shipping – so you'll just have to pick and choose those which interest you the most. Space-obsessed kids will enjoy the capsule that rocketed to the moon in 1969 and simulator rides; chronomaniacs can examine a clock dating from 1392; dads can get close to a crashed Formula 1 car and in the 'Who am I?' gallery, visitors can see a reconstructed 2,000-year-old skeleton. There's also a giant IMAX screen (24 metres wide) showing 3-D films that'll make you jump. Plus, the Dana Centre in the museum's annex hosts live debates on controversial science, scientific art installations, experiments and stand-up comedy for grown-ups.

SPENCER HOUSE

- ❶ 27 St James's Place, SW1A 1NR
- ✆ Tel: 020 7499 8620 (24-hour information), 020 7514 1958; www.spencerhouse.co.uk
- ◉ Green Park
- ❹ £9

Despite the rather strict and snooty visiting rules, this 18th-century private palace is still worth a visit. Built between 1756 and 1766 for the first Earl Spencer – a relative of Diana, Princess of Wales – the eight restored rooms reflect the Spencers' passion for entertaining and art. On the ground floor, the Dining Room (with its chandelier, thick carpet and paintings) and the Palm Room (named after its carved, gilt palm trees) are the most impressive rooms. A stone staircase leads you upstairs – the Great Room, a large ballroom, is by far the most striking. Outside, the half-acre garden backs onto Green Park.

VAULT

- ❶ 150 Old Park Lane, W1K 1QZ
- ✆ Tel: 020 7629 0382, 020 7514 1700; www.hardrock.com
- ◉ Hyde Park Corner
- ❹ FREE

You needn't be a dinner guest at the Hard Rock Cafe to check out its permanent exhibition of rock and pop memorabilia in the restaurant's basement – which also happens to be the Queen's former bank vault. Items on display include the costume and guitar of Guns 'N' Roses' Slash, from the band's 'November Rain' video; Madonna's bustier from her 1990 Blonde Ambition tour; John Lennon's hand-corrected lyrics to 'Instant Karma'; and the museum's most popular exhibit, Jimi Hendrix's custom-made Flying V guitar. Visitors are allowed to touch some of the exhibits, such as signed guitars by Oasis, Red Hot Chilli Peppers and Black Sabbath, and staff are happy to give free guided tours.

VICTORIA & ALBERT MUSEUM (V&A)

- ❶ Cromwell Road, SW7 2RL
- ✆ Tel: 020 7942 2000; www.vam.ac.uk
- ◉ South Kensington
- ❹ FREE (permanent collections)

As this museum displays artefacts from all over the world from the past 3,000 years, it might be an idea to visit several times, viewing a different floor each time. The museum's 15 collections focus on art and design and cover everything from Asian Buddhist sculptures, psychedelic digital art displays and Vivienne Westwood platform shoes to a Parisian harp dating from 1785. Exhibitions are varied and interactive, with hands-on areas, workshops, demonstrations and talks. A new addition is the Theatre and Performance Gallery, a collection that was previously housed in the Theatre Museum in Covent Garden until its closure due to lack of space. Here, through 200-year old posters, programmes, puppets, film footage and over 3,500 stage costumes and props, all stages of a performance are examined, from its initial concept and stage and costume design to audience's reactions on the opening night. Look out for Peter Townshend's smashed guitar from a 1970's The Who performance, the flying harness from the first *Peter Pan* production in 1904, Margot Fonteyn's tutu worn in the 1964 production of *Swan Lake* and the human skull used in the Royal Court's 1980 version of *Hamlet*, later signed by the cast. Outside is the John Madejski garden; in the middle of the lawn is a stone-paved courtyard which has water jets children will love.

WELLCOME COLLECTION

- ❶ *183 Euston Road, NW1 2BE*
- ⊕ *Tel: 020 7611 2222; www.wellcomecollection.org*
- ⊖ *Euston*
- ❹ *FREE*

This modern museum explores the concepts of health, illness, life and death from a medical, scientific and artistic perspective. There are two permanent collections. Medicine Man has a range of objects collected by the founder, Henry Wellcome, such as chastity belts, artificial eyeballs, Napoleon's toothbrush and enema syringes; Medicine Now exhibits medical and scientific artworks dating from 1936 (the year Wellcome died). Highlights include a map made from mosquitoes and a collection of images taken by Ellie Harrison, who photographed everything she ate before eating it, for one year. There is also a temporary gallery; past exhibitions include Life Before Death – a display of intimate photos of terminally ill patients before and after their death, and a collection of skeletons found on digs around London.

THE WIENER LIBRARY INSTITUTE OF CONTEMPORARY HISTORY

- ❶ *4 Devonshire Street, W1W 5BH*
- ⊕ *Tel: 020 7636 7247; www.wienerlibrary.co.uk*
- ⊖ *Regent's Park*
- ❹ *FREE*

After Alfred Wiener, a German Jew, fled Germany in 1933, he set up an office dedicated to collecting information about Nazi Germany, which was the beginning of the Wiener Library. Its extensive collection now includes interviews of Holocaust survivors, original newspapers, photographs of everyday Jewish life, the rise of anti-Semitism, refugees, the Holocaust and post-war trials of Nazi war criminals.

▼ NORTH

CHURCH FARMHOUSE MUSEUM

- *Greyhound Hill, Hendon, NW4 4JR*
- *Tel: 020 8359 3942; www.churchfarmhousemuseum.co.uk*
- *Hendon Central*
- *FREE*

This museum, which has eight rooms open to the public, is housed in a former farmhouse dating from 1660. It contains a reconstructed 1820's kitchen, an 1890's laundry, an 1850's dining room, plus a display of 20th-century toys, puzzles and games children can play with. There are also changing exhibits and a small outdoor garden with a pond, fruit trees and a small children's maze.

FREUD MUSEUM

- *20 Maresfield Gardens, NW3 5SX*
- *Tel: 020 7435 2002; www.freud.org.uk*
- *Finchley Road*
- *£5*

This three-storey Hampstead house was once home to the psychoanalyst Sigmund Freud. The ground floor and first floor now serve to display his family's collection of Egyptian, Greek, Roman and Chinese artefacts – the most popular piece, of course, being his psychoanalytic couch.

THE JEWISH MUSEUM

- *129–31 Albert Street, Camden, NW1 7NB*
- *Tel: 020 8371 7373; www.jewishmuseum.org.uk*
- *Camden Town*
- *£6.50*

Following a two-year renovation, the museum is estimated to reopen in January this year. Visitors will realize that there's a lot more to Jewish history than the Holocaust. The museum covers Jewish history, religion and immigration from 1066 to the modern day, and includes ceremonial art and photography exhibitions.

MARYLEBONE CRICKET CLUB (MCC) MUSEUM

- *Lord's Cricket Ground, St John's Wood, NW8 8QN*
- *Tel: 020 7616 8500, 020 7616 8595 (tours); www.lords.org*
- *St John's Wood*
- *£3 museum, £14 tour*

The museum charts the 400-year history of cricket, from the time it was an informal game on a village green to becoming a major international event. Cricket fans will be interested to see photographs, paintings and, of course, the Ashes urn, which Australia gave to the England cricket captain in 1883.

▼ SOUTH

THE BRAMAH MUSEUM OF TEA AND COFFEE

- ❶ *40 Southwark Street, Bankside, SE1 1UN*
- ⊕ *Tel: 020 7403 5650; www.teaandcoffeemuseum.co.uk*
- ❷ *London Bridge*
- ❸ *£4*

This museum explores the social impact behind the UK's 400-year tea and coffee trade. Through prints, maps and old photographs you'll discover how tea was produced in the plantations of east Asia, India and Sri Lanka and how it found its way to sitting rooms across Britain. When you've finished looking around, stop for afternoon tea in the tea room, and admire the floral teacups.

CLINK PRISON MUSEUM

- ❶ *1 Clink Street, SE1 9DG*
- ⊕ *Tel: 020 7403 0900; www.clink.co.uk*
- ❷ *London Bridge*
- ❸ *£5*

This educational museum opened 20 years ago on the site of the UK's first women's prison (1151–1780), which burned down in an arson attack and later became a men's prison. There are seven areas in the museum's only room; these explore crime and punishment, the history of Southwark and former inmates. The display of torture devices will make you squirm.

DESIGN MUSEUM

- ❶ *28 Shad Thames, Bermondsey, SE1 2YD*
- ⊕ *Tel: 020 7940 8790; www.designmuseum.org*
- ❷ *London Bridge*
- ❸ *£8.50*

In 1989, this museum moved from the basement of the V&A Museum to a former warehouse on the South Bank. Since its conception, it has hosted exhibitions based around contemporary fashion and graphic design, architecture, ceramics and furniture. The museum has two galleries, as well as an outdoor glass tank, all of which host eight different exhibitions a year – its most popular show to date was a collection of shoes by Manolo Blahnik.

FAN MUSEUM

- ❶ *12 Crooms Hill, Greenwich, SE10 8ER*
- ⊕ *Tel: 020 8305 1441; www.fan-museum.org*
- ❷ *Cutty Sark DLR*
- ❸ *£4*

Inside these two Grade II-listed Georgian town houses is a collection of 3,500 fans dating from the 11th century. It's a small museum – just two galleries – but it manages to pack in fans made from ivory, mother of pearl, tortoiseshell and paper, some of which are carved and decorated with silver, gold and precious stones. The first gallery is permanent and the second gallery changes three times a year. The museum also organizes fan-making workshops and there's a delightful Orangery, which serves afternoon tea.

FASHION AND TEXTILE MUSEUM

- ❶ *83 Bermondsey Street, Southwark, SE1 3XF*
- ⊕ *Tel: 020 7407 8664; www.ftmlondon.org*
- ◎ *London Bridge*
- ❹ *£6.50*

Since 2003, this iconic museum has livened up Bermondsey Street with its brightly painted orange-and-pink exterior. British designer Zandra Rhodes founded the museum to celebrate fashion, textiles and jewellery design. Past exhibitions have focused on the little black dress, the evolution of underwear and style mag *i-D*; the museum also runs book signings, talks and workshops where you can turn an old jumper into a hat or make your own brooch.

FLORENCE NIGHTINGALE MUSEUM

- ❶ *St Thomas's Hospital, 2 Lambeth Palace Road, SE1 7EW*
- ⊕ *Tel: 020 7620 0374; www.florence-nightingale.co.uk*
- ◎ *Waterloo, Westminster*
- ❹ *£5.80*

Florence Nightingale (1820–1910) dedicated her life to nursing and this museum dedicates itself to her. Known as 'the lady with the lamp' for her role in caring for Crimean War veterans, Nightingale later fought to improve healthcare standards in hospitals, campaigned for free healthcare and set up the Nightingale Training School for Nurses. At the time of writing, the museum was planning a £1 million development project to prepare for the centenary of Nightingale's death in 2010.

GARDEN MUSEUM

- ❶ *Lambeth Palace Road, SE1 7LB*
- ⊕ *Tel: 020 7401 8865; www.gardenmuseum.org.uk*
- ◎ *Lambeth North*
- ❹ *£6*

This museum, formerly known as the Museum of Garden History, was founded in 1977 in the old St Mary-at-Lambeth parish church. After a refurbishment, it reopened in November 2008 with a new timber interior. Inside, there's a permanent gallery upstairs and a temporary one downstairs, where you can learn about British gardeners through private archives, photographs and paintings. There's also a small 17th-century-inspired knot garden in the grounds, where plants and flowers are chosen for their historic significance. In the summer, delightful evening concerts are held in the garden, which is on the River Thames opposite the Houses of Parliament.

HORNIMAN MUSEUM

- 100 London Rd, Forest Hill, SE23 3PQ
- Tel: 020 8699 1872; www.horniman.ac.uk
- Forest Hill BR, then bus 176, 185, 197, 356, P4
- FREE

This fascinating museum dates from the 1860s, when Frederick John Horniman, a tea trader, began collecting artefacts on his travels. Its five permanent collections now display exhibits from as far afield as Uzbekistan, Mongolia and Cameroon. Visit the Natural History Gallery to see stuffed and dissected animals; the Centenary Gallery for its African masks and torture chair; and the African Worlds Gallery, with its Egyptian mummies dating from 1570 to 1070BC. The basement has an aquarium with British pond life, Fijian reef fish and poisonous blue frogs, and there's a garden, too (see p.202).

IMPERIAL WAR MUSEUM

- Lambeth Road, SE1 6HZ
- Tel: 020 7416 5320; www.iwm.org.uk
- Lambeth North
- FREE

However much Nazi Germany was drummed into you at school, you're bound to learn more in the Imperial War Museum's permanent Holocaust exhibition. There's also a 'children's war' section, fighter planes you can touch and a replica of an underground bunker in the Blitz Experience gallery. While the museum is interactive, with hands-on displays, videos and phones you can pick up and listen to, it is still text-heavy. So it's best to visit several times over a few months – ideally not during school time if you want to read in peace.

THE OLD OPERATING THEATRE MUSEUM AND HERB GARRET

- 9a St Thomas Street, Southwark, SE1 9RY
- Tel: 020 7188 2679; www.thegarret.org.uk
- London Bridge
- £5.60

There's something appealing about this ramshackle collection, which is at the top of a spiral staircase inside a dusty church attic. The church was once part of the old St Thomas's Hospital, but it was boarded up when the hospital moved, and the attic remained hidden until it was rediscovered 100 years later, in 1956. It's now a museum dedicated to making visitors squeamish. With the help of artefacts such as a wooden operating table and gruesome photos, visitors to the operating theatre – built in 1822, before anaesthetics and antiseptic – can imagine the agony of an operation. The herb garret is also a main draw, with its stock of medicinal herbs and faded labels explaining their health properties.

▼ EAST

GEFFRYE MUSEUM

- ❶ *136 Kingsland Road, E2 8EA*
- ⊕ *Tel: 020 7739 9893; www.geffrye-museum.org.uk*
- ⊜ *Old Street, then bus 243*
- ❺ *FREE*

Amid the council estates and cheap Vietnamese restaurants on Kingsland Road, you might not expect to come across former almshouses dating from the 18th century. So, visitors to the two-storey Geffrye Museum and its 1.5-acre grounds will be pleasantly surprised. As you progress through the ground floor, you pass a permanent display of 11 period rooms in chronological order, which explore how the interiors of British middle-class homes have changed since 1600. Starting with a 17th-century dining room, you'll be guided past a typical Georgian town house drawing room, a 1930's lounge, an open-plan 1960's living room and a modern, converted loft. At the back of the house there's a lovely landscaped garden with a greenhouse and walled herb garden.

MUSEUM OF CHILDHOOD

- ❶ *Cambridge Heath Road, E2 9PA*
- ⊕ *Tel: 020 8983 5200; www.vam.ac.uk*
- ⊜ *Bethnal Green*
- ❺ *FREE*

Set in a stunning glass-and-iron building, this museum's marble mosaic floors in its central hall will impress you as soon as you enter. Interactive displays cover 3,000 square metres over two floors – plenty to keep both adults and children occupied for an afternoon. The exhibitions explore how toys and games were invented, how they're influenced by gender roles and the extent of children's imagination. The museum's permanent galleries are divided into three sections. Highlights from the Moving Toys exhibition include mechanical dancing monkeys, a Hornby train track, robots and a rocking horse. The Creativity area encourages children to use their imagination with Victorian tea sets, a dressing-up area and a Meccano play table. The Childhood section has dolls' houses dating from 1673, a sandpit children can play in and Punch and Judy booths, as well as a dance area with a free jukebox. There is also a lively events programme.

MUSEUM OF IMMIGRATION AND DIVERSITY

- ❶ *19 Princelet Street, E1 6QH*
- ⊕ *Tel: 020 7247 5352; www.19princeletstreet.org.uk*
- ⊜ *Algate East, Liverpool Street*
- ❺ *FREE*

Built in 1719, this Grade II-listed house has, in its time, been home to a family of French silk-weavers who escaped persecution at the hands of Louis XV; the site of a synagogue built in its garden in 1869; a community centre in which anti-fascist marches were planned; and, more recently, a house at the heart of the Bengali community. So, it's apt that it now houses the Museum of Immigration and Diversity, which brings to life the influence of the ethnic groups who have immigrated to the East End through a modest exhibition of immigrants' testimonials and photographs. The museum is under threat due to lack of funding, so its opening hours are sporadic – call ahead if you plan to visit.

MUSEUM OF LONDON

- 🄾 150 London Wall, EC2Y 5HN
- 🄾 Tel: 020 7001 9844; www.museumoflondon.org.uk
- 🄾 Barbican, St Paul's, Moorgate
- 🄾 FREE

This fascinating museum brings to life the history of London with reconstructed street scenes, original artefacts found on archaeological digs and a new interactive touch-screen map. The museum has two floors. The lower galleries, which tell the story of London and its people from 1666 to the present day, will reopen this March following a £20.5 million refurbishment programme. Highlights include the City Gallery, which is home to the Lord Mayor's Coach. In the Sackler Hall you can access the museum's collections online, and there is also a 230-seat auditorium for lectures and film screenings. One of the more poignant displays includes a memorial book dedicated to the 52 people who died in the July 2005 bombings. The upper galleries explore London from prehistoric times to 1666. Here you can swot up on Roman London, medieval London and the Vikings, and how a small bakery fire managed to devastate the city. A Victorian pleasure garden is also planned, which will have trees lit with tea lights, plus mannequins dressed in gowns and masks.

MUSEUM OF LONDON DOCKLANDS

- 🄾 West India Quay, Canary Wharf, E14 4AL
- 🄾 Tel: 020 7001 9844; www.museumindocklands.org.uk
- 🄾 Canary Wharf, West India Quay DLR
- 🄾 £5 for annual ticket

This Grade I-listed Georgian building was once a warehouse used to store the sugar, rum and coffee brought to Britain from Caribbean plantations. Now, this museum's 12 permanent galleries and temporary displays explore the 2,000-year history behind the River Thames: from Roman and Saxon times and the emergence of the docks to the impact of the Blitz and the area's regeneration in the past 20 years. Highlights include harrowing sketches of slaves on a treadmill, an opium pipe, a mummified rat found in St Katherine's Docks and debris left over from the ruins of the Blitz. Exhibitions strive to be interactive and children in particular will enjoy guessing the smell of the spices, tea and wine in the Warehouse of the World gallery, as well as exploring Sailortown, a reconstruction of Wapping's maze of 19th-century lanes.
Insider info: in 2006, a private exorcism ceremony was held within the museum to expel evil spirits.

SUTTON HOUSE

- 🔂 2–4 Homerton High Street, Hackney, E9 6JQ
- 🌐 Tel: 020 8986 2264; www.nationaltrust.org.uk
- 🔵 Hackney Central BR
- 🔴 £2.90

This Tudor house and courtyard has certainly had a chequered history since it was built in 1535. As you walk around the oak-panelled rooms, with their Tudor windows and original stone fireplaces, displays explain the history of the house and who has lived there – Henry VIII's secretary of state, merchants and Victorian schoolteachers. A trade union then took it over, but when they abandoned it the building was left to ruin – it was actually home to squatters in the 1980s, who left their mark in graffiti in the attic. In the early 1990s it underwent a renovation, and it's now a National Trust property. Special events include piano concerts, children's craft workshops, poetry classes and walking tours of Hackney. It also hosts regular displays of contemporary art by local artists.

WHITECHAPEL BELL FOUNDRY

- 🔂 32–4 Whitechapel Road, E1 1DY
- 🌐 Tel: 020 7247 2599;
  www.whitechapelbellfoundry.co.uk
- 🔵 Aldgate East
- 🔴 FREE; £10 for a tour

The foundry has been making bells since 1570 – it even made Big Ben, in 1858. At this small museum you'll realize there's quite a lot to bells – there are displays on clock bells, tower bells and turret bells, as well as information on campanology. Tours run every Saturday, but booking ahead is advised.

THE WOMEN'S LIBRARY

- 🔂 London Metropolitan University, 25 Old Castle Street, E1 7NT
- 🌐 Tel: 020 7320 2222;
  www.londonmet.ac.uk/thewomenslibrary/
- 🔵 Aldgate East, Aldgate
- 🔴 FREE

The Women's Library moved to its current location in 2002, but its history goes back to 1926, when the less-catchy Library of the London Society for Women's Service was set up. It aims to examine British women's lives in the past, present and future, by exploring women's rights over suffrage and reproduction, the family and home, education and employment. Past exhibitions include Between the Covers, which looked at how women's magazines from the 17th century reveal changes in women's aspirations, while What Women Want explored women's achievements since gaining the vote. There's a lively events calendar that includes talks by artists, guided tours and performances.

▼ WEST

FULHAM PALACE

- ❶ *Bishops Avenue, Fulham, SW6 6EA*
- ⊕ *Tel: 020 7736 8140; www.fulhampalace.org*
- ⊖ *Putney Bridge*
- ❶ *FREE*

This museum is housed in a Grade I-listed building that dates from 1495, when it used to be a summer retreat for the bishops of London. While the grounds opened to the public in 1974, the palace didn't open till 1992. Since then, the museum's three rooms have showcased local-history displays and artefacts relating to the building's history and architecture, as well as contemporary art exhibitions in its art gallery. The palace is set in 13 acres of woodland, sweeping lawns and botanic gardens – a walk around the grounds takes about 15 minutes.

MUSEUM OF BRANDS, PACKAGING AND ADVERTISING

- ❶ *2 Colville Mews, Lonsdale Road, Notting Hill, W11 2AR*
- ⊕ *Tel: 020 7908 0880; www.museumofbrands.com*
- ⊖ *Notting Hill Gate, Ladbroke Grove, Westbourne Park*
- ❶ *£5.80*

This museum is a shrine to advertising, managing to turn the mundane – from a comic, magazine or Kellogg's cornflake packet – into a significant cultural artefact worthy of study, exploring how the rise of brands from Victorian times have set trends and influenced our lives. Past exhibitions have explored, among other things, the 'make do and mend' attitude of wartime Britain and what today's generation could learn from it; 'the art of the biscuit tin'; and old sweet wrappers – remember Opal Fruits and Marathons?

NATIONAL ARMY MUSEUM

- ❶ *Royal Hospital Road, Chelsea, SW3 4HT*
- ⊕ *Tel: 020 7881 2455 (recorded information), 020 7730 0717 (switchboard); www.national-army-museum.ac.uk*
- ⊖ *Sloane Square*
- ❶ *FREE*

This museum has thousands of weapons, plus 10 frostbitten fingers from a Mount Everest explorer. But it's not all about blood and gore – the museum looks in depth at the human cost of war, through first-hand oral accounts from World War I veterans, factory workers and prisoners of war. There are four permanent galleries: the Making of Britain 1066–1783 gallery, which looks at the beginnings of the British Empire; the Changing the World gallery, which explores the expansion and defence of British trade from 1784–1904; the World Wars gallery; and the Modern Army gallery, where you can put your military skills to the test and learn jungle survival techniques.

THEATRE, CINEMA & COMEDY

What is it about going to the theatre that gives you a natural high? If anyone knew, they'd bottle it and make a million. If West End musicals aren't for you, then head to Islington to catch a play in a theatre-pub, or go to a comedy club (*see* pp.154–5) or see a dance performance at Sadler's Wells (*see* p.156). Alternatively, if you're craving popcorn, but don't want to spend £10 on a barrel's worth at a big-name cinema, then consider some of London's independent picture houses.

(N.B. Prices are guides only, for one adult ticket – contact the venues directly for further details.)

▼ CENTRAL

BFI IMAX

- ❶ *1 Charlie Chaplin Walk, Southbank, Waterloo, SE1 8XR*
- ⊕ *Tel: 0870 787 2525 (box office); www.bfi.org.uk*
- ⊜ *Waterloo*
- ❸ *£8.75–£15 IMAX; £27 all-nighters; £20 opera screenings*

Recall the last time you were frightened out of your wits and imagine that fear magnified 20 times. That's how you will feel watching great white sharks dart towards you or dinosaurs leap out of the screen at the IMAX. At 20 metres high and 26 metres wide, the BFI IMAX screen is the UK's biggest, making whatever it is you're watching a thrilling experience – whether it's the latest Harry Potter film in 3-D, a U2 concert recorded live or a *Madame Butterfly* opera. The single auditorium has seats for just under 500 housed within a modern multi-storey, glass cylinder. The venue also hosts film festivals.

THE COCHRANE THEATRE

- ❶ *Southampton Row, WC1B 4AP*
- ⊕ *Tel: 020 7269 1606 (box office); www.cochranetheatre.co.uk*
- ⊜ *Holborn*
- ❸ *£8–12*

It's little wonder that the Cochrane hosts such cutting-edge dance, comedy and opera, once you know it's owned by the University of the Arts London. The university has links with Camberwell College of Art, Central Saint Martins College of Art and Design, Chelsea College of Art and Design, London College of Fashion and London College of Communication, and all of the theatre's shows are performed by the colleges' fashion, design and drama students.

CURZON SOHO

- 𝟢 *99 Shaftesbury Avenue, W1D 5DY*
- ⊕ *Tel: 020 7292 1686; www.curzoncinemas.com*
- ⊘ *Leicester Square*
- ⊕ *£12*

Curzon Soho is one of five Curzon cinemas across London. The cinema has three screens for 120, 133 and 249, all of which show a diverse mix of art-house films, shorts, cult classics and documentaries. It also hosts monthly film festivals, such as the Smoking Cabinet, which is dedicated to early burlesque; monthly midnight screenings; and live music in its underground bar – you might spot celebs here in among media types. As well as film, the venue is dedicated to hosting monthly art exhibitions, which tend to show photography and paintings that are linked in some way to the films on show. The other cinemas in the brand are Renoir Cinema in Camden, Curzon Mayfair, Chelsea Cinema and Curzon Richmond. Not sure which one to visit? Well, in the words of one Curzon exec, 'Renoir is the home of the more hardcore foreign-film-goer; Mayfair is our most prestigious site, with a more genteel clientele; Chelsea is a 700-seater which plays the best in art house alongside the likes of *Quantum of Solace*, while Richmond is a friendly, local neighbourhood cinema outside of central London.'

ICA

- 𝟢 *Nash House, The Mall, SW1Y 5AH*
- ⊕ *Tel: 020 7930 3647 (box office), 020 7930 0493 (switchboard); www.ica.org.uk*
- ⊘ *Charing Cross, Picadilly Circus*
- ⊕ *£8 cinema; £5 all cinema seats all Monday; £15 Q&A sessions*

Established in 1947 by a collection of creative types, the Institute of Contemporary Arts aims to make the arts accessible to everyone. The venue has two cinema screens that show experimental world cinema (with subtitles), shorts, documentaries and film festivals – the auditoria have a capacity for 45 and 185. The cinema also regularly hosts Q&A sessions with directors and actors, such as Dennis Hopper and Hanif Kureishi. As well as a cinema, the venue has a theatre, known for its new music – it hosted both Franz Ferdinand's and the Scissor Sisters' debut London gigs. It seats 80 but can fit up to 360 for its stand-up gigs; in the past, The Clash and the Stone Roses performed here. There are also two galleries (see p.124), a bookshop, bar and cafe.

TOP THEATRE TIPS

Theatre tip: Look for cheap tickets in the special-offer section on www.theatremonkey.com. It alphabetically lists every major theatre (not fringe) in London, every theatre offer and how to take advantage of it.

Theatre tip: For 16–25 year olds, visit www.anightlessordinary.org.uk for free theatre tickets for performances at 12 London venues, including **The Bush Theatre** (see p.161), **Royal Court Theatre** (see p.163), **Soho Theatre** (see p.153), **Theatre Royal Stratford East** (see p.160) and **Tricycle Theatre** (see p.156).

Cinema tip: Major discounts at the 14 Vue cinemas across London are available from www.lastminute.com. Tickets cost £4.99 for any film showing Monday to Thursday; just book before 4pm.

Comedy tip: The best comedians head to Edinburgh in August, so think twice before splashing out on tickets for comedy in the capital around this time.

PEACOCK THEATRE

- ❶ Portugal Street, WC2A 2HT
- ⊕ Tel: 020 7863 8268; www.peacocktheatre.com
- ◉ Holborn, Temple
- ❹ £10

This theatre, which seats 1,000, is run by the same group as Sadler's Wells in Islington (see p.156). Yet while Sadler's Wells is known for its highbrow dance performances, the Peacock Theatre hosts more commercial West End shows, such as acrobatics and musicals.

PRINCE CHARLES CINEMA

- ❶ 7 Leicester Place, WC2H 7BY
- ⊕ Tel: 020 7494 3654; www.princecharlescinema.com
- ◉ Leicester Square
- ❹ £1.50–£3.50 members; £4–£5 non-members; £15 singalongs

Considering its location – on a side road just off Leicester Square – this cinema is dirt-cheap; if you're a member (£12 a year), your ticket will cost you less than your bus fare to get here. The cinema has two screens, which show a variety of European films, not-quite-new mainstream blockbusters and singalong events, which cost extra. It also organizes Q&A sessions with directors, or you could do an all-nighter and watch three films back-to-back.

REGENT'S PARK OPEN-AIR THEATRE

- ❶ Open Air Theatre, The Ironworks, Inner Circle, Regent's Park, Camden, NW1 4NR
- ⊕ Tel: 0844 375 3460 (enquiries); 0844 826 4242 (box office); www.openairtheatre.org
- ◉ Regent's Park, Baker Street, Great Portland Street
- ❹ £10–£40
- ▣ Jun–Sep

This delightful alfresco theatre, which seats 1,240, makes an ideal setting for a cultured summer evening of Shakespeare or other classic plays. The venue also holds comedy and music events.

SCREEN ON BAKER STREET

- ❶ 96–8 Baker Street, W1U 6TJ
- ⊕ Tel: 0870 066 4777, 020 3145 0565 (venue manager); www.everymancinema.com
- ◉ Baker Street
- ❹ £10

The two screens at this cinema, which have seats for 85 and 77, show independent and mainstream films. As with all of the cinemas in the Everyman chain, it has a small bar, which allows you to take drinks into the auditoria.

SHAKESPEARE'S GLOBE

- ❶ 21 New Globe Walk, Bankside, SE1 9DT
- ⊕ Tel: 020 7902 1400; 020 7401 9919 (box office); www.shakespeares-globe.org
- ◉ Mansion House, London Bridge
- ❹ £5 standing tickets; £12–£33 seating tickets

Everything about this theatre – its water-reed thatched roof, wooden benches and circular stone courtyard – is a careful reproduction of the open-air playhouse that was built on this site in 1598; its designers meticulously studied written accounts, sketches and old building contracts of the original. Here you can watch Shakespeare plays as well as plays by contemporary writers and occasional operas and Greek dramas. You can also join a tour of the globe; listen to talks by actors, directors and designers; or watch a stage-reading show – where performers act out scenes while reading from the scripts. The single-stage auditorium seats 1,380. *Insider info: 10 thatchers used 800 bundles of sedge from the Norfolk Broads to re-thatch the roof in 2008.*

SOHO THEATRE

- ❶ 21 Dean Street, W1D 3NE
- ⊕ Tel: 020 7478 0100; www.sohotheatre.com
- ◉ Tottenham Court Road, Oxford Circus
- ❹ £10 under-26s; £15–£20 adults

After 41 years, this theatre in the centre of Soho has established itself as a pioneer in new writing. It has a main house for 144 and a studio for 85. As well as showing independent, world cinema and cabaret acts, it's popular for its late-night comedy – regular stand-up comedians include Russell Brand and Eddie Izzard. The venue also hosts talks and workshops. Soho Theatre encourages under-26s to visit by giving away free tickets most nights – availability depends on the show.

▼ NORTH

CLERKENWELL THEATRE

- ❶ *Exmouth Market Community Centre, 24 Exmouth Market, Islington, EC1R 4QE*
- ⊕ *info@teninabedtheatre.org; www.teninabedtheatre.org*
- ◒ *Angel, Farringdon*
- ❹ *£7.50*

This intimate theatre, with a capacity for just 60, hosts a variety of events from bingo and cabaret to alternative theatre by up-and-coming actors. It also hosts stand-up comedy – Alex Zane, Mark Dolan and Trevor Lock have all performed here. It occasionally hosts New Writing Sunday, too, organized by Ten in a Bed Theatre, which gives new writers the chance to get their scripts into the public domain; shows are free for EC1 residents if you can prove your postcode.

EVERYMAN BELSIZE PARK (AKA SCREEN ON THE HILL)

- ❶ *203 Haverstock Hill, Belsize Park, NW3 4QG*
- ⊕ *Tel: 0870 066 4777; www.everymancinema.com*
- ◒ *Belsize Park*
- ❹ *£12*

Like its Everyman Hampstead sister, this cinema shows mainstream films, screenings of live opera and ballet performances from the Royal Opera House and films especially for parents and babies. It also runs kids' programmes on Saturdays, which combine U and PG-cert films with 15 minutes of games and activities for young children – call ahead for details.

EVERYMAN HAMPSTEAD

- ❶ *5 Holly Bush Vale, NW3 6TX*
- ⊕ *Tel: 0870 066 4777; www.everymancinema.com*
- ◒ *Hampstead*
- ❹ *£12*

There are two screens at this cinema; both of which have spacious chairs with cushions. You'll need to book in advance for the second room, though, as it also has comfy red velvet sofas made for two – ideal for a romantic date. As well as showing mainstream films, the venue hosts film festivals, screenings of live opera and ballet performances from the Royal Opera House and films especially for parents and babies. *(N.B. Latecomers won't be allowed in.)*

HEN & CHICKENS

- ❶ *109 St Pauls Road, Highbury, N1 2NA*
- ⊕ *Tel: 020 7704 2001; www.unrestrictedview.co.uk,*
  www.myspace.com/henandchickenstheatre
- ◒ *Highbury & Islington*
- ❹ *£5–10*

This theatre-pub is easy to find as it's right on Highbury Corner, just two minutes' walk from the tube station. The pub downstairs is usually busy with people listening to the jukebox over a few pints; there's a mix of locals and after-work drinkers here, who appreciate the friendly, welcoming bar staff. The pub empties once the performances start, because it's the theatre's new writing and comedy that is the real draw. Established 25 years ago, the 54-seat theatre hosts mostly light-hearted sketches by artists such as Anil Desal, the stand-up chameleon – on one night, he impersonated 52 famous people in 52 minutes.

JACKSONS LANE

- ❶ 269a Archway Road, Highgate, N6 5AA
- ⊕ Tel: 020 8341 4421; www.jacksonslane.org.uk
- ❸ Highgate
- ❹ £10–£15 for shows, prices vary for other events

Housed in a red-brick Gothic church, this multi-arts venue has one theatre with a capacity for 160. Performances include contemporary circus shows, ballet, live music, animation and puppetry. The former church also has four dance and rehearsal studios (see p.227).

KING'S HEAD

- ❶ 115 Upper Street, Islington, N1 1QN
- ⊕ Tel: 020 7226 8561; www.kingsheadtheatre.org
- ❸ Angel, Highbury & Islington
- ❹ £17.50–£20

This pub's been going since the 19th century (see p.176) – but the small fringe theatre at the back wasn't added until 1970. Many a famous actor began treading the boards here: Victoria Wood, Hugh Grant, Shane Richie and Maureen Lipman have all made an appearance at one point. The theatre crams in about 120 on benches and puts on a mix of classic and contemporary material, mostly plays and musicals. Joanna Lumley and Sir Tom Stoppard are patrons.

PHOENIX

- ❶ 52 High Road, East Finchley, N2 9PJ
- ⊕ Tel: 020 8444 6789 (box office), 020 8883 2233 (info); www.phoenixcinema.co.uk
- ❸ East Finchley
- ❹ £6–£9

Built in 1910, this is the oldest continually run cinema in the country, and the projectionist has been working here for the last 50 years. The single-screen cinema, which seats 255, shows mostly art-house, foreign and specialist films, some of which have live music. Patrons Michael Palin, Ken Loach and Victoria Wood also give occasional talks. A £1,050,000 refurbishment of this art deco, Grade-II listed building is expected to be finished this year, which will see the addition of a cafe and new terrace bar.

SADLER'S WELLS

- 🛈 *Rosebery Avenue, Islington, EC1R 4TN*
- ⊕ *Tel: 020 7863 8198; www.sadlerswells.com*
- ⊜ *Angel*
- 💲 *£10–£50*

This modern theatre hosts martial arts, opera, puppetry and circus performances, though its heart lies with dance – anything from tango to flamenco. Past shows have included the *Nutcracker!* directed by Matthew Bourne, who also worked as a choreographer on the *Mary Poppins* musical. There are two stages; with seats for 180, the Lilian Baylis Studio is more suited to intimate performances, whereas the Sadler's Wells Theatre has a capacity for 1,568. The theatre launched a global dance contest lasting throughout 2009 to uncover talented dancers. Entrants post their performances on the theatre's YouTube channel in the hope to win the chance to perform on the Sadler's Wells' stage – the winners will perform on-stage in 2010.

SCREEN ON THE GREEN

- 🛈 *83 Upper Street, Islington, N1 0NP*
- ⊕ *Tel: 0870 066 4777; www.screencinemas.co.uk*
- ⊜ *Angel*
- 💲 *£9*

It may be smaller than the Vue nearby, but here you get the full retro experience of wine gums in a box and red velvet flip-up seats – just don't expect an interval where you can buy ice cream. There's just one screen, with 300 seats. As well as documentaries and foreign films, the cinema organizes occasional Q&A sessions with directors, such as Quentin Tarantino and Spike Lee; live video link to the Royal Opera House shows; and, for hardcore film buffs, all-nighters. You can also watch classic TV series – *The Magic Roundabout*, anyone? A refurbishment is planned for this year.

TRICYCLE

- 🛈 *269 Kilburn High Road, NW6 7JR*
- ⊕ *Tel: 020 7328 1000 (box office), 020 7328 1900 (information line); www.tricycle.co.uk*
- ⊜ *Kilburn*
- 💲 *£10–£20 theatre; £8 cinema; £7 life-drawing classes*

This theatre/cinema shows new and independent releases on its only screen, with seats for 300. Arrive early on Tuesday evenings and Saturday matinees and the first 20 seats are sold on a pay-what-you-can basis. The Tricycle also hosts classic and contemporary plays on its one stage (with seats for 230), such as a modern-day interpretation of *Twelfth Night*. It has a lively children's programme, too, so kids can take part in acting, mime and dance workshops, or listen to storytelling and music. There's also a small gallery, which hosts life-drawing classes and exhibits the work of the artist in residence.

▼ SOUTH

CLAPHAM PICTURE HOUSE

- ❶ *76 Venn Street, SW4 0AT*
- ⊕ *Tel: 0871 704 2055; www.picturehouses.co.uk*
- ◉ *Clapham Common*
- ❹ *£8.50–£10.50 non-members*

There are four screens in this Clapham branch of the City Screen chain. While the cinema shows all the mainstream films, it tries to be alternative and show left-of-centre films as well. Afterwards, stop for snacks and a drink in the cinema's stylish red-and-black split-level bar.

THE EXHIBIT

- ❶ *12 Balham Station Road, Balham, SW12 9SG*
- ⊕ *Tel: 020 8772 6556; www.theexhibit.co.uk*
- ◉ *Balham*
- ❹ *£5 cinema ticket*

You won't find cramped chairs in here – instead, cuddle up to cushions while reclining on one of 12 brown leather sofas made for two. The intimate setting is perfect for a date, or you can hire the room for a private party. The cinema has a drinking licence, so you can sip cosmopolitans while watching a chick flick, or share a bottle of red over an arty French film. Boys, if that's not for you, then go along to a screening of the football World Cup or Six Nations rugby instead.

GREENWICH PICTURE HOUSE

- ❶ *180 Greenwich High Road, Greenwich, SE10 8NN*
- ⊕ *Tel: 020 8853 0484 (office), 0871 704 2059 (box office); www.picturehouses.co.uk*
- ◉ *Greenwich DLR*
- ❹ *£6–£10*

This five-screen cinema shows blockbusters, shorts and foreign-language films, documentaries and live opera via satellite from The Royal Opera House. It also has music and comedy events, and the basement, which seats 53, is available for private hire.

MENIER CHOCOLATE FACTORY

- ❶ *53 Southwark Street, SE1 1RU*
- ⊕ *Tel: 020 7907 7060; www.menierchocolatefactory.com*
- ◉ *London Bridge*
- ❹ *£20–£25*

Alas, this is a chocolate factory no more. Yet this theatre, restaurant and rehearsal venue, which opened in 2004, still has original wooden beams, cast-iron columns and exposed-brick walls dating from 1870.

OVAL HOUSE THEATRE

- 52–4 Kennington Oval, SE11 5SW
- Tel: 020 7582 0080; www.ovalhouse.com
- Oval
- £12

Two theatres make up the Oval House, both of which show plays and musicals. Its urban writing is popular with the black community. The theatre is very disability-friendly; there are screens for wheelchair users to watch the first-floor shows, and shows are accompanied by subtitles or British sign language.

RITZY PICTURE HOUSE

- Brixton Oval, Coldharbour Lane, SW2 1JG
- Tel: 020 7326 2615, 0871 704 2056; www.picturehouses.co.uk
- Brixton
- £6.50–£8.50 non-members

Built in 1910, this five-screen cinema still has some of its original features. These days, though, the cinema has all mod cons and broadcasts live shows from the Royal Opera House via satellite, as well as hosting annual film festivals.

UP THE CREEK

- 302 Creek Road, Greenwich, SE10 9SW
- Tel: 020 8858 4581; www.up-the-creek.com
- Cutty Sark DLR, Greenwich DLR/BR
- £6–£15

This comedy club is popular with hen and stag dos. There are comedy and disco nights on weekends; the music ranges from soul and funk to house and dance.

UNUSUAL CINEMA EXPERIENCES

★ SECRET CINEMA

- www.secretcinema.org

Secret Cinema organizes monthly screenings in locations you wouldn't normally expect – from a derelict theatre to a children's playground or a city farm. All the info is hush-hush; members only find out the details on the day.

★ THE PAPER CINEMA

- www.thepapercinema.com

This cinema uses sketches drawn onto cardboard, intricately cut shapes and poised lights to breathe life into a cast of marionettes. The cinema travels around the UK and Europe, and occasionally hosts 'gigs' at Shunt (see p.170).

▼ EAST

ARCOLA THEATRE

- 27 Arcola Street, E8 2DJ
- Tel: 020 7503 1646 (box office), 020 7503 1645 (office); www.arcolatheatre.com
- Dalston Kingsland BR
- £14–£18

Housed in a converted textile factory, the Arcola Theatre has been putting on shows by pioneering new writers, as well as classic drama, music and comedy performances, since 2000. It has two small studios. On Tuesday evenings, this fringe theatre runs an innovative 'pay what you can' scheme, although seats are limited. As well as performances, every week the theatre runs a free drama class for teens, a Turkish-language acting class, plus acting and writing classes for over-50s. Capoeira dance classes are held on Tuesdays and Thursdays 7–9pm (£7).

HACKNEY EMPIRE

- 291 Mare Street, E8 1EJ
- Tel: 020 8985 2424 (box office), 020 8510 4500 (office); www.hackneyempire.co.uk
- Hackney Central BR; Bethnal Green, then bus 106, 254
- FREE–£22.50 events; £10 bespoke tours

Charlie Chaplin, Stan Laurel, Louis Armstrong, the Greek soprano Maria Callas and Cliff Richard have all performed at this theatre since it opened in 1901. You can still see some original features, such as a statue of the Greek muse of music, Euterpe, adorning the front of the theatre. After a stint as a bingo hall, the theatre reopened as a performance venue and now puts on plays, concerts and operas, as well as pantomimes, burlesque and comedy shows in a tiered auditorium. If you're interested in the theatre's history, or want a glimpse of the dressing rooms backstage, book a tour of the Empire.

JONGLEURS

- 221 Grove Road, Bow, E3 5SN
- Tel: 0844 499 4062 (option two); www.jongleurs.com
- Mile End, Bethnal Green
- £13–£14

This national chain has 15 comedy clubs, four of which are in London (Bow, Battersea, Camden and Watford). While the club's use of 'corporate comedians' sounds about as far from spontaneous comedy as you can get, there's no denying this club's popularity with all age groups. Housed in a restored Victorian warehouse, Bow Jongleurs has two floors with a capacity for 300, with space for a further 250 in its bar. It has an outdoor terrace, too, along Bow Wharf. As well as comedy nights, it hosts quiz nights, gigs and themed parties.

RICH MIX

- *35–47 Bethnal Green Road, E1 6LA*
- *Tel: 020 7613 7498; www.richmix.org.uk*
- *Old Street, Liverpool Street*
- *£7*

Housed in a former garment factory, this three-screen cinema opened in 2006. It shows a mix of new releases, independent and world cinema and films targeted specifically at families; parent and child screenings are available. The centre also has a lively cultural programme, which includes live music, theatre shows, film-making and dance workshops and children's storytelling sessions.

SILENT CINEMA

- *Various*
- *Tel: 0844 477 1000 (bookings), 020 7961 1234 (Andaz Hotel); www.silent-cinema.co.uk*
- *£10*

This is such a simple idea; we can't believe it's not been done before. If you're fed up with teenagers talking loudly in the cinema, trying to be funny, then give the Silent Cinema a try – everyone in the audience wears wireless headphones, so you can watch the film in peace, sort of. The film is projected onto a cinema-sized screen. The event is monthly, and screenings are usually themed films, ranging from *The Shining* on Hallowe'en to *Casablanca* on Valentine's Day.

STRATFORD EAST PICTURE HOUSE

- *Gerry Raffles Square, Salway Road, Stratford East, Stratford, E15 1BX*
- *Tel: 087 1704 2066; www.picturehouses.co.uk*
- *Stratford BR*
- *£7*

This modern, four-screen cinema shows new releases as well as independent films. It tries to cater to everyone – as well as autism-friendly screenings and parent and child screenings, over-60s can watch a matinee performance every Wednesday for £2, which includes free drinks in the cinema's cafe.

THEATRE ROYAL STRATFORD EAST

- *Gerry Raffles Square, Stratford, E15 1BN*
- *Tel: 020 8534 0310; www.stratfordeast.com*
- *Stratford*
- *£3–£19*

Built in 1881, this Grade II-listed building still has some original Victorian features, such as its red-and-gold decor. There's just one stage, with seats for 460 in the auditorium. The theatre shows mostly new plays, many of which have ethnically diverse themes – although its pantomimes are its most successful shows. The venue's vibrant bar has entertainment every day of the week.

▼ WEST

THE BUSH

- ❶ *Shepherd's Bush Green, W12 8QD*
- ⊕ *Tel: 020 8743 5050; www.bushtheatre.co.uk*
- ⊜ *Shepherd's Bush*
- ❹ *£15*

With just 81 seats, The Bush is one of the smallest studios in London. Yet established actors and playwrights who may have begun their career at this theatre still perform here, including names such as John Simm, Joseph Fiennes and Sheridan Smith of *Two Pints of Lager...* fame. The Bush is particularly known for its new writing; Lucy Kirkwood and Ben Schiffer, both writers on TV series *Skins*, have worked here.

CINÉ LUMIÈRE

- ❶ *Institut Français, 17 Queensberry Place, SW7 2DT*
- ⊕ *Tel: 020 7073 1350; www.institut-francais.org.uk*
- ⊜ *South Kensington*
- ❹ *£9*

If you want to brush up on your language skills, come and watch a film at the Institut Français. While it was founded in 1910 to promote French culture, the institute's 300-seat cinema shows a mix of French, European and world cinema classics and new releases, all of which are in their original language (with subtitles). Special events may see actors and directors making an appearance. On Sundays the cinema shows French classics only.

THE ELECTRIC CINEMA

- ❶ *191 Portobello Road, W11 2ED*
- ⊕ *Tel: 020 7908 9696; www.electriccinema.co.uk*
- ⊜ *Ladbroke Grove, Notting Hill Gate*
- ❹ *£12.50 front seats; £14.50 seats at back with footrests; £30 sofas at back*

This one-screen cinema, dating from 1910, has many of its original features: old-fashioned fire buckets, a domed ceiling and plaster alcoves give the venue a touch of theatrical glamour. It shows mostly blockbusters. Occasional special events have included male models dressed in bowties serving cosmopolitans and canapés on Oscar night. On Mondays the cinema hosts parent and child screenings at 11am and films with subtitles (and sound) for the hard of hearing at 3pm. Come on a Sunday if you want to see classics, such as *Wuthering Heights*, or double bills – usually two films linked by their director or main actor. You can watch the first film, then have a drink in the bar before returning to watch the second. *Insider info: John Christie, who is thought to have murdered seven women and one child in the Rillington Place murders, used to be a projectionist here in the late 1940s.*

THE GATE PICTURE HOUSE

- ➊ *87 Notting Hill Gate, W11 3JZ*
- ⊕ *Tel: 0871 704 2058; www.picturehouses.co.uk*
- ◒ *Notting Hill Gate*
- ➍ *£6–£11*

While The Gate's building dates from 1861, when it was a restaurant and brothel, it didn't open as a cinema until 1911. Despite World War II bombs ruining the domed roof, the auditorium's Edwardian plasterwork survived. The cinema became The Gate as we know it in 1974, and since then it has shown avant-garde and experimental films. It also screens films for parents with children, and on Saturdays at 10am it hosts children's activities followed by a film.

HAM HOUSE OPEN-AIR THEATRE

- ➊ *Ham Street, Ham, Richmond-upon-Thames TW10 7RS*
- ⊕ *Tel: 020 8940 1950; www.nationaltrust.org.uk*
- ◒ *Richmond, then bus 371*
- ◒ *£16 theatre; £6.50 cinema*

This 17th-century manor (*see p.221*) shows plays such as *Twelfth Night* in its open-air theatre in summer. At the time of writing, the house was planning to open an open-air cinema, too, to show mainstream films.

HEADLINERS COMEDY CLUB

- ➊ *George IV Pub, 185 Chiswick High Road, W4 2DR*
- ⊕ *Tel: 020 8566 4067; www.headlinerscomedy.com, www.georgeIV.co.uk*
- ◒ *Turnham Green*
- ➍ *£12*

After a £250,000 makeover, a rundown warehouse at the back of an old pub turned into this comedy club. From 8.30pm on Thursdays, Fridays and Saturdays, up-and-coming and established comedians, such as Steve Best, Jo Brand, Alan Davies and Matt Lucas, perform their latest gags.

HOLLAND PARK OPEN-AIR THEATRE

- ➊ *Ilchester Place, W8 6LU*
- ⊕ *Tel: 020 7361 3570 (enquiries), 0845 230 9769 (box office); www.ohp.rbkc.gov.uk*
- ◒ *High Street Kensington, Holland Park*
- ➍ *£10, £39.50, £47.50, £54 performances; £15, £20, £40 picnic tables*
  for up to four people

The open-air theatre in Holland Park is the perfect place to watch a *Hansel and Gretel* opera or listen to music by Mozart or Beethoven on a warm summer evening. The theatre, which has a capacity for 1,024, puts on six operas a year from June to August – visit the website above for details of this year's performances. A huge canopy shields the 18-metre stage, auditorium and the two bars in the foyer in case of rain. Make an evening of it and book a picnic table either on the terrace, the picnic deck, the Dutch garden lounge (which overlooks a formal garden) or the mezzanine, which has views of the park.

PUPPET THEATRE BARGE

- *Little Venice, W9 2PF*
- *Tel: 020 7249 6876; www.puppetbarge.com*
- *Warwick Avenue*
- *£10*

Set in a barge along a canal towpath is this 55-seat theatre, which has a regular programme of marionette-, rod- and shadow-puppet spectacles, such as *The Town Mouse and the Country Mouse*, *Little Red Riding Hood* and, its most popular, *Brer Rabbit Visits Africa*. It isn't high-tech – there's barely an attempt to hide the strings, and the costumes aren't fancy – but imaginative scripts, original music and special effects will charm both adults and children alike. A family ticket for four will cost around £37.

RIVERSIDE STUDIOS

- *Crisp Road, Hammersmith, W6 9RL*
- *Tel: 020 8237 1111; www.riversidestudios.co.uk*
- *Hammersmith*
- *£7.50 cinema; £7–£25 theatre*

Housed in a former Victorian warehouse, Riverside Studios has a long history – it opened as a cinema in 1934, was used as a BBC recording studio in the 1950s and *Top of the Pops* and *TFI Friday* were both filmed here. The single-screen auditorium seats 200 and shows blockbusters as well as double bills of European films. The venue also has two performance studios (one seats 400, the other 156), which present a mix of new writing and classical plays by established writers. The studios also host concerts, comedy and dance, as well as music festivals and art exhibitions. On warmer nights, get a drink from the bar and sit on the riverside terrace.

ROYAL COURT THEATRE

- *Sloane Square, SW1W 8AS*
- *Tel: 020 7565 5000 (box office); www.royalcourttheatre.com*
- *Sloane Square*
- *£15–£25*

Since its debut play in 1956, the Royal Court Theatre has been known for its new writing and world theatre. And you can bet any performance you see at this two-storey theatre will be challenging and thought-provoking – even in the radical 1960s the establishment conflicted with official censors. The theatre encourages scripts from writers from all walks of life, and encourages youths and ethnic minorities through its playwriting workshops. Theatre fanatics will enjoy browsing the bookshop, which sells a diverse range of plays – most of which have been produced by the Royal Court.

NIGHTLIFE AND MUSIC

Classical, industrial, funk or jazz – you can tap your feet to your favourite beat somewhere in London. Whether you're looking for comfy sofas, sleek cocktails or a jumping dance floor to accompany your tune of choice, you'll find it all here.

▼ CENTRAL

12 BAR CLUB

- ❶ 22–3 Denmark Place, WC2H 8NL
- ⊕ Tel: 020 7240 2622 (box office); www.12barclub.com
- ❷ Tottenham Court Road
- ❹ £5 after 11pm, or £5 one-off members fee

With room for 120 and a stage that struggles to fit two performers, this late-night bar feels intimate, as all live-music venues should. Acts range from solo blues or folk singers to rock and indie bands – all of whom write their own music. On Sundays, the bar hosts an open-mike night from 6pm.

ABSOLUT ICE BAR

- ❶ 31–3 Heddon Street, Mayfair, W1B 4BN
- ⊕ Tel: 020 7478 8910; www.belowzerolondon.com,
- ❷ Piccadilly Circus, Oxford Circus, Green Park
- ❹ £12.50; £16 Thur–Sat

The walls, bar top and tables in this bar are carved from ice taken from a Swedish river. Even your glass is made from ice, so you keep it throughout your allocated 40-minute time slot in the bar. The bar is kept at a constant -5°C and you're given gloves and a jacket before you enter.

ALL STAR LANES

- ❶ Victoria House, Bloomsbury Place, WC1B 4DA
- ⊕ Tel: 020 7025 2676; www.allstarlanes.co.uk
- ❷ Holborn
- ❹ £8.50 per person per game during peak hours

This 1950s Americana-themed bowling alley has four lanes and a diner. At weekends, dress up in a 1950s-style frock or suit and bow tie and get ready to jive (book ahead). There are also branches in Brick Lane and Bayswater.

THE BLACK GARDENIA

- 93 Dean Street, Soho, W1D 3SZ
- Tel: 020 7494 4955, 0872 148 2298; www.myspace.com/blackgardenia93
- Tottenham Court Road
- £2–£7

This cramped basement club in central Soho describes itself as 'Ronnie Scott's before the refurb' (see p.169). With its vintage microphone, piano and red walls, it's certainly got ambience. All the staff and many of the punters dress in vintage – hats, cravats and waxed moustaches for the men; tea dresses, cherry-red lipstick and stockings for the ladies. But they're not simply in fancy dress – they're dressed in pre-war fashion because that's their style. For a night of swing and jazz classics, jitterbug dancing, burlesque and cabaret, it's the place to go.

BLOOMSBURY LANES

- Tavistock Hotel basement, Bedford Way, WC1H 9EU
- Tel: 020 7183 1979; www.bloomsburybowling.com
- Russell Square
- £3–£7

There's more to this retro bowling alley than its eight lanes; live bands play on the stage, there are two karaoke rooms (book ahead), a 1950s-style American diner and a kitsch mini-cinema, where you can watch whatever film is playing for free. It's a popular dress-up night; so, girls, dress in your finest rock 'n' roll frocks, and, guys, slick back your locks with some heavy-duty hair gel.

COSTA DORADA

- 47–55 Hanway Street, W1T 1UX
- Tel: 020 7631 5117; www.costadoradarestaurant.co.uk
- Tottenham Court Road
- £29 the Spanish Experience

This Spanish restaurant hosts flamenco classes in its basement, as well as lively flamenco shows from Tuesday to Saturday. Once a month you can book the Spanish Experience to get you prepared for your next holiday; it includes a one-hour Spanish lesson, one-hour flamenco lesson and a tapas dinner in the restaurant on the ground floor.

COUSIN JILL'S KARAOKE LOUNGE

- 42 Albemarle Street (basement), Mayfair, W1S 4JH
- Tel: 020 7499 9969; www.cousinjills.com
- Green Park
- £350 for three hours for approx. 10 people, includes one champagne cocktail each on arrival

This stylish karaoke venue has three dimly lit rooms available for private hire. Choose from a list of 5,000 songs.

DARBUCKA

- 182 St John Street, EC1V 4JZ
- Tel: 020 7490 8772 (music lounge), 020 7490 8295 (restaurant); www.darbucka.com
- Farringdon, Angel
- £5 Fri, Sat

When Ahmad Mohammad moved to London from Syria in 1999, he brought his passion for music and cuisine with him. So, he opened this, a Syrian/Lebanese restaurant, which plays live global music in its basement lounge bar. Regular events include 'Chilli Fried', a dance night with DJs from India, Mali and Senegal, as well as the UK; 'Planet Egypt', which features Egyptian-style Raqs Sharqi belly dancers and the mellow sounds of solo bassist, Steve Lawson.

DOLLAR

- 2 Exmouth Market, Farringdon, EC1 4PX
- Tel: 020 7278 0077; www.dollargrills.com
- Farringdon
- FREE

A neon-red sign points you to the basement of this grill restaurant, on the corner of Exmouth Market. Downstairs, you can sit on cushions in cubbyholes under bare-brick archways and draw a curtain if you want some privacy. Dollar oozes decadence and glamour, but it's not pretentious at all; there's no charge to get in, you needn't reserve the private booths and there's certainly no dress code.

THE DRILL HALL

- 16 Chenies Street, WC1E 7EX
- Tel: 020 7307 5060; www.drillhall.co.uk
- Goodge Street
- £5–£17.50 performances

Built in 1882, The Drill Hall takes its name from the hall where the Bloomsbury Rifles used to practise. It's been a lesbian and gay multi-arts venue since 1977. It has a diverse performance programme, which includes cabaret, independent theatre and live gigs, which are held in its two drill halls. It also has four studios in which drama, tai chi, capoeira, ballroom and Latin dance classes are held.

FABRIC

- 77a Charterhouse Street, Clerkenwell, EC1M 3HN
- Tel: 020 7336 8898; www.fabriclondon.com
- Farringdon
- £10–£6

Since it was opened in 1999, Fabric has been internationally hailed for its sound system, lasers and DJs, such as Ricardo Villalobos, Richie Hawtin and Mathew Jonson, leading to *DJ* magazine voting it number one in the top 100 clubs in the world in 2008. Its reputation for its drum 'n' bass nights on Fridays and house on Saturdays has drawn crowds from all over the world, so expect to queue for everything. *Tip: with three floors and a labyrinth of walkways, keep an eye on your friends – once you've lost them, you won't find them again.*

G CASINO

- ❶ *3–4 Coventry Street, W1D 6BL*
- ☎ *Tel: 020 7287 7887; www.gcasino.co.uk*
- ❷ *Piccadilly Circus*
- ❹ *FREE entry; £25 per person (min. two) Straight Flush package; £30 per person (min. four) Full House package; £35 per person (min. six) Royal Flush package*

G casino has something other casinos don't: razzle dazzle. With its domed ceiling, columns and ornate balcony, there's still an air of pre-war glamour. The building dates from 1913, when it opened as the Rialto Cinema; it didn't open as a casino until 2002. There are 20 slot machines, 40 roulette machines, poker games and Black Jack roulette – the casino's most popular game. Packages include the Straight Flush, designed for gambling novices, which includes a drink, bar food, £5 slots vouchers and gaming chips; Full House, with its Black Jack and Roulette tuition, and Royal Flush, which includes a mini tournament.

GOLD BAR

- ❶ *125 Stoke Newington Church Street, N16 0UH*
- ☎ *Tel: 020 7254 0882*
- ❷ *Angel, then bus 73, 476*
- ❹ *FREE (at time of writing)*

This two-storey lounge bar fits in well with the Stokey scene. On the ground floor, the mismatched furniture, local artists' work and ivy garden attract arty twenty-somethings. Downstairs has no windows and a low ceiling, which makes the space feel dingy, although the two candle-lit caves at the back give the room character – they used to be storage alcoves for a tobacco company in World War II. There's a second bar in the basement, a dance floor for 40 and a DJ.

GREEN CARNATION

- ❶ *5 Greek Street, W1D 4DD*
- ☎ *Tel: 020 7434 3323 (reservations line); www.greencarnationsoho.co.uk*
- ❷ *Tottenham Court Road*

With its velvet chaise longues and Oscar Wilde quotes on the walls, there's an old boys' club feel to this decadent gay bar. Downstairs is another matter: smoke machines, lasers and pumping house and disco remind you you're still in Soho.

GUANABARA

- ❶ *Parker Street, WC2B 5PW*
- ☎ *Tel: 020 7242 8600; www.guanabara.co.uk*
- ❷ *Holborn, Covent Garden*
- ❹ *£5 Wed, Thur, Sun after 9pm; £10 Fri, Sat*

Guanabara is one of London's few nightclubs that plays live music every night. Come here to learn samba or Brazilian ballroom; listen to jazz; see a capoiera performance; or watch groups playing tambourines, cuicas and berimbaus on stage to Brazilian tunes in front of a crowd of 600. On weekend nights the club is busy but there's still room to move, and there's a feel-good vibe not matched in other big clubs: here, everyone leaves their big-city attitude at the door.

LONDON COLISEUM

- *St Martin's Lane, Trafalgar Square, WC2N 4ES*
- *Tel: 0871 911 0200; www.eno.org*
- *Charing Cross*
- *Various*

Home of the English National Opera, this spectacular 2,350-seat auditorium hosts both ballet and opera performances, such as the Birmingham Royal Ballet's *Sylvia* and the classic *Madame Butterfly*. Operas are sung in English.

LONDON STONE

- *109 Cannon Street, EC4N 5AD*
- *Tel: 020 7626 8246*
- *Cannon Street, Bank*
- *FREE*

This novelty gothic basement pub certainly brings character to an area rather dominated by chain bars. Gargoyles, dusty books and mad-scientist potions decorate the shelves on the wall and, if you order a cocktail, it'll come in a test tube. It's named after an ancient stone on the same street.

LUCKY VOICE

- *52 Poland Street, W1F 7NH*
- *Tel: 020 7439 3660; www.luckyvoice.com*
- *Oxford Circus*
- *£20–£120*

Make your own music at this popular yet pricey karaoke chain. As in Japan, here you hire a private room for you and your mates to belt out your fave tunes. Rooms come with tambourines, bongo drums and, if you're lucky, cowboy hats and wigs. There's a second branch in Islington (020 7354 6280).

MADAME JOJO'S

- *8–10 Brewer Street, W1F 0SE*
- *Tel: 020 7734 3040; www.madamejojos.com*
- *Piccadilly Circus, Oxford Circus*
- *£5 Trannyshack Wed 10.30pm; £10 Magic Night first Fri of every month 7pm*

While this compact cabaret club is right next door to Soho's sex alley, inside it's more camp than seedy. The two-tier venue means you can grab a drink at the bar and stand on the balcony to watch the stage and dance floor below. The club is the new home of Trannyshack – kitsch drag acts and a catwalk finale – and there is Magic Night on the first Friday of every month.

PIGALLE CLUB

- 🄀 *215–17 Piccadilly, W1J 9HN*
- 🌐 *Tel: 020 7734 8142 (after 6pm); www.thepigalle.co.uk*
- ⬤ *Piccadilly Circus*
- 💲 *£10 show; £45 dinner and show*

Since this 1940s cabaret club opened in 2007, its live jazz, jive and burlesque shows have drawn the likes of Kylie and Boy George. It's designed to resemble a wartime supper club, so diners are served by staff in 1940s attire as they eat on the mezzanine overlooking the stage. There's live cabaret one Wednesday a month, Motown night on Thursdays and a swing band on Saturdays.

RONNIE SCOTT'S

- 🄀 *47 Frith Street, Soho, W1D 4HT*
- 🌐 *Tel: 020 7439 0747; www.ronniescotts.co.uk*
- ⬤ *Tottenham Court Road, Leicester Square*
- 💲 *£26–£150*

A Soho institution, Ronnie's was opened by its namesake, the saxophonist, in 1959. The headliners tend to be major American performers – Bill Evans, Ella Fitzgerald and Nina Simone are among the jazz greats who have played here – while British artists are generally the support acts. The supper club was taken over in 2006 and much has been said about its change of style. Nevertheless, it's still a hugely popular live-music venue, and has ventured into other music genres, such as mambo and soul.

ROYAL OPERA HOUSE

- 🄀 *Covent Garden, WC2E 9DD*
- 🌐 *Tel: 020 7304 4000 (box office); www.roh.org.uk*
- ⬤ *Covent Garden*
- 💲 *£4–£480 ballet and opera; £10 tea dance; £9 1.5-hour backstage tour*

After the first two theatres on this site were destroyed by fire, the current opera house opened in 1858. The £178 million revamp in 2000 brought the theatre up to date with new technology and a modern atrium, although its stunning red-and-gold auditorium, which seats 2,250, kept its Victorian roots, so much so that it was used as a film set for *The Phantom of the Opera*. As well as opera, the venue hosts ballet performances by The Royal Ballet and visiting global national ballet companies. You can also learn the waltz, tango and cha cha cha at a tea dance; take a behind-the-scenes tour; or watch films in the cinema.

SALSA

- ❶ 96 Charing Cross Road, WC2H 0JG
- ⊕ Tel: 020 7379 3277; www.barsalsa.eu
- ● Tottenham Court Road, Leicester Square
- ❹ £4 admission after 9pm; £5 per one-hour dance lesson; £8 per two-hour dance lesson
- ▦ Salsa Mon, Wed-Sun; Samba Tues; Merengue and Lambada Fri; La Rueda Sun

If the thought of Latin dancing in public terrifies you, you needn't worry – if you go early in the evening there's hardly anybody watching and there are free beginners' classes on Fridays and Sundays. There are also classes for advanced students and, as the night goes on, the movers and shakers come out of the darker corners to show off their moves. It's fun even if you're only watching.

SHUNT

- ❶ Joiner Street, Bankside, SE1 9RL
- ⊕ Tel: 020 7378 7776; www.shunt.co.uk
- ● London Bridge
- ❹ £5 Wed, Thur; £10 Fri

A candle-lit tunnel leads into this arts venue within the London underground network. Off the main corridor there's a warren of 30 or so archways that host a changing programme of events – because curators alternate fortnightly, you never really know what to expect. As well as two theatres showing new writing, there's a gallery and a space reserved for live gigs. Elsewhere, there are three bars with a pool table and a couple of table-football tables, pinball machines and pianos, which anyone can play. There's also a fringe cinema for 150, which shows shorts, horror nights, film festivals and The Paper Cinema (see p.158). If you think that's unusual, wait until you see the plastic shark and try the maze.

SKETCH

- ❶ 9 Conduit Street, Soho, W1S 2XG
- ⊕ Tel: 020 7659 4500; www.sketch.uk.com
- ● Oxford Circus
- ❹ FREE (members bar after 9pm)

Despite the hype, this restaurant bar is decidedly unpretentious – early in the evening, anyway. On the ground floor, there's the parlour, which is by day a bohemian cafe, by night a buzzing members' bar for celebs et al. There's another, smaller bar downstairs in the shape of an igloo with a sunken bar in the middle that serves cocktails such as Bloody Sketch and Where's Mary?

ST MARTIN-IN-THE-FIELDS

- ❶ Trafalgar Square, WC2N 4JJ
- ⊕ Tel: 020 7766 1100; www.stmartin-in-the-fields.org
- ● Leicester Square, Charing Cross, Covent Garden
- ❹ £5 (jazz concerts)
- ▦ Lunchtime concerts 1pm; Evening concerts 7.30pm; Jazz concerts 8pm Wed

This 13th-century church (see p.214) has been hosting free music concerts for 60 years. If you're in the area at lunchtime, pop in to experience their concerts promoting new talent. Alternatively, attend one of their two-hour evening concerts by candlelight. Performances vary from Beethoven, Brahms and Chopin to choirs singing a capella, harpists and the odd ceilidh band on the pipes. If it's jazz you're after, jazz nights are held downstairs in the restored crypts.

SWAP-A-RAMA RAZZMATAZZ

- ❶ Favela Chic, 91–3 Great Eastern Street, EC2A 3HZ
- ✆ Tel: 020 7613 4228; www.myspace.com/swaparamarazzmatazz, www.favelachic.com
- ◉ Old Street
- ❹ £3 before 9pm; £5 after 9pm

Just as you find yourself slipping into trance mode to wild DJ tunes at this monthly Swap-A-Rama event, a horn will blow, indicating it's time to swap a piece of clothing – so don't go wearing your favourite jeans. Be prepared for anything; you might end up going home wearing a baseball cap, tutu and string vest. It's happened before...

TART

- ❶ 117 Charterhouse Street, Smithfield, EC1M 6AA
- ✆ Tel: 020 7253 3003; www.tartbar.co.uk
- ◉ Farringdon
- ❹ FREE

Cakes and cocktails combined is every woman's dream, so Tart hits the spot with its sickly sweet cocktails. Try the lemon meringue pie, made from vodka and lemon curd, decorated with a slice of meringue, or the rhubarb crumble custard (rum, Frangelico, rhubarb purée and custard). But it's the wall art that gets people talking, with creepy doll canvases and racy wallpaper bordering on porn. There's a restaurant serving British food at the back, too.

WIGMORE HALL

- ❶ 36 Wigmore Street, W1U 2BP
- ✆ Tel: 020 7935 2141 (box office); www.wigmore-hall.org.uk
- ◉ Bond Street, Oxford Circus
- ❹ £3–£30

This renowned concert venue was built in 1901, in the art-nouveau style, and many of the original features can still be seen. The stalls and balcony seat 537. The hall hosts varied performances, including evening chamber concerts, evening recitals and lunchtime and Sunday morning concerts. You can expect to hear jazz, classic pieces composed before 1600 and music written by living composers. The Amadeus Quartet, Elisabeth Schwarzkopf and the King's Consort have all performed here, as well as Julia Fischer on the violin.

SEVEN ALTERNATIVE NIGHTS OUT

★ 1 FETISH NIGHT: TORTURE GARDEN

🛈 *Various venues; office: 111 Cremer Business Centre, 37 Cremer Street, E2 8HD*
☎ *Tel: 020 7613 4733; www.torturegarden.com*
🛈 *Various*

Up to 2,600 people attend each of these monthly fetish balls. If you're not sure what to expect, then try to imagine the fantasies of those 2,600 people and dress accordingly. If you go wearing a gas mask and nipple tassles, a PVC catsuit or simply hot pants and a chain around your neck, you'll fit right in.

★ 2 STITCHING NIGHT: STITCH AND BITCH

🛈 *Various venues, usually Harrisons, 15–19 Bedford Hill, SW12 9EX*
☎ *Tel: 020 8675 6900 (venue); www.stitchandbitchlondon.co.uk,*
   www.harrisonsbalham.co.uk
🚇 *Balham*
🛈 *FREE*

Laura Davis, Lauren O'Farrell and Georgia Reid set up this knitting group in 2005. It's since expanded, and now the girls run knitting sessions across London every two weeks. They also organize themed knits, such as sock surgery, and special events, such as guerilla knitting or yarn bombing. So if you've noticed a bollard wrapped up in a stripy pink knit, now you know why.

★ 3 TEA DANCE NIGHT: VIVA CAKE TEA DANCE

🛈 *Various venues, usually St Aloysius Social Club (see p.178)*
☎ *www.myspace.com/vivacakebitches*
🚇 *Euston*
🛈 *£7*
▧ *Sat 4.30pm–Sun 1am*

If you're fed up with clubs so noisy you have to play charades, this tea dance offers something different. Starting in the afternoon, you can help yourself to tea and snacks while you play dominoes and cards, have your future read by a tarot reader, or try your luck in a bingo game. There's also a beauty bar that runs all night long. Later in the evening, grab a partner for the dance classes, then dance to live bands playing 1960s swing, jazz and rock 'n' roll.

★ 4 CEILIDH NIGHT: CEILIDH CLUB

🛈 *Various venues, including: Cecil Sharp House, 2 Regent's Park Road, NW1 7AY*
🚇 *Camden Town*
🛈 *Hammersmith Town Hall, King Street, W6 9JU*
🚇 *Hammersmith, Ravenscourt Park*
☎ *Tel: 0131 672 3123; 0844 477 1000 (box office); www.ceilidhclub.com*
🛈 *£12.50–£14.50*

If you secretly enjoyed barn dancing at school, then go along to a ceilidh – a Scottish country-dancing knees-up. The Ceilidh Club runs dances every few weeks, usually at the locations above. All the moves are explained at the beginning so it won't matter if you've never done it before, plus there's a bar to give you Dutch courage. You'll pick up The Gay Gordons and Strip the Willow in no time. The event also runs raffles and occasional storytelling and poetry reading sessions. (N.B. There's a £1 discount if you wear tartan.)

★5 GOTH NIGHT: FESTIVAL OF SINS

- *The Purple Turtle, 65 Crowndale Road, Camden, NW1 1TN*
- *Tel: 020 7383 4976 (venue), 078 3718 0268 (event);*
  www.festivalofsins.com; www.purpleturtlecamden.co.uk
- *Mornington Crescent*
- *£5 before 9.30pm; £7 after 9.30pm (£6 with flyer)*

On the second Saturday of every second month, dress up in your best fetish and goth gear and celebrate the seven deadly sins. Each event is themed around a different one: lust, gluttony, greed, sloth, wrath, envy and pride (at the time of writing, they were planning to add an eighth). Performances may include a striptease, pole dancing, a drag queen or a fashion show, with 1970s porn clips or mesmerizing graphic-art video installations in the background.

★ 6   RETRO DANCE NIGHT: HULA BOOGIE

- *Venue: South London Pacific, 340 Kensington Road, SE11 4LD (see pp.184–5).*
- *Tel: 020 8672 5972 (event); www.missaloha.weebly.com*
- *Kennington*
- *£7; £40 five-week beginner's jive course*

Liven up your Sunday nights with Hula Boogie, held on the third Sunday of every month. A 30-minute drop-in jive class starts at 7.30pm, followed by a night of 1930s, 1940s and 1950s swing, jive and rock 'n' roll. You can also take a five-week jive course on Tuesdays, learn the Hawaiian hula or master the fast-paced hand jive, bunnyhop or the stroll from the 1950s. In August, the event includes an Elvis tribute.

★ 7   ARTS AND CRAFTS NIGHT: HUNGA MUNGA

- *Various venues, including the Bethnal Green Working Men's Club (see p.187)*
- *www.hungamunga.co.uk, www.moondoglovesyou.com*
- *Various*

At this monthly event, Hunga Munga provide everything you might want (beads, glitter, paint and fuzzy felts) to create your own papier-mâché masterpiece or knitted woolly hat. Meanwhile, live bands play folk, jazz and glam-rock in the background, and special events are organized throughout the night. So you might play games, join in with a paint-a-thon, listen to stand-up comics or take part in a music quiz.

▼ NORTH

BARRIO NORTH

- ❶ *45 Essex Road, Islington, N1 2SF*
- ⊕ *Tel: 020 7688 2882; www.barrionorth.com*
- ◉ *Angel*
- ❹ *£5 dance lessons; £15 rum and tequila tasting events*

Inspired by Latin cultures, at Barrio you can try up to 30 types of rum and 20 types of tequila, as well as San Miguel beer on tap or crisp, golden Sol from Mexico. It also does a range of cocktails with names such as Brazilian Wax (blackberry, lemon and cachaca, made from sugarcane) and Carnaval Queen (passionfruit, ginger and champagne). Sit at the bar and graffiti the tiles or get comfy in a 1970s caravan, which the owner bought from eBay for £100. In fact, much of the decor in the bar is reclaimed – you may recognize the stools from science labs at school. During the week the bar has live bands and tango and flamenco dance classes on Tuesdays, with DJs playing at weekends. Barrio also hosts rum and tequila tasting events every few months, where you'll learn about the history of the drink's production and get to taste five or six different types.

THE BOSTON MUSIC ROOM AND THE DOME

- ❶ *178 Junction Road, Tufnell Park, N19 5QQ*
- ⊕ *Tel: 020 7272 8153; www.bostonarms.co.uk,*
  www.dirtywaterclub.com
- ◉ *Tufnell Park*
- ❹ *£5–£10 open-mike nights*

A friendly pub, the Boston Arms is popular with locals for its lively events programme. In the main bar, which accommodates about 150, Friday nights are for karaoke and Irish bands play live every Saturday. The venue has two other rooms; the Boston Music Room fits 200 and the Dome has capacity for 500. From Sunday to Thursday these rooms host a battle of the bands, where groups play anything from 1960s covers, punk, rhythm and blues and – what the Boston Arms does best – rock 'n' roll. Come on Fridays to hear four or five bands – the White Stripes played here in their early days. On Saturdays the two rooms are for private hire only.

EGG

- ❶ *200 York Way, N7 9AP*
- ⊕ *Tel: 020 7609 8364; www.egglondon.net*
- ◉ *King's Cross*
- ❹ *£8–£15*

This club's AstroTurf garden – complete with palm trees, canopies, plant pots and wrought-iron garden furniture – is its main draw; that, and the breakfast it serves for those still here in the morning. Egg has dance floors on each of its three levels, which fit up to 1,400 revellers. The one in the loft is the smallest. It mostly plays house and dance music, and hosts occasional special events, such as a Venetian masked ball or catwalk shows.

FREEMASONS ARMS

- *32 Downshire Hill, Hampstead Heath, NW3 1NT*
- *Tel: 020 7433 6811; www.freemasonsarms.co.uk, www.londonskittles.co.uk*
- *Hampstead Heath, Belsize Park*
- *£10 per player for private skittles events; 50p per game for members (plus £6 membership fee)*

In the basement of this countrified gastropub is a one-lane bowling alley, designed for the ancient game of Old English Skittles. Rather than rolling a ball, players hurl a 'cheese' – a wooden block resembling an oversized Minstrel – at nine pins, from almost 6.5 metres away. If you think it sounds easy, wait until you see how far apart the skittles are. The London Skittles club hosts member-only nights on Tuesdays, starting at 8pm, and Saturdays from 6pm (individuals can join in); the rest of the time the alley is open to the public.

THE GREEN

- *74 Upper Street, Islington Green, N1 0NY*
- *Tel: 020 7226 8895; www.thegreenislington.co.uk*
- *Angel*
- *FREE*

This compact gay bar can get very busy, so on weekend nights it feels rather cramped. On Thursdays, when the lights go down, 1980s pop is cranked up – The Green has even been known to host musical singalong events. On the first Friday of every month, the bar hosts 'Sink the Pink', a camp fancy-dress evening with pop classics and free cake, and, every Saturday, it hosts 'Prestige' night, when a drag queen plays house. Plants, wifi and bar food make it a laid-back, straight-friendly option in the daytime.

THE GREEN NOTE

- *106 Parkway, Camden, NW1 7AN*
- *Tel: 020 7485 9899; www.greennote.co.uk*
- *Camden Town*
- *£6*

This venue hosts live folk, blues, country and bluegrass from 9pm Wednesdays to Sundays, as well as occasional Tuesdays. Sunday evenings are open-mike. Past performances include Baby Dee on her harp; Africa to Appalachia, known for their banjo music; and the Texan accordionist, Ponty Bone. Amy Winehouse has also performed here. The small music room is at the back of the venue; there's a vegetarian restaurant at the front, which showcases artwork.

ISLINGTON ACADEMY

- ❶ N1 Centre, 16 Parkfield Street, Islington, N1 0PS
- ⊕ Tel: 020 7288 4400, 0844 477 2000 (box office); www.islington-academy.co.uk
- ⊖ Angel
- ❶ £4–£6 for club nights

This music venue holds gigs and club events for up to 800 people nearly every night. It hosts 'Headphone Disco' on the last Friday of every month, where revellers are given a set of wireless headphones and choose the music they want to listen to. Otherwise, go on 'I love the 90s' nights for soundtracks from classic 1990s films or on 'Club de Fromage' geek nights for the ultimate cheese fest.

JAZZ CAFE

- ❶ 5 Parkway, Camden, NW1 7PG
- ⊕ Tel: 020 7688 8899 (box office); www.jazzcafe.co.uk
- ⊖ Camden Town
- ❶ Events from around £8

Since it opened in 1990, the Jazz Cafe has been a Camden institution, hosting live performances by big names, such as American jazz and blues guitarist Robben Ford and Soul singer Jocelyn Brown. It doesn't just do jazz – it does anything from folk and blues to world music. It also gives up-and-coming bands a chance to perform, usually on Mondays. The main rooms have a capacity for 254 (the restaurant upstairs seats 90). Look out for well-known acts in the audience, as many of the musicians come to the cafe as guests. Prince, Scarlett Johansson and Keira Knightley have also been seen in the crowd.

KING'S HEAD

- ❶ 115 Upper Street, Islington, N1 1QN
- ⊕ Tel: 020 7226 8561; www.kingsheadtheatre.org
- ⊖ Angel, Highbury & Islington
- ❶ FREE

The working gas lamps you see here are originals, dating from when the pub was built in the 19th century. There's a theatre at the back (see p.155), and when the stage is not in use, live bands play jazz, blues and swing in the pub every Monday, Wednesday and Sunday. On weekends, DJs mix the latest tunes.

KINGS PLACE

- ❶ 90 York Way, N1 9AG
- ⊕ Tel: 020 7841 4860 (general enquiries), 020 7520 1490 (box office); www.kingsplace.co.uk
- ⊖ King's Cross
- ❶ Tickets from £9.50 (booking online is £2 cheaper than other bookings)

This 26,000-square-metre centre has two main concert spaces; the more formal Hall One, which is three floors high and seats 420; and Hall Two, a more intimate space for 220. It has events every night of the week: On Mondays it hosts discussions, debates and lectures, on Tuesdays there is music from contemporary classical and jazz to Indian and African music, plus film and dance shows in the halls. From Wednesday to Saturday, an artist or organization takes over and hosts whatever they want without restrictions, so you can see something different every week. On Fridays free jazz performances start at 5.30pm in the foyer. The venue also runs free weekly events, ranging from quiz nights to composing workshops. There are also three art galleries (see p.129).

KISS THE SKY

- 18–20 Park Road, Crouch End, N8 8TD
- Tel: 020 8347 6444; www.kisstheskybar.com
- Crouch Hill
- FREE

This laid-back bar, lit by church candles, fairy lights and a 1970s lampshade, has given Crouch End locals a place to relax since 2007. You'd be as comfortable here reading a book from its bookshelves, as you would playing Connect 4 with friends on a week night. It's livelier on Tuesdays, when it hosts acoustic nights, and on Sundays it has occasional DJs and country blues singers.

KOKO

- 1a Camden High Street, Camden, NW1 7JE
- Tel: 020 7388 3222; www.koko.uk.com
- Mornington Crescent
- £5–£25

The building that now houses Koko has undergone several transformations since it opened in 1900 as a music hall. Throughout its time it's been known for its live performances by artists capturing the zeitgeist – Charlie Chaplin, The Clash and the Eurythmics have all played here at one time, and it is where Madonna held her first UK performance. These days, you might expect to see names such as Katy Perry and Lily Allen. The stunning Victorian auditorium and balconies accommodate 1,500. Koko also hosts club nights and the monthly cheesy pop night Guilty Pleasures (www.guiltypleasures.co.uk).

LAUDERDALE HOUSE

- Waterlow Park, Highgate Hill, N6 5HG
- Tel: 020 8348 8716; www.lauderdalehouse.co.uk, www.waterlowpark.org.uk
- Archway, then bus 143, 210, 271
- £7 classical; £9 jazz; £13 cabaret

Built in 1582 on the hill of Waterlow Park (see p.197), Lauderdale House is an elegant music venue. On the ground floor, the house hosts Sunday morning classical concerts, jazz sessions, opera, acoustic and piano recitals, as well as cabaret with West End stars. It also runs music, dance, drama, art and writing workshops for adults and children.

THE OLD QUEEN'S HEAD

- 🛈 *44 Essex Road, Islington, N1 8LN*
- ☎ *Tel: 020 7354 9993; www.theoldqueenshead.com*
- ⊕ *Angel*
- 🎟 *£4 after 8pm*

Perennially popular, this stylish pub hosts burlesque, cabaret acts, live acoustic bands, music quizzes and book launches during the week. At weekends DJs get the dance floor going upstairs. It's open on Sundays, too, so you can read the papers on a Chesterfield leather sofa in front of a log fire. The same group runs Upper Street's Albert & Pearl, Clerkenwell's Queen Boadicea, The Westbury in Kilburn and Paradise by Way of Kensal Green (*see* p.92).

RYAN'S BAR

- 🛈 *181 Stoke Newington Church Street, N16 0UL*
- ☎ *Tel: 0872 148 0810*
- ⊕ *Angel, then bus 73, 476*
- 🎟 *Up to £5 for live music events, some events are FREE*

During the day, this is a family-friendly bar with a beer garden for 200 at the back, free wifi and a Thai menu. At night, Ryan's has DJs at the weekend, and live bands and solo singers during the week. It also shows major sports events live on its four TV screens.

SLIM JIMS

- 🛈 *112 Upper Street, N1 1QN*
- ☎ *Tel: 020 7354 4364; www.slimjimsliquorstore.com*
- ⊕ *Angel, Highbury & Islington*
- 🎟 *FREE*

Slam Jimi Hendrix or the Rolling Stones on the jukebox, order a Guatemalan rum on the rocks and pull up a bar stool in this atmospheric basement rock 'n' roll dive bar. But if you'd rather drink yourself into melancholy oblivion, pick one of the seven wooden booths, and ignore the buzz around you. Live acoustic bands and solo singers play Sunday to Thursdays, for an audience of 100, and burlesque evenings are held on the last Thursday of each month. You can also come here to watch Six Nations rugby on the big screen.

ST ALOYSIUS SOCIAL CLUB

- 🛈 *20 Phoenix Road, NW1 1TA*
- ☎ *Tel: 020 7388 4026*
- ⊕ *Euston*
- 🎟 *£7 Tapestry nights; £7 Tea dances*

This music bar hall/social club fits 200, and hosts stand-up comedians, old-fashioned tea dances (*see* p.172) and a Tapestry night (live bands). It also holds one-off events, such as bake-offs, burlesque acts or flamenco dance lessons.

FIVE TRADITIONAL BOOZERS

★ 1 THE SPANIARD'S INN, NORTH

- *Spaniard's Road, Hampstead Heath, NW3 7JJ*
- *Tel: 020 8731 8406*
- *Hampstead, then bus 21*

This tavern dates from 1585 – Dickens, Shelley, Keats and Byron were regulars in their day. Oak panelling, beams and creaking floors elude to its long history – ask the landlord about the pub's connection with highwayman Dick Turpin.

★ 2 DOG AND BELL, SOUTH

- *116 Prince Street, Deptford, SE8 3JD*
- *Tel: 0871 258 9753; www.thedogandbell.com*
- *Deptford BR, New Cross BR*

This backstreet pub is worth hunting out for its traditional qualities: real ales on tap, a billiards table, quizzes on Sunday evenings and no music.

★ 3 THE PALM TREE, EAST

- *Haverfield Road, Bow, E3 5BH*
- *Tel: 020 8980 2918*
- *Mile End*

Walking into this pub is like stepping back in time; it's cash only, they have old-fashioned cash registers, take about five people's orders at once and go at their own pace. *Insider info: when Frank Sinatra first came to London, he asked to be taken to a real East End boozer, and someone brought him here.*

★ 4 GUINEA, CENTRAL

- *30 Bruton Mews, Mayfair, W1J 6NL*
- *Tel: 020 7409 1728 (office), 020 7499 1210 (reservations); www.theguinea.co.uk*
- *Bond Street*

Dating back to the 15th century, this pub has kept its charming beamed ceiling, panelled walls and reputation for serving cask bitters and ales.

★ 5 BLUE POSTS, CENTRAL

- *81 Newman Street, Fitzrovia, W1T 3EU*
- *Tel: 020 7637 8958*
- *Goodge Street*

This proper old-fashioned pub has flower baskets outside, a dartboard on the ground floor and no music. There aren't many pubs like this left in central London. *Tip: there are a few pubs called Blue Posts in the area, so make sure you get directions to the right one.*

▼ SOUTH

ARCH 635

- 15–16 Lendal Terrace, Clapham, SW4 7UX
- Tel: 020 7720 7343; www.arch635.co.uk
- Clapham North
- £3 after 10.30pm

When everywhere else in Clapham is packed, head to Arch 635 – named after the railway arch it's under. You won't find a single chandelier here – instead, it's got exposed air vents, table football and four bold canvases hung above the bar. At the back there's space for a live band. The bar has a varied events calendar: Wednesdays are for karaoke; Thursdays host open-mike and poetry events on alternative weeks; and DJs play funky house and dance music at weekends.

BABEL

- 3–7 Northcote Road, Battersea, SW11 1NG
- Tel: 020 7801 0043; www.faucetinn.com
- Clapham Junction BR
- FREE

Even on a busy night, you're likely to get a seat on one of Babel's many sofas. But on Sundays you may find yourself standing up instead, tapping your feet to live jazz. The clientele here tends to be local.

THE BANK

- 31–7 Northcote Road, Battersea, SW11 1NJ
- Tel: 020 7924 7387; www.fullers.co.uk
- Clapham Junction BR
- FREE

Housed in a former bank, this restaurant/bar has kept its original white pillars and maintained a traditional theme with chandeliers and old wooden clocks and picture frames grouped together on the wall. The DJ on Saturdays gets the lively 200-strong crowd going with house music. Extra seating is provided on the pavement outside, protected from the elements by large canopies and heaters.

THE BEDFORD

- 77 Bedford Hill, Balham, SW12 9HD
- Tel: 020 8682 8940; www.thebedford.co.uk
- Balham
- £5 dance membership, then pay weekly: £5 line, £6 salsa, £7 swing, £6–£8 tango; six-week pole-dancing course, contact Pole People (see p.225); £13–£16 Banana cabaret

The Bedford dates back to the 1830s, when it opened as a hotel. It has since been a brothel, a courtroom, a live-music venue and an Irish pub, before becoming the pub it is now in the late 1990s. With three floors, five bars and room for 600, there's always something going on. Tuesdays see new comedy acts and established comedians trying out their latest gags; there's a quiz night on Wednesdays; Hoopla, an improvisation theatre club, meets at 8pm on Thursdays, and there are club nights and a comedy club at the weekend. Throughout the week dance classes are held in the ballroom, so you can learn swing, tango, salsa, plus line-and pole-dancing. The pub also hosts live music acts every night during the week – some of which are impromptu – as well as sports events projected onto the wall in the Globe Theatre on the ground floor.

BISON & BIRD

- ❶ *182 Clapham High Street, SW4 7UG*
- ⊕ *Tel: 020 7622 4436; www.bisonandbird.com*
- ❷ *Clapham Common*
- ❹ *FREE*

While this bar is owned by the same company that runs Mary Janes in EC3 (see p.189), each has their own identity. The B&B is huge, with two bars to satisfy its 400 capacity, so there's space to dance when the DJ plays at the weekend, and on Sundays, when there's live music. On warm nights, the glass doors at the front open up onto the street, where there are a few small tables, to make a space for smokers. Revellers won't be outside on match days, though, as they'll be watching the footie on the pub's four big TVs indoors. But this is no sports bar: it's got chandeliers made from entwined antlers, birdcages filled with church candles and arty photos in gilt frames grouped together on the wall. As for drinks, try the B&B house cocktail, a blend of Mercier NV champagne, vodka, black raspberry liqueur, pineapple juice and passion fruit.

BLACK CHERRY

- ❶ *21 Lordship Lane, East Dulwich, SE22 8EW*
- ⊕ *Tel: 020 8299 8877; www.blackcherrybar.co.uk*
- ❷ *East Dulwich BR*
- ❹ *FREE*

Black Cherry is a glamorous cocktail and champagne bar, which gives a nod to beer. Its signature cocktail is the black cherry caipirinha; a muddle of lime, syrup, Sagatiba Cachaca (a Brazilian cane sugar spirit) and black cherries, of course.

CORSICA STUDIOS

- ❶ *Units 4–5, Elephant Road, Newington, SE17 1LB*
- ⊕ *Tel: 020 7703 4760; www.corsicastudios.com*
- ❷ *Elephant and Castle*
- ❹ *£3; some events are FREE*

This independent, not-for-profit music and arts space has an eclectic live music programme ranging from drum 'n' bass to jazz. It also hosts changing art exhibitions in its two rooms.

THE FALCON

- ❶ *33 Bedford Street, Clapham, SW4 7SQ*
- ⊕ *Tel: 020 7274 2428; www.thefalconclapham.co.uk*
- ◉ *Clapham North*
- ❷ *FREE*

The highlight of The Falcon is its beer garden at the back, which has a bar of its own and 30 tables among potted plants. As well as heaters and fairy lights, quirky chairs give this pub garden a modern touch. More picnic tables are at the front, but they overlook the road. There's seating for 300 in total; inside has comfy sofas and papers on a Sunday.

THE FOX & HOUNDS

- ❶ *165–7 Upper Richmond Road, Putney, SW15 6SE*
- ⊕ *Tel: 020 8788 1912*
- ◉ *East Putney*
- ❷ *FREE*

With eight TV screens and one big screen, wherever you stand you'll have a decent view of the match that's playing. The pub has a capacity for 220, and still gets busy when big games are on.

THE GARRISON

- ❶ *99–101 Bermondsey Street, SE1 3XB*
- ⊕ *Tel: 020 7089 9355; www.thegarrison.co.uk*
- ◉ *London Bridge*
- ❷ *FREE*

Locals flock to this elegant gastropub on weekends. The ground-floor dining room, which seats 65, has grey, panelled walls, taxidermy and peeling-paint furniture, and looks like the front cover of *Country Living* magazine. The cinema room downstairs underwent a refurb last July; it's now bright and cosy, with bare a brick wall and exposed light globes. This room fits 20, and is often hired for film screenings and live sports events. On Sundays the pub holds a free cinema night, playing classic films and new releases.

GIGALUM

- ❶ *7–8 Cavendish Parade, Clapham Common Southside, SW4 9DW*
- ⊕ *Tel: 020 8772 0303; www.gigalum.com*
- ◉ *Clapham South*
- ❷ *FREE*

If you're bored on a Sunday evening and want a pick-me-up, Gigalum fits the bill. DJs play house music on Fridays, Saturdays and Sundays; during the week the bar hosts occasional wine tasting and speed-flatmating parties, where you can mingle with other flathunters. In summer, take advantage of the 12 picnic tables on the terrace at the front, which overlook the common.

HOLY DRINKER

- 59 Northcote Road, Clapham Junction, SW11 1NP
- Tel: 020 7801 0544; www.holydrinker.co.uk
- Clapham Junction BR
- FREE

Take a seat on one of the pews in this candle-lit cavern, and wait not for forgiveness but for your mate to bring over your beer. The Holy Drinker takes drinking to a higher level – just don't walk towards the light, as it's not heaven but a large projection screen and your shadow will get in the way of the film (art-house clips, mostly). A DJ plays funk, soul and dance on occasional Fridays and every Saturday.

LIQUORISH

- 123 Lordship Lane, East Dulwich, SE22 8HU
- Tel: 020 8693 7744; www.liquorish.com
- East Dulwich BR
- FREE

By day, Liquorish is a cool grey cafe with photos and canvases hanging on the wall and a wide selection of board games. At weekends, up to 150 hipsters pack into this trendy bar, drawn in by the DJ's R 'n' B, 1970s and 1980s tunes. The bar serves cocktails and bottled beer from Peru, Jamaica, Mexico, Kenya and Europe. Smokers – there's a courtyard at the back.

LOST SOCIETY

- 697 Wandsworth Road, SW8 3JF
- Tel: 020 7652 6526; www.lostsociety.co.uk
- Clapham Common
- £5 after 9pm, Fri–Sat

Once a 16th-century barn, Lost Society is now a large bar covering two levels. During the week, it's a stylish restaurant/bar, decorated with a gramophone, birdcage and peacock murals between the original beams in the ceiling. It hosts comedy nights, pub quizzes, cocktail classes and film nights Mondays to Fridays; weekends see resident DJs playing hip hop, disco, funk and house.

THE O2

- Peninsula square, SE10 0DX
- Tel: 020 8463 2000; www.theo2.co.uk
- North Greenwich

As well as an arena with a capacity for 20,000, which holds regular events, the O2 is home to indigO2, which fits in 2,200 for gigs, an 11-screen Vue cinema and 25 bars and restaurants.

OLIVER'S MUSIC BAR

- ❶ 9 Nevada Street, Greenwich, SE10 9JL
- ⊕ Tel: 020 8858 5855; www.myspace.com/oliversmusicbar
- ⊙ Cutty Sark DLR
- ❻ £3

Even if you've been before, you might walk past Oliver's, which is hidden downstairs next to the Spread Eagle and opposite Greenwich Theatre. This intimate, dimly lit piano bar is seedy for some, romantic for others, although most would agree that it's charming. It hosts live jazz performances most nights, and stays open well into the early hours.

THE RAILWAY

- ❶ 16 Blackheath Village, SE3 9LE
- ⊕ Tel: 020 8852 2390; www.therailwayblackheath.co.uk
- ❻ Blackheath BR
- ❻ FREE

There's room for 300 standing in The Railway, with an additional 50 on the patio at the back, and another 35 on the roof terrace, where you can smoke. When it's too cold to be outside you can huddle around the open fire inside. Considering its location, next to the station, The Railway is a good bet for an after-work drink – it has a wide range of ciders and ales. On Sunday evenings it hosts live bands playing indie, rock and jazz.

ROLLER DISCO @ RENAISSANCE ROOMS VAUXHALL

- ❶ Off Miles Street (opposite Arch no. 8), Vauxhall, SW8 1RZ
- ⊕ Tel: 0844 736 5375; www.rollerdisco.com
- ⊙ Vauxhall
- ❻ Thur £10; Fri £12.50; Sat–Sun £10

Boys, put on your dungarees and girls, don a ra-ra skirt, leg warmers and a headband for a night of cheese at this roller disco, which plays a mix of 1970s funk, 1980s pop, disco and house. Roller Motion on Sundays draws a different crowd as the music is R 'n' B and hip hop. There are two circular spaces; the front one is intended for wobbly skaters who like to cling onto the side; the back one is meant for the pros. But once everyone's had a few drinks it's a free-for-all.

SOUTH LONDON PACIFIC

- ❶ 340 Kennington Road, SE11 4LD
- ⊕ Tel: 020 7820 9189; www.southlondonpacific.com
- ⊙ Kennington
- ❻ £3.95 before 10pm; £5 after 10pm

Sitting on a wicker chair overlooking a tropical beach scene, with a Bahama Mama (rum, grenadine, lime, orange and pineapple) in hand, you could almost be in Hawaii. During the week, come here to play on the bar's pinball machine or have a game of Hawaiian table football; at weekends, special events, such as bingo, are held, or you can dance to pop, rock and funk. It also hosts Hula Boogie (see p.173), Oh My God I Missed You, and a new night, Hoodoo Voodoo, which comes with cave-girls, gorillas and sacrificial burlesque.

STAR & GARTER

- ❶ 4 Lower Richmond Road, Putney, SW15 1JN
- ⊕ Tel: 020 8780 2122; www.thestarandgarter.com
- ◉ Putney Bridge
- ❶ FREE

Built in 1787, the Star & Garter was once a hotel by the same name, and the ground floor used to be a boathouse. It's now an upmarket wine bar, with 100 types of wine on the menu. It hosts regular wine-tasting events and you can match the wine with cheese from the bar's walk-in cheese room. The biggest selling point is its riverside location. You can watch the Oxford and Cambridge boat race from here (see p.25) – on the benches on the riverbank outside. The bar also screens major sporting events on the big screen in the cellar.

SUGAR CANE

- ❶ 247 Lavender Hill, Clapham Junction, SW11 1JW
- ⊕ Tel: 020 7223 8866; www.thesugarcane.co.uk
- ◉ Clapham Common, Clapham Junction BR
- ❶ FREE

Tiki statues greet you as you enter this tropical bar, which serves up Hawaiian cocktails in coconut shells. Order the Island Princess (lychee, rose syrup, vodka and Barcadi) or a rum and pineapple at the grass-roofed bar, then head out to the leafy garden, which has five small tables. Alternatively, book one of their three bamboo tiki huts, each of which seat about 12. The rest of the bar is just as kitsch; with wooden masks, a globe-fish light and palm trees. On Friday nights DJs play a mix of hip hop, dance, funk and R 'n' B – Saturdays are reserved for Desert Island Disco, which plays tunes from the past five decades; it's the bar's busiest night, and popular with hen nights and birthday parties.

SUN & DOVES

- ❶ 61–3 Coldharbour Lane, Camberwell, SE5 9NS
- ⊕ Tel: 020 7733 1525; www.sunanddoves.co.uk
- ◉ Denmark Hill BR, Loughborough Junction BR
- ❶ FREE

If you want to feel cultured while you enjoy a drink, visit this Camberwell joint. It doubles up as an art gallery, displaying the work of local and international artists. It also holds events: on Tuesdays you can watch a film on their big screen, on Wednesdays take part in a quiz at 8pm, and on the first Thursday of every month you can bring along your own seven-inch vinyls to play. At the time of writing, there were plans to host live acoustic and jazz nights.

TOOTING TRAM AND SOCIAL

- ❶ *46–8 Mitcham Road, Tooting, SW17 9NA*
- ☎ *Tel: 020 8767 0278; www.antic-ltd.com/tooting/*
- ❸ *Tooting Broadway*
- ❹ *£4 for live music events*

Housed in an old tram-shed warehouse, this cavernous space still has many of the original features – cracked Victorian tiles line the walls. The 15-metre-high ceilings and exposed air-conditioning pipes give it an industrial warehouse feel, which is softened by moody lighting coming from the three chandeliers above. Live music events are held on the second Monday of every month. The music is diverse, so one month it could be an indie band (The Kooks played here in 2008), the next a solo pianist. At weekends there's a DJ, and even though there's no official dance floor, with a capacity for 350–400, there's space to dance. If you like the Tooting Tram, it's worth checking out the 10 other pubs run by the same group.

THE WOOLPACK

- ❶ *98 Bermondsey Street, SE1 3UB*
- ☎ *Tel: 020 7357 9269; www.woolpackbar.com*
- ❸ *London Bridge*
- ❹ *FREE*

Opposite the Fashion and Textile Museum (*see* p.144), you'll find this smart pub, which still has its original Victorian tiling, Baroque furniture and gilt mirrors. It's popular with locals who, on warmer days, can be found sipping real ale in the leafy garden at the back, which is dog-friendly. When the afternoon starts drawing in, the heated lamps under the canopy at the back of the garden come on, so you can sit out for a bit longer.

ZERO DEGREES

- ❶ *29–31 Montpelier Vale, Blackheath, SE3 0TJ*
- ☎ *Tel: 020 8852 5619; www.zerodegrees.co.uk*
- ❸ *Blackheath BR*
- ❹ *FREE*

This is a pub with a difference: you can choose to watch the footie or watch your pint being brewed before you drink it. All of Zero's beer is made on the premises, so you know it's fresh, and it doesn't have any additives, preservatives, sweeteners or artificial colours. There are four main types of ale available: slightly bitter pilsner, fruity pale ale, black lager and cloudier wheat ale. There's always a seasonal beer on the menu, too, which changes about once a month. In summer, try the mango beer, made with sweet mango purée. The staff is friendly and knowledgeable, and keen to give you a free tour of the microbrewery, which includes tastings (book ahead). There's a DJ at the weekend playing the latest R 'n' B and hip hop.

▼ EAST

BAR KICK

- ❶ *127 Shoreditch High Street, E1 6JE*
- ⊕ *Tel: 020 7739 8700; www.cafekick.co.uk*
- ⊜ *Old Street, Liverpool Street*
- ❸ *80p a game*

With 10 table-football tables, Bar Kick has more than any other bar in Europe. If all the tables are busy, watch the footie on TV – there are six TVs, plus a big screen, which show major sporting events. The bar also hosts comedy nights, cabaret and magic shows, ukulele jams and cinema nights. There's a smaller branch, Cafe Kick, on Exmouth Market (*see* pp.98–9).

BETHNAL GREEN WORKING MEN'S CLUB

- ❶ *44–6 Pollard Row, Bethnal Green, E2 6NB*
- ⊕ *Tel: 020 7739 2727 (venue); www.workersplaytime.net, www.ohmygodimissyou.com, www.myspace.com/grindagogo, www.myspace.com/creamrevue*
- ⊜ *Bethnal Green, then bus 8, 55*
- ❸ *£8 The Birthday Club; £6 before 10pm; £7 after Cream Revue*

This multi-arts venue is best known for the diverse events it hosts, each with a different theme. Look out for The Birthday Club, by Oh My God I Miss You, which will take you back to your childhood. It's got cake, jelly and ice cream, limbo dancing, the conga and 1950s and 1960s classics. It also hosts Grind a Go Go, a night of dancers on podiums, striptease and belly dancing; and Cream Revue, a swing and rock 'n' roll night with hula hoopers and flamenco dancers.

CAPTAIN KIDD

- ❶ *108 Wapping High Street, E1W 2NE*
- ⊕ *Tel: 020 7480 5759*
- ⊜ *Tower Hill, then bus 100; Shadwell DLR*
- ❸ *FREE*

From the street, this windowless building appears to be derelict, but cut through a courtyard and you'll arrive at a popular riverside watering hole. Take in the view from the large, leafy terrace: Canary Wharf skyscrapers to your left, the City to your right and ships moored on the river – but be warned; once you've downed a few pints of ale, there's only a low wall separating you from the water below. Inside, there are pews for seats and barrels for tables and a long oak table that suits groups. A stone floor, low, beamed ceiling and old photographs, paintings and maps of the River Thames hint at the history of this 17th-century building. A former ship-building warehouse, it was reinvented as a pub over 100 years ago, and named after a shipowner who was hung for piracy nearby in 1701 (hence the name of the upstairs restaurant, The Gallows).

CITY BUNKER

- ❶ *Cannon Workshops, Hertsmere Road, Canary Wharf, E14 4AS*
- ⊕ *Tel: 020 7537 7940; www.citybunker.co.uk*
- ◉ *Westferry DLR, West India Quay DLR*
- ❹ *£40 per hour indoor golf, Mon–Fri, £20 per hour indoor golf, Sat; £40 per 30-minute golf lessons; £70 per hour golf lessons; £40 per hour per table for poker*

This place is made for City boys and stag dos – you can host a game of poker or have poker lessons, play Wii games on a 3-metre by 4-metre screen, take one-to-one or group golf lessons and play indoor golf. The venue has five simulators, so, using a real golf club, you hit your ball towards a screen. Your ball drops to the ground but continues flying in the air in cyber space.

CLUB AQUARIUM

- ❶ *256–64 Old Street, EC1V 9DD*
- ⊕ *Tel: 020 7251 6136 (Aquarium), 0870 246 1966 (Carwash); www.clubaquarium.co.uk*
- ◉ *Old Street*
- ❹ *£15*

On Saturdays the club hosts Carwash nights, and 1970s costume is mandatory – so expect Bee Gee-esque dance moves, afros and drawn-on sideburns. But what makes this club different is its swimming pool (*see p.230*). A former gym, when the club opened in 1995, managers decided to keep the pool. Two oval portholes give those on the dance floor in the adjacent room a chance to gawp at bathers in the pool and jacuzzi. If you can't wait for your summer holiday and want to mix cocktails and disco with a splash about, Club Aquarium is for you.

DALSTON CULTURE HOUSE

- ❶ *11 Gillett Square, Dalston, N16 8JH*
- ⊕ *Tel: 020 7993 3643 (enquiries), 020 7254 4097 (reservations), 020 7923 9532; www.vortexjazz.co.uk, www.ochreworks.co.uk*
- ◉ *Dalston Kingsland BR*
- ❹ *£5–£12 (jazz club)*

Dalston Culture House is home to two great entertainment sources: Vortex Jazz Club and, on the ground floor, a bar called Ochre Works. The jazz club launched in 1987 and moved from Stoke Newington to its current location in Dalston in 2005. It hosts seven live performances a week, ranging from soul, reggae, jazz and gospel to solo saxophonists, such as Ingrid Laubrock. Most nights, though, you can see young, local artists performing on stage or on the grand piano. The club also organizes nights dedicated to open-mike and improvisation. As for Ochre Works, when the manager opened this bar in July 2008, she wanted to 'make it just like your front room, just cooler'. She's achieved what she set out to do. With its mishmash of furniture, retro coffee tables and 1970s plastic lampshades, this lounge bar is stylish, unpretentious and relaxed. So it's no surprise it draws a mixed age group – unlike most bars. It seats 30, but when the DJ is playing it can pack in up to 100.

LONDON SYMPHONY ORCHESTRA, ST LUKE'S

- ❶ 161 Old Street, EC1V 9NG
- ⊕ Tel: 020 7566 2871; www.lso.co.uk
- ⊖ Old Street
- ❹ Various

With its high ceilings, enormous windows and brick walls, the acoustics in the cavernous Jerwood Hall in St Luke's are an ideal home for the London Symphony Orchestra (LSO). Some of the best musicians in the world play here – as well as LSO performers, symphony orchestras on world tours stop by. But this Grade I-listed church doesn't just host classical performances. In between BBC Radio 3 lunchtime recitals, evening chamber concerts and the LSO recording soundtracks for *Star Wars: Revenge of the Sith* and *Harry Potter and the Goblet of Fire*, St Luke's has hosted gigs by Elton John, Sting and Michael Ball.

MARY JANES

- ❶ 124–7 Minories, EC3N 1NT
- ⊕ Tel: 020 7481 8195; www.maryjanesbar.com
- ⊖ Aldgate, Tower Hill, Tower Gateway DLR
- ❹ FREE

With its black-and-hot-pink colour scheme, Baroque gilt chairs, and mirrors grouped together on bare brick walls, Mary Janes oozes opulence and couldn't be sexier. If the seductive decor gets you in the mood, try their signature cocktail, Mary Janes Passion (passion fruit, pineapple juice, raspberry liqueur, vodka and rose champagne). The bar also serves a range of sweet-shop shooters – jam doughnut, toffee apple and bubblegum are favourites. For weekend nights, groups can book the theatre balcony in the Sky Bar; from there you can people-watch revellers on the ground floor or draw the red velvet curtains round you if you want some privacy...

THE NAG'S HEAD

- ❶ 9 Orford Road, Walthamstow, Upper Walthamstow, E17 9LP
- ⊕ Tel: 020 8520 9709
- ⊖ Walthamstow Central
- ❹ FREE

Hidden away in the village, this pub is popular with laid-back locals enjoying the four real ales on tap. It also serves Belgian fruit beers. In summer, sit in the conservatory or beer garden at the back and the landlord's cat will sleep at your feet.

RHYTHM FACTORY

- *16–18 Whitechapel Road, E1 1EW*
- *Tel: 020 7375 3774; www.rhythmfactory.co.uk*
- *Aldgate East*
- *£3–£15*

You have to walk through a lively cafe to reach the Rhythm Factory's two live-music venues, one of which has a stage. During the week, this is where unsigned bands play jazz, rock, indie and soul, and DJs play funk and hip hop. You might see a few familiar faces on stage, too, such as Pete Doherty. The venue also hosts frequent open-mike comedy nights, poetry readings and performance-art shows on Mondays, and an occasional dance night for people with learning difficulties. At the weekend, top DJs, such as Nicky Blackmarket, play drum and bass, dubstep, dance, techno and electronica till 7am. Its rough and ready student crowd and grubby interior won't suit everyone.

ROUGH TRADE EAST

- *Dray Walk, Old Truman Brewery, 91 Brick Lane, E1 6QL*
- *Tel: 020 7392 7788; www.roughtrade.com*
- *Aldgate East*
- *FREE*

What started out as a record shop specializing in US and Jamaican imports in 1976 became a label and then a music venue in 2007. As well as an indie record shop, with a decent selection of German indie music (krautpop), a cafe and exhibition space, the centre has a stage for live music. Live bands such as Blur and singer-songwriter Colin MacIntyre play indie and electronic gigs about three times a week, until 10pm. Get there early if you want to be near the front, as a queue snakes down the street.

SHOREDITCH HOUSE

- *Ebor Street, E1 6AW*
- *Tel: 020 7739 5040; www.shoreditchhouse.com*
- *Liverpool Street*
- *£700 annual membership fee*

The three main storeys of this exclusive members-only complex pretty much cover every type of entertainment you might want. On the fourth floor there's a two-lane bowling alley, and on the fifth floor there's a games room with a pool table, cards and dominoes; a big screen shows sporting events, and treatment rooms include a sauna, steam room and gym. Plus there are bars and dining rooms dotted all over the place. The rooftop is dominated with an outdoor heated pool and views of the gherkin and surrounds. When you're flirting with stylish twenty-somethings over a glass of champagne with the lights from the steaming pool glowing around you, or mingling with successful business types, you'll know you've made it. Beg, borrow or steal to get in.

▼ WEST

DI'ZAIN

- ❶ *277 New King's Road, Hammersmith, SW6 4RD*
- ⊕ *Tel: 020 7751 9711; www.di-zain.co.uk*
- ⊜ *Parsons Green*
- ❶ *FREE*

The three connecting rooms in this minimalist bar have a Japanese feel to them, what with their monochrome colour scheme, candles and design and lifestyle magazines on the tables. This makes the large free-standing mirror in the middle room all the more striking. It's a stylish bar; relaxed, chilled out and a good option for a glass of wine or champagne in the evening.

GARDEN BAR

- ❶ *41 Bramley Road, Notting Hill, W10 6SZ*
- ⊕ *Tel: 020 7229 1111; www.housebars.co.uk*
- ⊜ *Latimer Road*
- ❶ *FREE*

From the outside, Garden Bar seems like so many other London gastropubs – that is, until you enter the enormous garden at the back. It can seat 300 in its open-air and heated undercover areas so you barely need to bother moving all day. In August the pub takes part in the Portobello Film Festival, showing art-house and blockbuster films on the huge screen in the garden. The pub was once a blues bar and still hosts new bands and the odd celebrity on its stage – Noel Gallagher has made an appearance in the past.

TROUBADOUR

- ❶ *263–7 Old Brompton Road, SW5 9JA*
- ⊕ *Tel: 020 7370 1434; www.troubadour.co.uk*
- ⊜ *West Brompton, Earl's Court*
- ❶ *£7–£10*

Depending on the night you go, this basement club, beneath a 1950s coffee house, has a mix of acoustic acts, unsigned bands and DJs. In the 1960s, Jimi Hendrix, Joni Mitchell and Bob Dylan all played here, and most recently Pete Doherty, The Chemical Brothers, Katie Melua and Ben Mark, who co-writes Take That's songs, have performed. The club hosts a singer/songwriter night every Wednesday, which, in the words of the owner, 'is the anti-thesis of *The X Factor* – all our performers write their own music, sing their own music and play their own musical instruments'. There's room for 120 standing, or 60, if seated.

GREEN SPACES

Londoners are lucky – of the world's major metropolises, London also has to be one of the greenest. And the city's public green spaces are varied, too. As well as parks, hidden green squares and city farms, there's a generous smattering of lidos, reservoirs and woodland accessible on an Oyster card.

▼ CENTRAL

GREEN PARK

- 🄵 *Piccadilly, SW1A 2BJ*
- 🄼 *Tel: 020 7930 1793; www.royalparks.org.uk*
- 🄴 *Green Park*

If you're feeling lazy, or particularly British, hire one of the 2,000 stripy deckchairs in the north-east corner of the park, and while away a warm afternoon reading your paper.

HYDE PARK

- 🄵 *Serpentine Road, W2 2UH*
- 🄼 *Tel: 020 7298 2100; www.royalparks.org.uk*
- 🄴 *Hyde Park Corner, Marble Arch, Knightsbridge*

Each part of this vast 350-acre park has its own character. Families and lovers splash about on the Serpentine lake in rowing boats or sit on a bench watching rollerbladers skilfully weave round makeshift obstacle courses. The farther you get from the lake, the wilder the park gets – ideal for mass football games or walking your dog in the unkempt grass.

KENSINGTON GARDENS

- 🄵 *Kensington Gore, W2 2UH*
- 🄼 *Tel: 020 7298 2000; www.royalparks.org.uk*
- 🄴 *Lancaster Gate, Queensway, Bayswater*

On the western side of West Carriage Drive are Kensington Gardens, home to the Serpentine Gallery (*see pp.126–7*). This 275-acre park, with its ornamental flowerbeds, Round Pond and palace, has a more formal atmosphere than its sprawling neighbour, Hyde Park. The beautiful, golden Albert Memorial is in the south of the park.

REGENT'S PARK

- *Outer Circle, NW1 4NR*
- *Tel: 020 7486 7905; www.royalparks.org.uk*
- *Regent's Park, Baker Street*

A fourth of the park's 487 acres is vast open space, which attracts footballers and joggers. Couples and young families are drawn to the boating lake, which is also popular with resident swans. Nearby, the formal Queen Mary's Gardens in the park's inner circle have a serene atmosphere. In summer, over 30,000 roses of 400 varieties bloom here – kids will enjoy finding the rose with the funniest name.

ST JAMES'S PARK

- *Horse Guards Road, SW1A 2BJ*
- *Tel: 020 7930 1793; www.royalparks.org.uk*
- *St James's Park*

At 58 acres, this is one of the city's smaller royal parks, and you're never too far from the traffic surrounding it. Still, it's a pleasant place for a stroll – walk parallel to the Mall and do a loop of the lake, passing the bandstand, memorial garden flowerbeds and Duck Island along the way, or simply flop onto the grass and watch the world go by. In summer, the park bursts with colour.

10 BEST PICNIC SPOTS

Whether you want a birthday picnic party for 20 or a romantic champagne picnic for two, pick one of the spots below...

▶ **Alexandra Palace** (gardens), north (*see p.194*)

▶ **Horsenden Hill**, north (*see p.203*)

▶ **Greenwich Park** (hill), south (*see p.202*)

▶ **Horniman Museum** (gardens), south (*see p.202*)

▶ **Springfield Park**, east (*see p.205*)

▶ **Epping Forest**, east (*see p.204*)

▶ **Holland Park** (Japanese garden), west (*see p.209*)
   (*N.B. Picnics only permitted on the benches*)

▶ **Richmond Park** (in the long grass), west (*see p.210*)

▶ **St James's Park**, central (*see above*)

▶ **Green Park** (by the deckchairs), central (*see opposite*)

▼ NORTH

ALEXANDRA PALACE GARDENS

- ❶ *Alexandra Palace Way, Wood Green, N22 7AY*
- ⊕ *Tel: 020 8365 2121; www.alexandrapalace.com*
- ◉ *Wood Green, then bus W3*

On a sunny evening, grab a blanket and sit on the steep, sloping gardens at the front of Ally Pally, where you can admire the high-rise views of the Telecom Tower, the gherkin and Canada Tower. You can also play pitch and putt on a nine-hole course, explore 196 acres of woodland, meadows and conservation areas or hire a rowing boat on the lake behind the palace. Fishing is allowed (permit required).

BLUEBELL WOOD

- ❶ *Winton Avenue, Haringey, N11*
- ⊕ *Tel: 020 8489 5868; www.haringey.gov.uk*
- ◉ *Bounds Green; bus 184, 299, 102*

This one-hectare wood is home to a variety of wildlife, such as butterflies and the Wild Service tree, which is rare and usually found only in ancient woodland.

CAMLEY STREET NATURE PARK

- ❶ *12 Camley Street, NW1 0PW*
- ⊕ *Tel: 020 7833 2311; www.wildlondon.org.uk*
- ◉ *King's Cross*

The history behind this two-acre site, hidden behind King's Cross station, goes back 200 years. Set on the banks of Regent's Canal, the area was once used as a coal yard where boats would collect fuel. It then became derelict wasteland, until it was rescued in the 1980s. It opened as a nature reserve in 1985 and has been largely maintained by volunteers since then. It's divided into three areas: the pond, which attracts kingfishers and geese; a meadow, home to rabbits; and woodland, in which bats hide. A visitor's centre runs occasional free events, such as reed pulling, country crafts and poetry reading.

CLISSOLD PARK

- ❶ *Church Street, Stoke Newington, N16 9HJ*
- ⊕ *Tel: 020 7923 3660; www.clissoldpark.com*
- ◉ *Angel, then bus 73, 476*

There's a relaxed community feel to this 54-acre park. Locals come here to jog or to play cricket, ultimate Frisbee and tennis. There's also a dilapidated bowling green and two ponds. But the park is worth a visit even if you don't live nearby; kids will love the paddling pool in summer, the aviary, the butterfly tunnel and the farm animals. The highlight of the park is Clissold Mansion, a Grade II-listed building dating from the 1700s. Inside, local artists' work is displayed; outside, parasols deck the lawn, which overlooks a rose garden and nearby church.

FINSBURY PARK

- 1 Hornsey Gate, Endymion Road, N4 2NQ
- Tel: 020 7263 5001; www.haringey.gov.uk
- Finsbury Park, Manor House

Since 1869, this 112-acre park has provided north Londoners with a vast recreational space. It has a variety of sports facilities, including a sandy running track, skate park, American-football field, bowls club and basketball court, plus a lake, where you can hire boats, or stroll in the formal American Gardens.

FORTY HALL

- Forty Hill, Enfield, EN2 9EU
- Tel: 020 8363 8196; www.enfield.gov.uk
- Enfield BR, then bus W10, 191; Turkey Street

The Forty Hall estate dates from the medieval era, when the grounds were home to Elsyng Palace. The Grade I-listed Jacobean Hall has eight rooms open to the public for free, with local history displays, art and photography exhibitions. The grounds stretch across 260 acres and include an avenue of lime trees, woodland, informal rose gardens, a large ornamental lake and a fishing lake. There is also a peaceful walled garden. Keen walkers should note that footpaths connect the grounds with Whitewebbs Park (see p.197) and Hilly Fields Country Park.

HAMPSTEAD HEATH

- Highgate Road, NW5 1QR
- Tel: 020 7485 4491 (Parliament Hill Visitor Centre); www.cityoflondon.gov.uk
- Hampstead Heath, Golders Green, Gospel Oak BR

This massive 790-acre space is big enough to feel like you've got out of the city, even when everyone else has had the same idea. In the south of the park, Parliament Hill is a popular place to fly a kite and admire the London skyline. The much-loved ponds (see p.226) are to the east, with Kenwood House to the north. This former private home is now maintained by English Heritage, and hosts outdoor concerts by its lake in the summer. Golders Hill, in the heath's north-west corner, used to be the private grounds of a mansion but is now a walled flower garden. Nearby is the hill garden, which has a pergola as long as Canada Tower is tall. There's also a pond and animal enclosure with deer, goats and birds.

HIGHBURY FIELDS

- Highbury Place, Islington, N5 1AR
- Tel: 020 7527 2000; www.islington.gov.uk
- Highbury & Islington

At a modest 29 acres, this green is big enough for sporty types to jog a few laps round, but you wouldn't come here to get away from it all as the road circling the green is clearly visible. There are tennis, netball and basketball courts at the green's north end, plus an indoor swimming pool.

HIGHGATE WOOD

- Muswell Hill Road, N10 3JN
- Tel: 020 8444 6129; www.cityoflondon.gov.uk
- Highgate

Pick one of the walking trails weaving through this 28-hectare wood and enjoy a few hours exploring – the northern corner is dense with bluebells in spring.

LITTLE VENICE GARDENS

- Little Venice, Maida Vale, W9
- www.opensquares.org
- Warwick Avenue

Follow the canal through Little Venice and you'll meet a handful of hidden gardens: the ornamental Rembrandt Gardens; the tree-lined Formosa Garden; Cleveland Square and Little Venice Gardens, which bloom with roses in June.

MUSWELL HILL PLAYING FIELDS

- Coppetts Road, Haringey, N10
- Tel: 020 8489 5868; www.haringey.gov.uk
- East Finchley

This 10.4-hectare space has six football pitches, plus a separate space usually used for cricket.

PRIMROSE HILL

- Primrose Hill Road, Camden, NW3
- Tel: 020 7486 7905; primrosehill.com
- Chalk Farm

Here's the Primrose rule: you're not allowed to look over your shoulder until you're at the top of this 78-metre hill. That way, once you've reached its peak, you'll be surprised when you're met with a sweeping panorama of London. Spread a blanket and open a bottle of chilled champagne as you take in the view.

ST PANCRAS GARDENS

- Off Pancras Road, NW1
- Tel: 020 7974 1693; www.camden.gov.uk
- King's Cross

This tranquil cemetery beside St Pancras Old Church is worth seeking out if you want some time alone.

TRENT COUNTRY PARK

- Cockfosters Road, Barnet, EN4 0PS
- Tel: 020 8449 2459 (park), 020 8379 1000 (council); www.enfield.gov.uk
- Cockfosters

Strolling along an avenue of lime and oak trees with views of grassland, you'd hardly believe Trent Country Park is only 30 minutes from King's Cross. The park dates from the 1300s when it was used as a royal hunting ground. The grounds cover 413 acres, which include a 2-km cycle route, a 4.25-km horse-riding track, a Braille trail and a woodland walking circuit. A loop of the park takes about two hours on foot and passes by a butterfly meadow, rolling hills and a lake.

WATERLOW PARK

- ❶ *Highgate Hill, N6 5HG*
- ⊕ *Tel: 020 8347 9957, 020 7974 1693, 020 8348 8716 (Lauderdale House); www.waterlowpark.org.uk, www.lauderdalehouse.co.uk*
- ⊘ *Archway, then bus 143, 210, 271*

Compared to neighbouring Highgate Cemetery, this 20-acre park barely gets a look-in. But see it in a soft pinky-orange winter sunset with a light smattering of snow, and it'll look magical. Get a hot drink from the cafe in old Lauderdale House and stroll around the three ponds, which are fed by natural springs. *Insider info: shelters from the world wars are still buried under the park.*

WHITEWEBBS PARK

- ❶ *Whitewebbs Road, Enfield, EN2*
- ⊕ *Tel: 020 8379 1000; www.parkexplorer.org.uk*
- ❶ *Enfield BR, then bus W10; Crews Hill BR*

This 196-acre park was formerly the estate of a manor house; the present house was built in 1791. The grounds were made into a public golf course in 1931, though there's still a lake and plenty of woodland to explore. On rainy days you could visit the transport museum in the north-west corner of the park.

GET INVOLVED WITH GARDENING

★ BE A GUERRILLA GARDENER

- ⊕ *www.guerrillagardening.org*

The practice of transforming public green spaces under the cover of darkness is technically illegal, but if you're willing to risk arrest, then set up your own escapade or keep your ear to the ground for an organized dig.

★ WORK ON AN ALLOTMENT

- ⊕ *www.london.gov.uk/allotments*
- ⊘ *£40 per year for a full-sized 250-square-metre plot*

If you're interested in working on an allotment, get your name on a waiting list now, as it can take years to be awarded your own patch, depending on which borough you live in.

10 CITY FARMS

Health experts say stroking your furry pets can lower stress levels, cholesterol and blood pressure. But what are you to do if your flat isn't big enough to swing a cat? Well, you could head to one of London's city farms – here are 10 of the best.

★ 1 THE WOODLANDS FARM TRUST

- ● *331 Shooters Hill, Welling, Kent, DA16 3RP*
- ☎ *Tel: 020 8319 8900;*
  www.thewoodlandsfarmtrust.org
- ◎ *Welling BR, Falconwood BR*
- ❻ *FREE*

This 90-acre farm has a history going back 200 years, and much of its land is ancient woodland, streams and fields – which are still maintained by a horse and cart. Active types will be interested in the orienteering course that stretches across the farm; if that sounds like too much work, you could explore the organic garden in front of a Victorian farmhouse or meet the farm's Vietnamese pot-bellied pigs.

★ 2 MUDCHUTE PARK & FARM

- ● *Pier Street, Isle of Dogs, E14 3HP*
- ☎ *Tel: 020 7515 5901;*
  www.mudchute.org
- ◎ *Mudchute DLR*
- ❻ *FREE*

A panorama of grazing sheep with a backdrop of Canary Wharf skyscrapers is a strange one. Yet this 32-acre site – once destined to be high-rise blocks – now has steep, grassy banks, woodland and meadows that are home to llamas and donkeys, among other animals. The farm also has a nature trail, allotments and a riding school, which also caters for people with disabilities.

★ 3 FREIGHTLINERS FARM

- ● *Sheringham Road, N7 8PF*
- ☎ *Tel: 020 7609 0467;*
  www.freightlinersfarm.org.uk
- ◎ *Highbury & Islington*
- ❻ *FREE*

The farm's name comes from the disused railway goods vans that housed its animals when it first opened behind King's Cross station in 1973. The farm moved to its current location five years later, and now, as well as farmyard animals, it has a flower garden, an aviary and five beehives. The farm encourages visitors to adopt an animal or gain a qualification in beekeeping.

★ 4 HACKNEY CITY FARM

- ● *1a Goldsmiths Row, E2 8QA*
- ☎ *Tel: 020 7729 6381;*
  www.hackneycityfarm.co.uk
- ◎ *Liverpool Street, then bus 26, 48; Old Street, then bus 55; Bethnal Green*
- ❻ *FREE*

This farm makes the most of its 4.5 acres – as well as all the usual farm animals, which roam freely in fields, there are also degus and chinchillas. There is a small herb and vegetable garden, with pear, plum and apple trees and a sculpture garden at the front, with outdoor seating for 40. Inside, a cafe and restaurant seats a further 45 and serves Sunday roasts and Mediterranean dishes (£–££). At the back of the restaurant is a craft room, mostly used for pottery classes.

★ 5 SPITALFIELDS CITY FARM

- ❶ Buxton Street, E1 5AR
- ☎ Tel: 020 7247 8762;
  www.spitalfieldscityfarm.org
- ⊖ Whitechapel
- ❻ FREE

Come to this 1.3-acre site to toast marshmallows on an open fire while sitting on old railway-sleeper benches in the Bengal vegetable garden. Or perhaps a donkey ride or cookery class is more your thing? If none of those appeal, you can try your hand at milking a goat – just watch your aim.

★ 6 HOUNSLOW URBAN FARM

- ❶ Faggs Road, Feltham, Middlesex, TW14 0LZ
- ☎ Tel: 020 8831 9658;
  www.hounslow.info
- ⊖ Hatton Cross, then bus 90, 285, 490
- ❻ £4.25 adults; £2.75 children

This 29-acre farm has four Shetland ponies, two donkeys, two peacocks and two rheas.

★ 7 KENTISH TOWN CITY FARM

- ❶ 1 Cressfield Close, NW5 4BN
- ☎ Tel: 020 7916 5421;
  www.ktcityfarm.org.uk
- ⊖ Kentish Town, Chalk Farm
- ❻ FREE

Since 1972, this 4.5-acre site has provided a picnic area round its pond and a place for horse-riding lessons.

★ 8 STEPPING STONES FARM

- ❶ Stepney Way, Stepney, E1 3DG
- ☎ Tel: 020 7790 8204;
  www.steppingstonesfarm.co.uk
- ⊖ Stepney Green
- ❻ FREE

This farm may have a collection of animals that include two Kune Kune pigs, a chinchilla and pet rats – but its history is even more glamorous. Buried underneath its cow field is a 16th-century aristocratic mansion, Worcester House, which the farm's volunteers hope will be excavated. In the meantime, visitors can explore the ruins of an old Sunday School.

★ 9 VAUXHALL CITY FARM

- ❶ 165 Tyers Street, SE11 5HS
- ☎ Tel: 020 7582 4204;
  www.vauxhallcityfarm.org
- ⊖ Vauxhall
- ❻ FREE

The riding centre here has eight horses and offers lessons to people with disabilities and disadvantaged children. Covering less than an acre, this farm is one of the city's smallest, but it still has a community vegetable and herb garden and picnic facilities. Call in advance if you'd like a guided tour.

★ 10 HEATHROW SPECIAL NEEDS FARM

- ❶ Bath Road, Longford Village, Hillingdon, Middlesex, UB7 0EF
- ☎ Tel: 01753 680 330; www.heathrow specialneedsfarm.co.uk
- ⊖ Hounslow West, then bus 81
- ❻ £4 per 15-minute riding lesson

Formerly known as Spelthorne, this 12-acre farm welcomes volunteers to help out in its vegetable garden and farmyard. Otherwise the farm is not open to the general public; rather, it is dedicated to adults and children with special needs, giving them the opportunity to interact with farm animals and learn how to ride a horse.

▼ SOUTH

BATTERSEA PARK

- ❶ *Albert Bridge Road, SW11 4NJ*
- ⊕ *Tel: 020 8871 7530; www.batterseapark.org*
- ⊜ *Battersea Park BR*

Battersea Park shares its northern border with part of the River Thames, so rollerbladers can watch boats chugging up and down the river pass the Japanese Peace Pagoda. Also in the north of the 200-acre park is an old English garden, hidden behind a rusty gate and brick walls. Follow the road anti-clockwise and you'll cut through football pitches, ending up at the lake in the south-eastern corner of the park, where you can hire rowing boats in summer. A sub-tropical garden and a rosary garden border part of the lake.

BLACKHEATH

- ❶ *Shooters Hill Road, Blackheath, SE3*
- ⊕ *Tel: 020 8856 2232; www.greenwich.gov.uk*
- ⊜ *Blackheath BR*

How the heath got its name is disputed; some believe it was the site of a mass burial of plague victims in 1665, others argue it's a distortion of the words 'bleak' and 'heath'. Indeed, there is an element of bleakness to the common – on a grey day it resembles a seaside front in winter. Head here on a windy day, though, and this exposed common high on a hill is the best place in London to fly a kite.

BROCKWELL PARK

- ❶ *Dulwich Road, Herne Hill, Lambeth, SE24 0NG*
- ⊕ *Tel: 020 7926 6283 (park officer), 020 7926 9000 (council); www.brockwellpark.com*
- ⊜ *Herne Hill BR*

Brockwell Park offers a wide variety of sporting facilities – as well as a bowling green, there's a BMX track, tennis courts, volleyball court, free bowling green and an area for cricket. In summer, the lido is open (*see* p.228) and kids will love the miniature steam train. Also, within the park's 128 acres is a walled English herb garden, ponds, colourful flowerbeds and an old clock tower. There's a cafe in the centre of the grounds, on the ground floor of the Georgian Brockwell Hall, which has views of the park and surrounding area.

BURGESS PARK

- ❶ *Albany Road, Old Kent Road, Chumleigh Street, Wells Way, SE5 0RJ*
- ⊕ *Tel: 020 7525 1065; www.southwark.gov.uk*
- ⊜ *Elephant and Castle*

There's not much open space in Southwark, so Burgess Park gives locals a place to get some fresh air away from the kebab shops on Old Kent Road. Flat, grassy areas take up much of the 113-acre park, which received a £2 million cash injection last year. There's also a lake in which you can fish (permit required) and sports facilities – cricket and football pitches, cycling and go-karting tracks and a tennis centre. Farther into the park are Chumleigh Gardens, which are surrounded by old almshouses. There's a cafe inside the cottages and behind them is another well-kept garden, which is divided into Islamic, English, African/Caribbean, Mediterranean and Oriental areas, reflecting the borough's ethnic diversity.

CLAPHAM COMMON

- ❶ *Clapham Common North Side, SW4*
- ⊕ *Tel: 020 7622 5745; www.claphamcommon.org*
- ◉ *Clapham Common*

The Manor of Clapham first mentioned the common in 1086, in the Domesday Book. Since then, its 220 acres have been a popular place for south Londoners to relax. These days, locals go to jog, play football and tennis or to watch the summer music events (*see* p.48) or the November fireworks. For kids, there's a paddling pool at the Clapham High Street end; families will enjoy the cafes and a stroll around the common's three fishing ponds. There's a restored Grade II-listed bandstand, too.

CRYSTAL PALACE PARK

- ❶ *Crystal Palace Park, Thicket Road, SE20 8DT*
- ⊕ *Tel: 020 8778 9496; www.crystalpalacepark.org*
- ◉ *Crystal Palace BR*

Queen Victoria opened Crystal Palace Park in 1854, and, since its completion three years later, it has provided south Londoners with 200 acres of public space. There's a lake and a Victorian maze, renovated in 2009, which is, at 49 metres wide, the biggest in London. Rather unexpectedly, the park is home to 32 dinosaurs (of the stone variety), close to the lake. The Grade I-listed sculptures, which underwent a £4 million restoration programme in 2000, were built when the park opened. Real reptiles can also be found within the park, on the farm; there are snakes and lizards, as well as Kune Kunes (a hairy, chubby, breed of pig), small llama-like alpacas and Shetland ponies. A massive regeneration project began in 2009.

DULWICH PARK

- ❶ *Dulwich Village, SE21 7BG*
- ⊕ *Tel: 020 7525 2000; www.dulwichparkfriends.org.uk*
- ◉ *West Dulwich BR, then bus 176, 185; West Dulwich BR, then bus P4*

This peaceful 72-acre park in Dulwich Village has tennis courts, landscaped gardens and a lake in the middle. For the novelty, you could hire a recumbent bike and cycle in a reclined position around the park. Alternatively, visit the Pavilion Cafe, in the middle of the park, which has great views of the surrounding gardens.

GREENWICH PARK

- *Blackheath Gate, SE10 8QY*
- *Tel: 020 8858 2608; www.friendsofgreenwichpark.org.uk*
- *Cutty Sark DLR, Maze Hill BR*

Most tourists coming from Greenwich village climb the hill to the meridian line (from where Greenwich Mean Time – GMT – is measured from), outside the Royal Observatory. From there, take in views of Canary Wharf, the O2 and the Thames in the distance, as well as the National Maritime Museum and Old Royal Naval College below. But there's much more to the park. Have a snack at the Pavilion tea house and do a loop of the rest of the 183-acre gardens, admiring the flowerbeds, or feeding the ducks in the two ponds.

HORNIMAN MUSEUM GARDENS

- *100 London Road, Forest Hill, SE23 3PQ*
- *Tel: 020 8699 1872; www.horniman.ac.uk*
- *Forest Hill BR, then bus 176, 185, 197, 356, P4*

Rays of sunlight splice through the trees of this 16-acre garden, casting shadows across its sloping lawns. As well as over 150 banana trees in the African garden, there's a sundial, a small rose garden in summer and a sunken garden. At the top of the hill, near the bandstand, there's an animal enclosure with hens, geese and goats and an old well. Take a moment to relax here on a bench to take in the view of Canada Tower, Wembley Arch and Tower Bridge. The highlight is its stunning Victorian orangery, which is now a cafe.

PECKHAM RYE PARK

- *Strakers Road, SE15 3HU*
- *Tel: 020 7525 2000; www.southwark.gov.uk*
- *Peckham Rye BR*

Since 1894, locals have been able to stroll around 52 acres of themed gardens, woodland and meadows. There's also a stream and lake within the park, which is now Grade II-listed. Infants will enjoy the play area, and there is an adventure playground for older children and a BMX skate park. The park also has three football pitches and outdoor gym equipment, such as bench presses.

WANDSWORTH COMMON

- *207 Trinity Road, SW17 7HW*
- *Tel: 020 8871 6000; www.wandsworth.gov.uk*
- *Wandsworth Common BR*

Wandsworth Common covers 175 acres and stretches from Trinity Road on its east side to Bolingbroke Grove on its west. A railway line divides the grassy park in two, but trains pass by quite quietly. There are tennis courts, a bowling green, an exercise trail and a renovated children's play area next to a flower garden. At the edge of the park is Stock Pond, which is fringed by oak and birch trees.

WALKS AND BIKE ROUTES

★ THE CAPITAL RING

❶ *Tel: 020 7222 1234; www.tfl.gov.uk*
❷ *Woolwich Arsenal DLR*

Completed in 2005, this walking trail was designed to give walkers the chance to make the most of London's green belt. The length of the trail is disputed, but it's approximately 120km divided into 15 sections. The trail officially begins at Woolwich foot tunnel, and follows a clockwise direction, but walkers can start anywhere along the route. The track circles the whole of London – along the way walkers will pass Severndroog Castle, Eltham Palace and Richmond Park in the south, Horsenden Hill in the west, Highgate Wood in the north and Lea Valley in the east.

★ NEW RIVER WALK

❶ *Tel: 020 7527 4953 (Greenspace division); 078 2509 8457 (ranger);*
   www.london.gov.uk
❷ *Angel, Finsbury Park, Highbury and Islington*

The New River was built to transport drinking water from Hertfordshire to London's residents. You can now follow the 38-mile route from Islington all the way to Chadwell Springs in Ware. To start at the beginning, look for signs for the Round Pond off Rosebery Avenue near Sadler's Wells (see p.156). The route takes you to the New River Walk, which starts behind Embassy bar on Essex Road, Islington. As you pass a small waterfall gushing over rocks, you'll find it hard to believe you're just a few minutes' walk from the city's major bus routes. Continue on through Stoke Newington's Clissold Park (see p.194), past and do a loop of Hackney's two reservoirs, which are unfortunately blighted by ugly tower blocks and rubbish. The path then takes you through Finsbury Park (see p.195) and parallel to Cambridge Road in Enfield. Once you pass the M25, you'll be on the home stretch: Chadwell Springs.

★ REGENT'S CANAL WALK AND BIKE ROUTE

❶ *Tel: 020 7278 6612; 020 7261 0447; www.wildlondon.org.uk;*
   office: London Wildlife Trust, 80 York Way, N1 9AG
❷ *Various – including Paddington, Camden Town, Angel, Finsbury Park, Mile End*

The Regent's Canal stretches all the way from the Limehouse Basin in east London to the Paddington Basin in the west. Each part has a different ambience; the leafy stretch around Little Venice and Hampstead is a pleasant walk or cycle route, whereas the path leading from Hawley Lock in Camden, through Kentish Town and to St Pancras Lock, is unfortunately strewn with litter and graffiti. Turn left at the end of Broadway Market (see p.115) in the east and you can walk or cycle to Victoria Park (see p.205), then on to Mile End Park (see p.205).

▼ EAST

EPPING FOREST

- ℹ *High Beech, Loughton, Essex, IG10 4AF*
- ⊕ *Tel: 020 8508 0028; www.cityoflondon.gov.uk*
- ◉ *Chingford BR*

This forest is enormous – its 6,000 acres stretch from Manor Park in east London to beyond Epping in Essex. Once a royal hunting ground in medieval times, Queen Elizabeth's hunting lodge can still be seen in the centre. Over 50 km of horse-riding trails take you through the parkland, or you can walk past ponds and lakes in which you can fish. Further south is Hollow Pond, where you can hire boats for £10 an hour. There's also a golf course and 60 football pitches.

HACKNEY MARSHES

- ℹ *Homerton Road, E9 5PF*
- ⊕ *Tel: 020 8356 8467; www.hackney.gov.uk*
- ◉ *Hackney Wick BR*

If you want to get fit, then head here – along the canal footpath, there's an outdoor trail of gym apparatuses. The marshes also have an athletics track, 88 football fields and 3 rugby pitches. The River Lee runs through this 337-acre space, which also has a designated conservation area.

HAINAULT FOREST COUNTRY PARK

- ℹ *Romford Road, Chigwell, Essex, IG7 4QN*
- ⊕ *Tel: 020 8500 7353; www.hainaultforest.co.uk*
- ◉ *Hainault, then bus 247*

You needn't travel for hours to see highland cows, butterflies and bluebells – Hainault Forest, just 11 stops from Liverpool Street, has all of these. The forest dates from the mid-19th century, when it was part of a royal hunting ground. It opened to the public in 1906; since then, a farm and petting area, bridleways and a golf course have been added. The forest has an orienteering course, which crosses part of the 800-acre site. There are also rough paths you can follow past 300-year old lime, rowan and maple trees across grassy slopes and woodland. On a clear day the London Eye is visible, 13 miles away.

LEE VALLEY REGIONAL PARK

- ℹ *Office: Myddelton House, Bulls Cross, Enfield, Middlesex, EN2 9HG*
- ⊕ *Tel: 0845 677 0600; www.leevalleypark.org.uk*
- ◉ *Tottenham Hale, Canning Town*

This nature reserve stretches north over 26 miles, covering a massive 10,000 acres. As well as a series of reservoirs, there's a watersports centre that organizes windsurfing, designated fishing spots and riding trails. A towpath runs the length of the reserve, and doubles up as a cycle track for dedicated cyclists.

LONDON FIELDS

- *London Fields Westside, E8 3EU*
- *Tel: 020 8356 8428 ext 29 (parks and leisure), 020 8356 9674 (parks department); www.hackney.gov.uk*
- *London Fields BR*
- *£4 lido*

On a sunny Saturday you can combine a visit to the trendy Broadway Market (see p.115) with a laze about in London Fields. As well as tennis, football and cricket facilities, there's a lido in the north-west corner, and a children's play area. In spring you can eat your falafel wraps/crêpes/tuna baguette from the market on picnic benches under the cherry blossoms.

MILE END PARK

- *London Fields, Hackney, E8*
- *Tel: 020 7364 4147; www.towerhamlets.gov.uk*
- *Mile End*

This 75-acre park is more like several small parks in one, as each section has a different ambience. Sporty types will head straight to the field; children will enjoy the sandpit; and those looking for adventure will be interested in the electric go-kart track, climbing wall and areas for skating and BMX riding (see p.233). The park's formal terraced garden is much calmer, with its fountain and landscaped flowerbeds. There's also an ecology park and lake, as well as an arts pavilion hosting art exhibitions, workshops and poetry readings.

SPRINGFIELD PARK

- *Upper Clapton Road, Hackney, E5 9EF*
- *Tel: 020 8986 9674 ; www.hackney.gov.uk*
- *Clapton BR, then bus 393, 253, 254*

In 1905, the grounds of three private manors combined to create this park, which shares its eastern border with the River Lea. If you've followed the towpath along the Lea Valley, have a rest on the park's sloping lawns as you watch canal boats chugging by. Otherwise, follow the paths through the park's sweet chestnut, lime and mulberry trees to the pond and feed the ducks.

VICTORIA PARK

- *Victoria Park Road, E9 7BT*
- *Tel: 020 7364 7907; www.towerhamletsarts.org.uk*
- *Mile End, then bus 277, Bethnal Green*

Vicky Park looks a bit tatty these days, but still, with its lakes, bandstands and old pavilions, it's a nice enough place to stroll around. As well as a paddling pool and children's play area, kids will enjoy the deer enclosure near Grove Road. The park also has tennis courts and a bowling green. In summer, the 218-acre site hosts lively open-air festivals around the Chinese pagoda.

10 BEST CEMETERIES

Spooked by cemeteries? You shouldn't be, because London has some of the UK's most tranquil. Below are details of London's historical 'magnificent seven' (Kensal Green, West Norwood, Highgate, Abney Park, Nunhead, Brompton and Tower Hamlets), as well as a few others we recommend you visit.

★ 1 KENSAL GREEN CEMETERY

- ❶ Harrow Road, W10 4RA
- ☎ Tel: 020 8969 0152; www.kensalgreen.co.uk
- ⊖ Kensal Green

Established in 1832, Kensal Green is one of the oldest cemeteries in London. Since it opened, it's been a dedicated mixed-faith cemetery and is still operational today. Tours take you around the 72-acre space, leading you past the grave of book-lover W.H. Smith.

★ 2 WEST NORWOOD CEMETERY

- ❶ Norwood Road, West Norwood, SE27 9JU
- ☎ Tel: 020 7926 7999; www.fownc.org
- ⊖ West Norwood BR; Brixton, then bus 2, 196, 432

Consecrated in 1837, this cemetery later became known as 'millionaire's cemetery' for the quality of its mausolea. Wander around the site and you'll come across the crematorium in the middle of the grounds; it's the cemetery's highest point and has views across central London. You can find out more about the cemetery's history on the tours, which are held on the first Sunday of every month.

★ 3 HIGHGATE CEMETERY

- ❶ Swain's Lane, Highgate, N6 6PJ
- ☎ Tel: 020 8340 1834; www.highgate-cemetery.org
- ⊖ Archway

Since it opened in 1839, Highgate Cemetery has been one of London's most-loved cemeteries, attracting international visitors as well as locals. It is the site of George Eliot and Karl Marx's graves, and is still used for burials today.

★ 4 ABNEY PARK CEMETERY

- ❶ Abney Park Trust, South Lodge, Abney Park, Stoke Newington High Street, N16 0LN
- ☎ Tel: 020 7275 7557; www.abney-park.org.uk
- ⊖ Stoke Newington BR; Angel, then bus 73, 106, 149, 476

From its Church Street entrance, you'd think this cemetery was a small, scruffy park. Once inside, however, you're met with a warren of sandy paths that weave deep into 32 acres of woodland and past graves dating from 1840. The cemetery largely closed to burials in the 1970s, and has since been left to decay in the nicest possible way – it's now a tranquil nature reserve.

★ 5 NUNHEAD CEMETERY

- ❶ Linden Grove, SE15 3LP
- ☎ Tel: 020 7732 9535
- ⊖ Nunhead BR; Canada Water, then bus P12

Follow winding paths around the graves of wealthy locals in this peaceful cemetery, which dates back to 1840. Here you can peel back woodland that has overgrown decaying Grade II-listed memorials to find the names of former ship owners and MPs. The cemetery runs monthly tours for free on the last Sunday of the month. The two-hour tour explores the 52-acre site, taking in the partially restored chapel at the top of the avenue and the view of St Paul's from the hillside. Meet at the Victorian gate, Linden Grove, at 2.15pm.

★ 6 BROMPTON CEMETERY

ℹ *Fulham Road, SW10 9UG*
☎ *Tel: 020 7352 1201;*
  www.royalparks.org.uk
◉ *Fulham Broadway, West Brompton*

This 101-acre cemetery, which dates from 1840, is long and narrow and split in two by a central avenue. The walkway leads visitors past Emmeline Pankhurst's memorial (on the left) and up to a chapel, the exterior of which was filmed in *Golden Eye* (1995).

★ 7 TOWER HAMLETS
CEMETERY PARK

ℹ *Southern Grove, Bow, E3 4PX*
☎ *Tel: 020 8252 6644, 07904 186 981;*
  www.towerhamletscemetery.org
◉ *Mile End*

This 27-acre site opened as a cemetery in 1841; it's here you'll find the grave of John Willis, the owner of the Cutty Sark. It closed to burials in 1966, and was designated a local nature reserve a decade ago. Come in summer and you'll see up to 27 species of butterfly flitting about the reserve's six ponds.

★ 8 HAMPSTEAD CEMETERY

ℹ *69 Fortune Green Road, West Hampstead, NW6 1DR*

☎ *Tel: 020 7527 8300;*
  www.camden.gov.uk
◉ *West Hampstead BR*

This 26-acre space opened in 1876, just off Finchley Road. Points of interest include two Gothic chapels and the resting place of Lord Joseph Lister (1827–1912), the British surgeon accredited for promoting antiseptic.

★ 9 ST PANCRAS AND
ISLINGTON CEMETERIES

ℹ *High Road, East Finchley, N2 9AG*
☎ *Tel: 020 7527 8300;*
  www.camden.gov.uk
◉ *East Finchley, then bus 263*

With a combined space of 190 acres, these two cemeteries have joined to create London's largest burial ground – but if you get achy legs walking around, you can hop on the free bus that does a loop of the grounds on weekends. Established in 1854, the cemetery's woodland is abundant with wildlife, encouraged by the ancient Coldfall Wood next door.

★ 10 CITY OF LONDON CEMETERY

ℹ *Aldersbrook Road, E12 5DQ*
☎ *Tel: 020 8530 2151;*
  www.cityoflondon.gov.uk
◉ *Manor Park BR; East Ham or Wanstead, then bus 101*

You may be wondering how you missed a 200-acre cemetery in the middle of the city, but this cemetery is actually close to Epping Forest. The cemetery opened in 1854 and remains open for mixed-faith burials today. It contains a large memorial garden with 28,000 rose bushes that bloom in June.

▼ WEST

BUSHY PARK

- ❶ Hampton Court Road, Hampton, Middlesex, TW12 2EJ
- ⊕ Tel: 020 8979 1586; www.royalparks.org.uk
- ◉ Teddington BR, Hampton Wick BR, Hampton Court BR

Of all of the royal parks, this one is probably the least well known, although, after Richmond, it's the second largest, at 1,099 acres. There are several entry points, and the park is roughly divided in two by Chestnut Avenue and a large fountain. To the west of the fountain is a long avenue of lime trees, which run parallel to Longford River. If you follow the river, you'll pass through woodland; branch off to your right and you'll find yourself on one of the park's many walking trails snaking through fields in which 320 deer roam. The eastern part of the park is much the same, and it is also home to a skate park, allotments, a cricket ground and royal paddocks. Plus, there are three connecting ponds in the middle, one of which is used for sailing model boats.

CHELSEA PHYSIC GARDEN

- ❶ 66 Royal Hospital Road, SW3 4HS
- ⊕ Tel: 020 7352 5646; www.chelseaphysicgarden.co.uk
- ◉ Sloane Square
- ❹ £8

Sloane-ranger types and those in the know often choose this garden as a wedding venue. The gardens were created in 1673, but weren't open to the public until 1983. If you want to simply visit, then you can either look around them on your own or join a free tour. Guides lead groups of up to 20 on informative tours around perfume and aromatherapy gardens, a world medicine garden, beehives and past a statue of Dr Hans Sloane – the man credited for introducing the recipe for milk chocolate into Britain.

GUNNERSBURY PARK

- ❶ Gunnersbury Park, Ealing, W3 8LQ
- ⊕ Tel: 020 8992 1612; www.hounslow.gov.uk
- ◉ Acton Town

This 200-acre park dates from the 1700s, but it wasn't open to the public until 1925. The Large Mansion within the grounds has been the home of Gunnersbury Park Museum since 1929, and displays costumes, fine art and two early 19th-century horse-drawn carriages. From the museum, you can follow a 2.9-km circuit clockwise around the grounds, passing another property, known as Small Mansion, and an orangery, built in 1836 (which is closed to the public). Continue on to Potomac fishing lake in the southern corner of the park, and you'll see a temple dating from 1760, Italian gardens and a round boating pond in the north. Sports facilities include 36 football pitches, 14 tennis courts and pitch and putt, so you can easily spend a whole day there.

HOLLAND PARK

- *Ilchester Place, W8 6LU*
- *Tel: 020 7938 8170; www.rbkc.gov.uk*
- *High Street Kensington*

If you're coming from the High Street Kensington end, you'll pass playing fields on your left as you walk towards Holland Open-Air Park Theatre (see p.162) and Holland House, which was built in 1605. Continue past an orangery and you'll enter formal gardens brimming with colourful flowers – look out for peacocks strutting around. Nearby there's a lawn that's popular with sunbathers in warmer months, and around the corner, a manicured Japanese garden and pond, which is the park's real draw. Watch out for the ferocious gardener – you'll endure his wrath if you step on the grass.

KENSINGTON ROOF GARDENS

- *99 Kensington High Street, W8 5SA*
- *Tel: 020 7937 7994 (to organize a visit), 020 7368 3971 (to hire the gardens); www.roofgardens.virgin.com*
- *High Street Kensington*

Pink flamingos belong more in a tropical zoo than London's West End. But they can be found in a 1.5-acre garden only 30 metres above the high street. The Roof Gardens were created in 1936 and opened to the public two years later. Spanish, Tudor and Woodland gardens cover the sixth floor of what was Derry and Tom's department store, now a Grade II-listed building. The Spanish garden is the largest, with its cobbled pathway winding round a courtyard. A trellis-covered tunnel, used for barbecues, leads visitors into an outdoor dining area in the Tudor garden. The most interesting features here are those most easily overlooked: a face carved into a brick wall, a wishing well and a hunting-scene carving almost covered by plants. Around a corner is the Woodland garden, with its carp pond, humped wooden bridge and cherry blossom tree.

KEW GARDENS

- *Royal Botanic Gardens, Kew, Richmond, Surrey, TW9 3AB*
- *Tel: 020 8332 5655; www.kew.org*
- *Kew Gardens*

Kew Gardens was founded in 1759 by George III's mother, and became a UNESCO World Heritage Site in 2003. You could easily spend a whole day exploring all of the garden's 300 acres, and it would be a shame not to. There's plenty to see and do whatever time of year you go. Hide behind trees in a snowball fight in dense woodland in winter, stroll parallel to the Thames in summer or see cherry blossoms bloom in February near Temperate House. The 4,880-square-metre glasshouse, built in 1859, is one of many stunning buildings within the grounds. The Chinese pagoda in the southern corner of the garden is particularly scenic. Another highlight is the 18-metre-high tree-top walkway, which has views for miles.

OSTERLEY PARK

- ❶ *Jersey Road, Isleworth, TW7 4RB*
- ⊕ *Tel: 020 8232 5050; www.nationaltrust.org.uk*
- ◎ *Osterley*

At the heart of this 357-acre landscaped park and farmland is Osterley House, a National Trust manor. Three lakes split the park in two – the middle one has the best views of the house. Follow the Nine Acre path from the car park and you'll do a loop of most of the grounds, which takes about an hour. You'll first pass a meadow on your left, where you can meet friendly Shetland ponies – some aren't much bigger than a dog. Continue to the north and west of the house and you'll come across tranquil pleasure grounds, which are at their best in summer when they burst with colour. The stables next to the manor show a short film of what life at Osterley Park used to be like in the 16th century. The grounds are also home to a former World War II rifle range.

RICHMOND PARK

- ❶ *Richmond upon Thames, Surrey, TW10 5HS*
- ⊕ *Tel: 020 8948 3209; www.royalparks.org.uk*
- ◎ *Richmond, then bus 65, 371*

Known for its deer, this 2,360-acre wild expanse is London's biggest royal park, and it's made for lying in the long grass with your lover. More active types could hike through the park's woodland; make sure you visit the Isabella plantation and King Henry VIII's mound, so called because he used to hunt there. From there you'll see St Paul's Cathedral to the east, 16 km away, and a panorama of the Thames Valley to the west. Alternatively, cycle along the park's bike tracks or fly a kite on Corretts Copse. Guided tours can also be arranged. If you're lucky, your guide might explain how Spankers Hill got its name... *Tip: if you came by car, remember which gate you parked near.*

WWT LONDON WETLAND CENTRE

- ❶ *Queen Elizabeth's Walk, Barnes, SW13 9WT*
- ⊕ *Tel: 020 8409 4400; www.wwt.org.uk*
- ◎ *Hammersmith, then bus 283; Barnes BR, then bus 33, 72*
- ❹ *£9.50*

Unless you're a keen bird spotter or insect enthusiast, you probably won't be interested in the labels detailing the rare wildlife seen here. Still, this 105-acre space is a family-pleaser with its series of lakes, marshes and wetland meadows connected by boardwalks and paths. There are six viewing hides dotted around so you can bird watch – come in winter to see birds migrating over 3,000 km from Siberia. Included in your ticket are guided tours, on which you'll learn about bird migration and what lies beneath the ponds. There's also an adventure area for children; kids will love zooming down the 20-metre zip wire, climbing on the boulder wall and exploring giant water vole tunnels.

RIVER AND CANAL CRUISES

To get the most out of a trip along the Thames, you need to pick the right company, season and section of the river. The western strip is undoubtedly more picturesque, but the eastern end, while mostly dotted with cranes and building yards, does take you past some fascinating industrial heritage. For an alternative boat trip, consider a jaunt along London's canal network. You can either join a small group or charter your own canal boat for parties of up to 12.

★ LONDON CANAL CRUISES

❶ *Various routes. Office: 63 Salisbury Road, High Barnet, Hertfordshire, EN5 4JL*
⊕ *Tel: 020 8440 8962; www.londoncanalcruises.com*

Charter a canal boat with London Canal Cruises and you can choose the route you take, and be served lunch and afternoon tea onboard, too. Otherwise you can opt for their usual route, which starts from City Road near Angel tube station and heads north to Kensal Green and Stonebridge. Included in the price is a trip to the London Canal Museum, plus you get to pass through the centre of London Zoo – so you can see the aviary and wild African hunting dogs.

★ THAMES RIVER SERVICES

❶ *Westminster Pier, Embankment, SW1A 2JH*
⊕ *Tel: 020 7930 4097; www.thamesriverservices.co.uk*
⊝ *Westminster*

This company operates from Westminster Pier and heads east to the Thames barrier. You'll take in sights such as Canary Wharf, the O2 and the changing urban landscape, as well as the National Maritime Museum in Greenwich.

★ WALKERS QUAY

❶ *250 Camden High Street, NW1 8QS*
⊕ *Tel: 020 7485 4433; www.walkersquay.com*
⊝ *Camden Town*

From April to October, join a cruise along Regent Canal, starting from Camden Lock. The route goes through a lock and past some of the city's most expensive houses. It continues past London Zoo and Regent's Park and into Maida Vale.

★ WESTMINSTER PASSENGER SERVICES ASSOCIATION

❶ *Westminster Pier, Victoria Embankment, SW1A 2JH*
⊕ *Tel: 020 7930 2062; www.wpsa.co.uk*
⊝ *Westminster*

This company also leaves from Westminster Pier, sailing west in the direction of Hampton Court Palace. It stops off at Richmond and Kew along the way, and operates in warmer months only.

SIGHTS

This chapter focuses on the best sights London has to offer, from British icons, such as the House of Parliament and the London Eye, to less well-known sights, including St Sofia's Greek Cathedral, which have shorter queues. If you're looking for art galleries and museums, please see the relevant chapters.

▼ CENTRAL

BUCKINGHAM PALACE AND SURROUNDS

- ℹ️ *The Mall, SW1A 1AA*
- 🌐 *Tel: 020 7766 7300; www.royalcollection.org.uk*
- 🚇 *Green Park, St James's Park*
- 💷 *£7.50–£29.50*
- ▪️ *State rooms: only open to visitors over the summer, from late Jul to end of Sep*

If you pay the full amount, you can see Buckingham Palace, the State Rooms, the Queen's Gallery and the Royal Mews; for an extra fee you can also visit Clarence House. Built in 1703, the palace has 600 rooms – but on the tour you only get to see 19. Still, the ones you do see are grand. The State Rooms are decorated with paintings by Rembrandt and Rubens, elaborate plasterwork, porcelain and sculptures, and are used to entertain guests on ceremonial business. On your way out you'll pass through the garden and lake at the rear of the palace. At the time of writing, plans were in place for summer tours around the whole 39-acre lawns.

You can also see part of the Royal Collection in the Queen's Galleries: the jewellery, furniture, silverwork and armour collected over the past 500 years by kings and queens. Look out for the limited-edition Fabergé eggs.

The Royal Mews, or working stable, is for true royalists who can't get enough of behind-the-scenes at the palace. While the horses are not always on view, you may spot one or two, as well as the gold state coach, which you will recognize from the Queen's golden jubilee celebrations in 2002. The tour takes 45 minutes.

Down the mall is Clarence House, home to Charles and Camilla, William and Harry. You only get to see the five rooms downstairs, used for official guests.

HOUSES OF PARLIAMENT

- ℹ️ *Parliament Square, SW1A 0AA*
- 🌐 *Tel: 0870 906 3773 (tours), 020 7219 3000 (switchboard); www.parliament.uk*
- 🚇 *Westminster*
- 💷 *FREE tours year round for UK residents, if booked in advance through your MP;*
  £7 for 75-minute tours everyday during summer, except Sundays

Ever wondered why the Lords' seats are red and the Commons' are green? Red was the colour of royalty and green dye was cheaper, apparently. On a tour of

Parliament you'll also find out that you can post a petition to the Parliament and, once it's received, it'll go in the petition bag behind the speaker's chair in the Commons. Your guide may also tell you that, originally, the speaker's chair was designed as a toilet so the speaker could 'just go' during a debate, which otherwise would have had to have stopped if he'd needed to relieve himself; the speaker would simply pull a curtain around his chair, and the MPs would talk among themselves to hide any embarrassing noises. You'll visit the corridors in which MPs vote, too – they have eight minutes to walk to the 'aye' corridor if they vote yes, or the opposite corridor if their vote is 'no'. The tour will then lead you through the Lords' debating chamber and into the Queen's robing room, where Her Majesty gets dressed in ceremonial robes before making the Queen's speech.

LONDON AQUARIUM

- ❶ *County Hall, Riverside Building, Westminster Bridge Road, South Bank, SE1 7PB*
- ⊞ *Tel: 020 7967 8000; www.londonaquarium.co.uk*
- ◉ *Waterloo*
- ❸ *£8.25*

Following a revamp earlier last year, the aquarium reopened in March 2009. The centre has 14 zones, which exhibit 400 species, each dedicated to a different sea. Highlights include the stingray pool, 'Nemo' clown fish, watching the sharks being fed (Tuesdays, Thursdays and Saturdays) and the piranhas in the tropical freshwater area. Visitors may be disappointed not to see great white sharks, dolphins or whales, but there's still plenty to entertain – a major highlight is one of the aquarium's main two tanks, the Atlantic. The Pacific tank is also popular, as visitors can see zebra, nurse and sandtiger sharks (which are also known as ragged tooth sharks because their teeth are visible, even when their mouth is closed).

LONDON EYE

- ❶ *Riverside Building, Westminster Bridge Road, South Bank, SE1 7PB*
- ⊞ *Tel: 0870 500 0600; www.londoneye.com*
- ◉ *Waterloo*
- ❸ *£17; £27 fast-track*
- ▦ *Flights operate every 30mins: 10am–8pm Jan–May, Oct–Dec; 10am–9pm Jun, Sep; 10am–9.30pm Jul, Aug*

It takes 30 minutes for each of the Eye's 32 capsules to do one loop, which gives you enough time to take in the scenes 135 metres below you. From the Eye, you'll be able to see Big Ben, the Houses of Parliament, St James's Park and Buckingham Palace. The best time to go is at dusk, when you get the best of both worlds – you'll see the sights in the day, the sun set over the Thames, then London's lights flicker on. Themed flights with champagne, chocolate tasting, canapés and beauty treatments are also available. If you want to avoid queuing for up to four hours, then book ahead. The trouble is, the fast-track tickets are pricey, and you can't guarantee sunshine. It's your call.

THE MOVIEUM OF LONDON

- County Hall, Riverside Building, Westminster Bridge Road, SE1 7PB
- Tel: 020 7202 7040; www.themovieum.com
- Waterloo
- £17 on the door; £12 online

Here you can have your 15 minutes of fame on the red carpet and play with props you'll recognize from *Star Wars*. You'll learn how a script jumps off the page and onto the screen and take part in workshops on how to draw cartoons. The Movieum strives to be interactive, so as well as playing a keyboard in the sound studio and starring in your own film, you can hop on a vintage car and 'drive' through London's streets (the attraction's most popular exhibit). The Movieum is also worth a visit to explore the former site of the General London Council, which dates from 1912. The council's 220-seat marble debating chamber still hosts occasional special events, and can be seen on *Harry Potter and the Order of the Phoenix* (2007). *Insider info: the building is said to be haunted by the grey lady ghost who may have a connection to the prison cells in the basement (not open to the public).*

RIPLEYS

- The London Pavilion, 1 Piccadilly Circus, W1J 0DA
- Tel: 020 3238 0022; www.ripleyslondon.com
- Piccadilly Circus
- £21.90

It may be a tourist trap but it's still lots of fun – who isn't just a bit curious to see a chewing-gum sculpture of The Beatles or a model of Tower Bridge made from 264,345 matchsticks? You might also like to see the man with two pupils in each eye, Marilyn Monroe's make-up case, a rock from the moon and the shrunken heads of a tribe's enemies. All of the 800 items on display, many of which were collected by the attraction's founder, Robert Ripley, during his travels in the 1920s and 1930s, are original and genuine – although you may find that hard to believe.

ST MARTIN-IN-THE-FIELDS

- Trafalgar Square, WC2N 4JJ
- Tel: 020 7766 1100; www.stmartin-in-the-fields.org
- Leicester Square, Charing Cross, Covent Garden
- FREE

A church has stood on this spot since at least 1222, although this particular church dates back to 1726. A £36 million restoration project has just been completed. It has transformed the courtyard in front and revamped the vaults underneath. The church is open for services and for visitors – you can look around on your own or go on a tour to explore the crypt and vaults. It also has a gallery that displays changing exhibitions, ranging from displays about the history of St Martin's and prints by local and international artists, to paintings by homeless people. The venue has a lively music programme (see pp.170–1), too.

WELLINGTON ARCH

❶ *Hyde Park Corner, W1J 7JZ*
⊕ *Tel: 020 7930 2726; www.english-heritage.org.uk*
⊖ *Hyde Park Corner*
❸ *£3.50*

Not to be confused with the three-arched Marble Arch near the corner of Oxford Street and Edgware Road, Wellington Arch has a single arch and was completed in 1830. It was originally built as an entrance to Hyde Park and was known as Green Park Arch. It was located on a narrow road opposite the park's Triumphal Screen (the park's main entrance) but, once Victoria Station opened, the arch caused traffic jams, so it was moved, block by block, to its current location. You can walk up through the arch's three floors, which host an exhibition about its history, to the top, where you can see the Houses of Parliament below.

WESTMINSTER ABBEY

❶ *20 Dean's Yard, SW1P 3PA*
⊕ *Tel: 020 7222 5152; www.westminster-abbey.org*
⊖ *St James's Park*
❸ *£15*

Not to be confused with Westminster Cathedral (*see below*) near Victoria, the abbey is the striking Gothic building close to the House of Parliament. It dates from 1245, under the reign of King Henry III, but there's been a place of worship on this site since AD 960. The abbey is best known for its connection to royalty: it has been the coronation church since 1066, when William the Conqueror was crowned, and, in 1952, the world watched as 27-year-old Elizabeth Windsor became Queen. It is still an active place of worship, although visitors are welcome (except on Sundays). You can take a tour, on which you'll learn the history behind the 13th-century paintings, stained-glass windows and artefacts on display; or you can wander around at your own pace – don't miss the tombs of Henry III, Charles Darwin, Isaac Newton and the poet Geoffrey Chaucer.

WESTMINSTER CATHEDRAL

❶ *42 Francis Street, SW1P 1QW*
⊕ *Tel: 020 7798 9055; www.westminstercathedral.org.uk*
⊖ *Victoria*
❸ *FREE*

Before the cathedral was built, the land on which it stands was the site of a fairground, maze and pleasure garden, as well as a ring for bull-baiting. It then became wasteground before Tothill Fields mixed prison was built here in 1834. John Francis Bentley didn't start building the cathedral until 1895. Influenced by historic Mediterranean architecture, Bentley designed the red-brick tower, domes and balconies, as well as the 126 marbles and mosaics inside – left unfinished after he died from tongue cancer. The cathedral is still active and holds seven masses a day, attracting 8,000 visitors a week.

▼ NORTH

LORD'S CRICKET GROUND

- ❶ St John's Wood, NW8 8QN
- ⊕ Tel: 020 7616 8500 (switchboard), 020 7616 8595 (tours); www.lords.org
- ⊖ St John's Wood
- ❹ £14 tour; £3 museum

The Marylebone Cricket Club was founded in 1787, but only moved to its current location in 1814. You can take a tour of the grounds, which includes a trip around the museum (see p.142), a visit to the dressing rooms and a chance to see the best views of the turf from inside the media centre. You will also be guided around the turf, which slopes 200 metres, so players have to adjust their game.

MADAME TUSSAUDS

- ❶ Marylebone Road, NW1 5LR
- ⊕ Tel: 0870 999 0046; www.madame-tussauds.co.uk
- ⊖ Baker Street
- ❹ £25; £87 family ticket

This waxworks museum is well worth a visit. Learn how Madame Tussauds went from making death masks to replicas of famous people, and how the models are made. It takes about two hours to walk around the 13 different zones, which display 300 figures. Highlights include Nicole Kidman, dressed in a full-length red gown, Barack Obama inside the Oval Office and the Queen.

ST SOPHIA'S GREEK CATHEDRAL

- ❶ Moscow Road, Bayswater, W2 4LQ
- ⊕ Tel: 020 7229 7260; www.stsophia.org.uk
- ⊖ Bayswater
- ❹ FREE

This memorable cathedral was completed in 1879. It was bombed during the blitz but has been repaired to its former glory, so you can see Italian and Greek marble, alabaster columns and a mosaic of Jesus Christ and the 12 apostles on the ceiling of the dome. It's still an active place of worship.

ZSL LONDON ZOO

- ❶ Outer Circle, Regent's Park, NW1 4RY
- ⊕ Tel: 020 7722 3333, 020 7449 6269 (keeper for a day); www.zsl.org
- ⊖ Baker Street, Camden Town
- ❹ £13.90 winter; £16.80 summer; £260 keeper for a day; £165 per half day

Since it opened in 1828, London Zoo has given Londoners the chance to see bearded pigs, anteaters, hissing cockroaches and bird-eating spiders. If you'd like to get even closer to the animals, you can try being a zookeeper for a day. You'll do everything from mucking out the zebra dens to feeding the meerkats.

▼ SOUTH

GOLDEN HINDE GALLEON

- *St Mary Overie Dock, Cathedral Street, SE1 9DE*
- *0870 011 8700; www.goldenhinde.com*
- *London Bridge*
- *£6 visit; £7 tours; £39.95 sleepovers*

A revered sea captain and explorer, Sir Francis Drake sailed around the world, returning to Britain in 1580 in the *Golden Hinde*. This is a replica of Drake's 16th-century ship, complete with cannons, ropes and a red-and-yellow canopy. As well as sleepovers on the deck, the ship also organizes children's pirate days, treasure hunts, storytelling, and tours led by guides dressed in Tudor costumes.

LONDON BRIDGE EXPERIENCE & LONDON TOMBS

- *2–4 Tooley Street, London Bridge, SE1 2PF*
- *Tel: 0800 043 4666; www.londonbridgeexperience.com*
- *London Bridge*
- *£21.95 (up to 50% discount available online)*

This attraction will entertain those interested in the history of London Bridge and its surrounds. On the ground floor, which is dedicated to the London Bridge Experience, visitors pass through Victorian, Viking and Druid areas, meeting Charles Dickens and the keeper of heads along the way – the keeper used to guard the bridge's spiked gateway, which was decorated with the heads of criminals. You are then given a hard hat before exploring the catacombs underground – be prepared for 'ghosts' to jump out and scare you. This is also where the skeletons of 80 adult and child plague victims were discovered in an excavation before the attraction opened in 2008. *Insider info: the tombs are said to be haunted by the screaming Shadow Man and a ghostly woman, Emily, who has been seen hiding in the tombs' corners; members of staff refuse to be left alone in the tombs, and one resigned out of fear.*

THE LONDON DUNGEON

- *Tooley Street, London Bridge, SE1 2SZ*
- *Tel: 020 7403 7221; www.thedungeons.com*
- *London Bridge*
- *£21.95 (up to 50% off available online)*

Make no mistake; this attraction is genuinely very scary. As you make your way around the dungeons, be prepared to be terrified out of your wits by actors jumping out of the shadows when you least expect, ghost-like special effects and a boat ride in the dark that will leave you dripping with sweat after you plummet backwards in the dark. Feel the floor give way beneath you in Extremis: Drop Ride to Hell and lose yourself in the mirrored tunnels of the Labyrinth of the Lost. Tours last between one and one-and-a-half hours. *Tip: go midweek and book through their website and the entry charge drops to half price.*

THE PAINTED HALL

- *Old Royal Naval College, Greenwich, SE10 9LW*
- *Tel: 020 8269 4747; www.oldroyalnavalcollege.org*
- *Cutty Sark DLR*
- *FREE*

In 1698, Sir Christopher Wren, of St Paul's fame, built this spectacular sailor's dining room on the site of King Henry VIII's palace. James Thornhill then took 19 years to paint it – he was later knighted for his efforts. Since then, the hall has been used as a pensioner's hospital and to exhibit naval art – before the artworks moved to the nearby National Maritime Museum in the 1930s. It was also used as a dining room for the Royal Navy until 1998. It's open to the public, so you can view the masterpieces yourself. The painting on the ceiling of King William and Queen Mary, cherubs and angels is arguably the grandest – you can look at it through the mirrors on the ground if you don't want to strain your neck.

ROYAL OBSERVATORY AND PLANETARIUM

- *Blackheath Avenue, Greenwich, SE10 8XJ*
- *Tel: 020 8312 6565; www.nmm.ac.uk*
- *Cutty Sark DLR*
- *FREE observatory; £6 planetarium*

Housed in Flamsteed House on top of Greenwich Hill, the Royal Observatory was built in 1675 for Charles II. It's the place to come if you're curious about stars, space and time, or want to touch a 4.5 billion-year-old meteorite or see the seventh largest telescope in the world. Arrive at lunchtime and you will see a ball rising slowly up a mast on top of the house; it starts climbing at 12.55pm, reaches the top at 12.58pm and falls at 1pm – you can set your watch by it. As well as the meridian line, a highlight is the camera obscura, or darkened chamber, where you will see a close-up moving panorama of Greenwich, the Thames, the National Maritime Museum and the Royal Naval College projected onto a table by a lens reflecting images from a rotating mirror. You can also visit London's only planetarium, which shows documentaries and educational films in its dome.

SOUTHWARK CATHEDRAL

- *London Bridge, Bankside, SE1 9DA*
- *Tel: 020 7367 6700, 020 7367 6734 (tours); www.dswark.org*
- *London Bridge*
- *FREE*

There's been a place of worship on this site since AD 606. Parts of the existing cathedral date back 800 years, making it London's oldest Gothic cathedral, although most of the cathedral was rebuilt following fires in the 13th century. It is still an active place of worship – there are five services a day – but you can look around. Look out for a memorial to Shakespeare within the grounds; his brother, Edmund, is buried here. Outside, the cathedral garden has benches, so you can buy a picnic at Borough Market (*see pp.96–7*) next door and eat it in the garden.

▼ EAST

MONUMENT

- ❶ Monument Street, EC3R 8AH
- ⊕ Tel: 020 7626 2717; www.themonument.info
- ⊖ Monument
- ❸ £3

Following a £4.5million restoration project, the memorial to those who died in the 1666 Great Fire of London re-opened in February 2009. The restoration took 18 months. Christopher Wren designed the column, which is 61.5 metres high – the same distance from the monument to the outbreak of the fire in Farriner's bakery in Pudding Lane. Visitors can climb 331 steps to a viewing platform at 49 metres; from there, there's a 360-degree view of the city. Perversely, you can now see the view from the top at the bottom, via a live video link.

ROYAL MAIL MOUNT PLEASANT SORTING OFFICE

- ❶ Farringdon Road, Islington, EC1R 4SQ
- ⊕ Tel: 020 7239 2311 (office), 020 7239 2252 (free tours)
- ⊖ Farringdon
- ❸ FREE

If you call ahead, you can take a tour around the sorting office's 37 km of underground tunnels, which cover 7.5 acres between Whitechapel and Paddington. The tunnels were built to deliver post and were also used as an air-raid shelter in World War II, although one flooded after it was bombed.

ST AUGUSTINE'S TOWER

- ❶ The Narroway, off Mare Street, Hackney, E8 4RP
- ⊕ Tel: 020 8986 0029; www.hhbt.org.uk
- ⊖ Bethnal Green, Hackney Central BR
- ❸ FREE

This Grade I-listed tower is the oldest building in Hackney. It's all that remains of the 13th-century parish church of St Augustine, which was demolished in 1798 after its congregation had grown too big to fit. The tower now hosts occasional displays of local artists' work, and visitors can climb the 135 steps to the top.

ST PAUL'S CATHEDRAL

- ❶ Ludgate Hill, EC4M 8AD
- ⊕ Tel: 020 7246 8357, 020 8778 6308 (bell ringing and bell tours); www.stpauls.co.uk
- ⊖ St Paul's
- ❸ £11 includes crypt and upper galleries

After the third cathedral on this site was destroyed in the Great Fire of London, Sir Christopher Wren started building St Paul's in 1675. The cathedral is still active, but you're allowed to explore the nave and the crypt and see the high altar.

However, climbing the 520 narrow steps of the cathedral's spiral staircase is by far the highlight. As you pass other breathless visitors, there's a sense of camaraderie, and midway you reach the dome. Here you can whisper into the wall and send your whisper echoing over to the other side. Once you've got your breath back, you can climb up to the Stone Gallery, then on to the Golden Gallery at the top, where you're met with a fantastic view of London, in all directions. The £40 million refurbishment of St Paul's, which began in 2001, is due to be completed in 2011. After it is finished, the cathedral will be cleaner, better lit and have more educational facilities. The Triforium Gallery, which currently has restricted access, will open in 2012.

TOWER BRIDGE

- *SE1 2UP*
- *Tel: 020 7403 3761; www.towerbridge.org.uk*
- *Tower Hill*
- *£7 exhibition; £6 group tour*

Completed in 1894, this iconic bridge is made from 11,000 tons of steel, Cornish granite and Portland stone. It's free to walk across, but if you want to learn more about the bridge's history you can visit the exhibition. You'll also get chance to see the original engine rooms and stroll across high-level walkways that lead from one end of the bridge to the other – you can see as far as Shooters Hill on Hampstead Heath. Otherwise there are group tours, which guide you underneath the riverbed, to working steam rooms and the bridge control rooms. *Insider info: in 1952, a double-decker bus leaped from one side to the other when the bridge began to rise by mistake.*

TOWER OF LONDON

- *Tower Hill, EC3N 4AB*
- *Tel: 0844 482 7777; www.hrp.org.uk*
- *Tower Hill*
- *£17*

William the Conqueror began building the tower in the 1070s, and more buildings were added later – the stone tower that can be seen today looks much like the tower of the 1350s. The tower is a former prison (the Kray twins were held here for a night) and site of execution – Henry VIII's wives Anne Boleyn and Catherine Howard as well as Lady Jane Grey were all executed here. It was also a place of torture – on display is a crushing device, manacles and a stretching rack, on which Guy Fawkes was probably tortured. But what most of the 2 million people who visit each year come to see are the crown jewels. The jewels date from 1660; Charles II had them made after Cromwell melted down the old ones. You can see bracelets, rings and swords made from sapphires, emeralds and rubies; and crowns, such as the St Edward's crown, which has 440 semi-precious stones, and was last used for the Queen's 1953 coronation. *Insider info: one of Cromwell's lieutenants is said to have hidden £20,000 gold coins in the tower, but the treasure has never been found.*

▼ WEST

HAM HOUSE

- ❶ *Ham Street, Ham, Richmond-upon-Thames TW10 7RS*
- ⊕ *Tel: 020 8940 1950; www.nationaltrust.org.uk*
- ❸ *Richmond, then bus 371*
- ❹ *£9.90 house and garden; £3.30 garden*

Dating from 1610, this house was given to the National Trust in 1948. Now visitors can explore 29 of the rooms inside the house, from the Hall Gallery (formerly the Great Dining Room) and North Drawing Room to the Great Staircase. The manor is set within 18 acres of formal gardens along the banks of the Thames. Stroll along an avenue of 250 trees, visit the cherry garden on the east side of the house and pass by the orangery, which is now a restaurant. In summer, the house hosts open-air concerts within the grounds (*see* p.162).

HAMPTON COURT PALACE

- ❶ *East Molesey, Surrey, KT8 9AU*
- ⊕ *Tel: 0844 482 7777 (palace), 020 3166 6471 (gardens); www.hrp.org.uk*
- ❸ *Hampton Court BR*
- ❹ *£14*

Henry VIII's stunning palace, which actually dates from the 11th century, covers a massive six acres – and that's just the building. Highlights include the Great Hall, characterized by its high, arched roof, wooden beams and tapestries on the walls; and the Tudor Kitchens, which were built to feed up to 600 people twice a day. They're still used today for live cooking demonstrations – on the first weekend of every month, chefs recreate medieval recipes using traditional cooking methods. The ornate Chapel Royal is also still in use, for weddings, funerals and religious ceremonies.

OSTERLEY PARK

- ❶ *Jersey Road, Isleworth, TW7 4RB*
- ⊕ *Tel: 020 8232 5050; www.nationaltrust.org.uk*
- ❸ *Osterley*
- ❹ *£8.40 house and garden*

This square, red-brick Tudor mansion has 4 towers and 70 rooms over 3 floors, 32 of which are open to the public. Most have views of the extensive grounds (*see* p.210). The house was built in 1576, then redesigned and brought up to date between 1760 and 1780 for a wealthy banking family, the Childs. Visitors can explore the manor's extravagant rooms, starting with the impressive entrance hall, which has alcoves, statues, a patterned stone floor and fireplaces adorned with the Child's family crest. But it's the tapestry room that is by far the most spectacular. Here you can see ornate candle-sticks, tapestries decorated with pictures of animals, musical instruments and flowers, and furniture upholstered in a similar design.

FITNESS & BEAUTY

Sport and fitness isn't just about football, tennis or going for a run. If you're bored of your gym routine, why not try capoeira, zorbing or sword fighting? Then you can have a pampering spa treatment without feeling the slightest bit guilty.

▼ CENTRAL

BERKELEY HOTEL

- Wilton Place, Knightsbridge, SW1X 7RL
- Tel: 020 7235 6000; www.the-berkeley.co.uk
- Knightsbridge, Hyde Park Corner

This pool, on the hotel's seventh floor, is West London's only rooftop pool. It's open to the public for a hefty daily rate of £65, which also permits access to the gym, sauna and steam room. The pool is a modest 1 metre, 20 cm deep, but wins points for its roof, which slides open in warm weather.

CITISKATE

- Various venues. Office: Citiskate London, Suite 22, 2 Lansdowne Row, W1J 6HL
- www.citiskate.co.uk

If you can get going but don't know how to stop, try a couple of one-to-one skating lessons, which are held in Hyde, Kensington and Battersea parks. Alternatively, four- and five-week group courses are available for beginners in Victoria and Hyde Park. Once you've mastered the basics, join the roller stroll, a mass 11-kilometre skate that starts at 2pm every Sunday from the east side of Serpentine Road (it's free). And if you can manage hills, you can progress to the Friday night skate event – it runs every week – or join in a game of roller football.

CITY GOLF CLUB

- 40 Coleman Street, EC2R 5EH
- Tel: 020 7796 5960; www.citygolfclubs.com
- Bank, Moorgate
- £80 per booth per hour (maximum eight golfers)

In City Golf Club you can book a booth and whack a regular golf ball towards a computer screen. Your ball passes through sensors that detect its speed and distance before it hits the screen and falls to the floor, while the virtual course picks up your shot.

ES PHYSICAL HEALTH

- ❶ *22 Harley Street, W1G 9PL*
- ⊕ *Tel: 020 7907 1900; www.esph.co.uk*
- ◒ *Oxford Circus*
- ❹ *£59–£125 isokinetics; £38–£69 massage; £59 per 30-minute physiotherapy session; £87 per 45-minute physiotherapy session (includes acupuncture)*

This upmarket physiotherapy centre aims to prevent illness as well as treat it, using a range of therapies, such as massage, acupuncture, hydrotherapy and isokinetics (the testing and strengthening of muscles). It also offers electrotherapy – a pain-free treatment which involves heating an injured body part to increase blood flow to the area, accelerating the healing process. There's a second branch in East Dulwich (020 8696 2493), which has a gym run by physiotherapists, as well as pilates, yoga and circuit-training classes.

JO HANSFORD

- ❶ *19 Mount Street, Mayfair, W1K 2RN*
- ⊕ *Tel: 020 7495 7774; www.johansford.com*
- ◒ *Bond Street*
- ❹ *£17–£200+; available from 8.30am*

On bad hair days, have a breakfast blow-dry at Jo Hansford. It takes 40 minutes and includes tea, coffee and toast.

KI LONDON

- ❶ *25 Queen Anne Street, W1G 9HT*
- ⊕ *Tel: 0845 459 1025; www.kiglobal.org*
- ◒ *Oxford Circus*
- ❹ *£40*

Don't come here expecting soothing whale music; rather, as your therapist pummels you during an acupressure massage, they'll release a screeching whistling sound resembling a boiled kettle. This unique technique originated from South Korea. By pressing on the body's 'energy points' in the head, shoulders, limbs and stomach, the therapist (or *ki* master) will loosen energy blockages and transmit *ki* (energy). Those who try it say it helps with ME, arthritis and asthma. It can also reduce stress and relieve pain.

LONDON BICYCLE TOUR COMPANY

- ❶ *1a Gabriel's Wharf, 56 Upper Ground, South Bank, SE1 9PP*
- ⊕ *Tel: 020 7928 6838; www.londonbicycle.com*
- ◒ *Waterloo*
- ❹ *£4 first hour, then £3 per hour to hire; £19 per day to hire; £15.95–£18.95 tour*

If you don't have a bike or the one you own is still in your parents' shed, then rent one out for the day. The company also runs three-hour bike tours in east, west and central London.

LONDON SCHOOL OF SAMBA

- *Waterloo Action Centre, Baylis Road, SE1*
- *Tel: 020 7394 7539; www.londonschoolofsamba.co.uk*
- *Waterloo*
- *£7 members; £8 non-members*

No maps are required for this school, which is behind Waterloo station; just follow the beat of drums instead. Step inside and even nervous types won't fail to crack a smile at this colourful, warm Brazilian dance and drumming school, which feels like Notting Hill Carnival on repeat. If you're keen to get involved, try a class or help fix the performer's costumes worn at the carnival.

QUEEN'S ICE AND BOWL

- *17 Queensway, Bayswater, W2 4QP*
- *Tel: 020 7229 0172; www.queensiceandbowl.co.uk*
- *Queensway, Bayswater*
- *£10 ice skating plus £1.50 skate hire; £6.50 bowling per person per game; £6.50 karaoke per person per hour*

With its ice rink for 1,000 skaters, 12 bowling lanes and 2 karaoke rooms for 12 to 25 people, this centre is popular with teenagers and families.

URBAN GOLF

- *33 Great Pulteney Street, Soho, W1F 9NW*
- *Tel: 020 7434 4300; www.urbangolf.co.uk*
- *Piccadilly Circus*
- *£20–£55 per simulator per hour*

If you've always wished you could swing your clubs at lunchtime, but you don't live anywhere near St Andrews, then let St Andrews come to you. At this virtual golf course, you can try your hand at indoor simulations of international golf courses. As well as a putting green, there are six simulators, and up to eight people can play. All levels are catered for – there's even a golf academy. Afterwards, you can meet fellow golfers in the licensed clubhouse for a post-game drink. There's a second branch, Urban Golf Smithfield, in the east.

VERTICAL CHILL

- *Tower House, 3–11 Southampton Street, Covent Garden, WC2E 7HA*
- *Tel: 020 7395 1010; www.vertical-chill.com*
- *Covent Garden*
- *£50 ice climbing lessons for beginners; £35 climbing, supervision and equipment for experienced climbers; £25 climbing and supervision for experienced climbers*

Wow. If you always dreamed of being an explorer, then at least you can pretend to be one when climbing this 8-metre wall of ice. Lessons last one hour and suit anyone, whether you want to increase your body muscle or just impress your mates with an unusual hobby. Wrap up warm – it's -12ffC in there.

FIVE BEST STRIPTEASE CLASSES

★ 1 BURLESQUE BABY

ℹ Various venues
⊕ *Tel: 020 3287 5164; www.burlesquebaby.com*
💷 *Burlesque: beginner's course £60, intermediate course £99; striptease: course £99*

Whether you want to learn burlesque, striptease or pole-dancing, Burlesque Baby has a range of courses, all accompanied by jazz music and rock 'n' roll.

★ 2 POLE PEOPLE

ℹ Various venues
⊕ *Tel: 020 7737 7447; www.polepeople.co.uk*
💷 *Pole-dancing: class £18, course £140; burlesque: class £18, course £120*

While Pole People specializes in pole-dancing, it offers classes, courses and parties in burlesque and musical theatre as well.

★ 3 POLE SECRETS

ℹ Various venues
⊕ *Tel: 07738 741 114; 01622 204 808; www.polesecrets.com*
💷 *Pole-dancing: class (for up to three people) £97.75, course £126.50; aerial trapeze: intensive workshop £50.00, course £90.00*

Here you can opt for private pole-dancing or burlesque lessons or take part in group classes. Pole Secrets also offers aerial courses so you can learn how to fly on a trapeze or dance in the air holding on to lengths of silk.

★ 4 POLESTARS

ℹ Various venues
⊕ *Tel: 020 7274 4865; www.polestars.net*
💷 *Pole-dancing: class £20, course £140; burlesque: class £20, course £100; can-can: class £20, course £100*

Polestars offers tuition in burlesque, pole-dancing and can-can dancing. It also has themed parties such as belly dancing, Bollywood and cocktail-making.

★ 5 LONDON SCHOOL OF STRIPTEASE

ℹ Workshops: LA Fitness, Golders Green, 152–4 Golders Green Road, NW11 8HE
  Taster classes: Danceworks, 16 Balderton Street, W1K 6TN
⊕ *Tel: 07958 314 107 (Jo King); www.lsos.co.uk*
⊖ *Brent Cross (LA Fitness); Bond Street (Danceworks)*
💷 *Burlesque: class £10/15, course £240; striptease: workshop £60, course £240*

Cabaret performer and choreographer Jo King runs various burlesque and striptease workshops, such as Undress to Impress and Glamour Puss.

▼ NORTH

ALEXANDRA PALACE ICE RINK

- ❶ Alexandra Palace Way, Wood Green, N22 7AY
- ⊕ Tel: 020 8365 4386, 020 8888 2955 (dance lessons); www.alexandrapalace.com
- ◉ Wood Green, then bus W3
- ❹ £6.50 Mon–Fri, £8 Sat–Sun public skating

This ice rink has a capacity for 1,250, including tiered seating for 741 spectators. It hosts regular discos on ice, and lessons for adults and children as young as two years old. The centre also organizes ballet and tap lessons in a mirrored dance studio, which overlooks the ice.

THE CASTLE CLIMBING CENTRE

- ❶ Green Lanes, Stoke Newington, N4 2HA
- ⊕ Tel: 020 8211 7000; www.castle-climbing.co.uk
- ◉ Finsbury Park, then bus 106
- ❹ £11 per visit for registered climbers (£4 one-off registration fee); £59 monthly pass

Of all the indoor rock-climbing centres in the UK, this former water-pumping station – complete with turrets and a 36.5-metre tower you can abseil down – has to be one of the most dramatic. Built in 1856 to supply fresh water to east London, you can still see the original exposed-brick arches and cast-iron columns. With over 1,000 square metres of wall surface reaching a height of 12.5 metres and 450 routes and courses designed for children and adults, the centre is suitable for all levels, whether you just want to give it a go or you're an experienced climber looking for a challenge. Climbers wishing to abseil down the tower can abseil from the inside or outside.

FLOATWORKS

- ❶ 1 Thrale Street, SE1 9HW
- ⊕ Tel: 020 7357 0111; www.floatworks.com
- ◉ London Bridge
- ❹ £40 per one-hour float

Floatworks opened nine tanks in 1993, making it the world's largest floatation centre. The tanks resemble a jacuzzi, but with a hatch. Once the hatch closes, you're left alone, floating in salty water, in a silent, dark space. It won't suit everybody, but it is said to induce a state of relaxation similar to meditation.

HAMPSTEAD HEATH PONDS

- ❶ Hampstead Heath, NW3
- ⊕ Tel: 020 7485 4491
- ◉ Hampstead

For a true back-to-nature experience, head to these spring-fed ponds, which were designed for swimming in the late 19th century (see p.195).

HENDON YOUTH SPORTS CENTRE CLIMBING CENTRE

- 🏠 *Marble Drive, NW2 1XQ*
- ☎ *Tel: 020 8455 0818; www.hysc.co.uk*
- 🚇 *Brent Cross*
- 💷 *£17.50 instructed climbing session; £8.30 per visit for experienced climbers*

This climbing centre is best for beginners and intermediate climbers. It has 12 routes across a single climbing wall, which reaches a height of 18 metres. It also organizes children's parties, and there's a small cave for children to play in.

JACKSONS LANE

- 🏠 *269a Archway Road, Highgate, N6 5AA*
- ☎ *Tel: 020 8341 4421; www.jacksonslane.org.uk*
- 🚇 *Highgate*
- 💷 *£3–£10*

A former Gothic church, Jacksons Lane is now a modern multi-arts venue that hosts over 50 courses for adults, teens and children. As well as a theatre (*see* p.155), the centre has four dance and rehearsal studios. Here you can learn and practise street, jive and belly dancing, as well as capoeira, fencing, juggling and African drumming. Life drawing, acting classes and circus skills classes are also available. Many of the classes are drop-in sessions.

MOVING EAST

- 🏠 *St Matthias Church Hall, Wordsworth Road, Stoke Newington, N16 8DD*
- ☎ *Tel: 020 7503 3101; www.movingeast.co.uk*
- 🚇 *Angel, then bus 73, 476*
- 💷 *£7 for a one-hour dance/martial art class*

This dance, martial arts and complementary medicine centre, housed in a former church hall, has a range of classes for children and adults, such as judo, aikido and contact improvization – a dance form similar to capoeira. After all that back-cracking in judo class, braver types might want to have a treatment – try *chavutti thirumal* (Indian rope massage), which involves being trampled on by a practitioner who is holding on to a rope.

SWISS COTTAGE SPORTS CENTRE CLIMBING CENTRE

- 🏠 *Adelaide Road, Camden, NW3 3NF*
- ☎ *Tel: 020 7974 2012 (sports centre), 084 5363 1144 (climbing centre); www.climblondon.co.uk*
- 🚇 *Swiss Cottage*
- 💷 *£17.50 instructed climbing session; £8.30 per visit for experienced climbers*

A vast glass wall on one side of this sports centre overlooks the road outside, so passers-by can watch climbers attempting the 14-metre lead wall inside. This rock-climbing centre has over 60 routes – new routes are added every month, so regulars won't get bored.

▼ SOUTH

BROCKWELL PARK

- ❶ Herne Hill, Lambeth, SE24 0NG
- ⊕ Tel: 020 7274 3088; www.brockwell-lido.co.uk
- ◎ Herne Hill BR
- ❹ £5.20 lido, May–Oct; £11 sports centre per day

Opened in 1937, you can still see some of the original features of this art deco lido, such as the square clock. The pool is 50 metres by 27 metres. Next to the lido is a modern sports centre, with a gym, four dance studios, a steam room and sauna, as well as a hydrotherapy pool that fits 12. There is no indoor pool.

DULWICH THERAPY ROOMS

- ❶ 47 Lordship Lane, East Dulwich, SE22 8EP
- ⊕ Tel: 020 8299 4232; www.dulwichtherapyrooms.co.uk
- ◎ East Dulwich BR, then bus 40

This 'integrated health centre' offers alternative treatments, such as maternity reflexology, hot stone massage and Hopi ear candling. It also offers Chinese medicine, homeopathy consultations and classes, and even yoga for children.

INDOOR URBAN SPORTS

- ❶ 72–4 Tooley Street, SE1 2TF (and separate entrance on 47 St Thomas Street)
- ⊕ Tel: 07872 179 303; www.indoorurbansports.com
- ◎ London Bridge
- ❹ Urban cricket per team per game £59.99 (plus £100 registration); urban football per team per game £54.99 (plus £100 registration); urban beach sports per team per game £54.99

Got the urge to play beach volleyball? Well, you can, at this 3,000-square-metre sports centre in Southwark. As well as two five-a-side football pitches and two cricket fields – the 'grass' is actually Burmatex carpet – Indoor Urban Sports has a 15- by 25-metre beach made with 90 tons of deep white sand. Book ahead if you want to play; sports on offer include volleyball, touch rugby and football.

LABAN

- ❶ Creekside, Greenwich, SE8 3DZ
- ⊕ Tel: 020 8691 8600; www.laban.org
- ◎ Cutty Sark DLR
- ❹ £82.50 for an 11-week course

This dance school is known for its contemporary-dance courses and is the largest purpose-built dance centre in the world. Its evening dance classes for adults range from classical ballet and contemporary dance to jazz. The school also teaches yoga and pilates. *Insider info: you might spot some fashionistas here – designers Margaret Howell and Zandra Rhodes have attended events here.*

THE LONDON FLOAT CENTRE AT COMMON SENSE

- ❶ 7 Clapham Common Southside, SW4 7AA
- ⊕ Tel: 020 7720 4952; www.londonfloatcentre.com
- ◑ Clapham Common
- ❹ £45 for one-hour float

This floatation centre opened 21 years ago and is open 24 hours a day, so you can float in salty water all night if you want to. Customers enter one of four small rooms in which they can stand as well as float. Shiatsu and rolfing, both types of massage, are among the alternative therapies also available.

POD LONDON

- ❶ Salmons Lane, Whyteleafe, Surrey, CR3 0HB
- ⊕ Tel: 0845 430 3322; www.zorbing.co.uk
- ◑ Whyteleafe South BR
- ❹ £49.95 for two people per run; £84.95 for two people per two runs

Imagine being strapped into a giant transparent ball and launched down a hill. That's zorbing. The Pod London track, set in woodland, is a 150-metre route that you hurtle down inside an inflatable ball, before splashing into a pool at the end. It doesn't come cheap, but it's tons of fun. The track is far out from central London, but it's not difficult to get to – trains leave from London Bridge every 10 minutes. (N.B. When you enquire about prices, ask how many 'rolls' you get.)

RED CARPET TREATMENTS

- ❶ 16 The Pavement, Clapham Common, SW4 0HY
- ⊕ Tel: 020 7627 8547
- ◑ Clapham Common

This small salon is decorated like a boudoir, with a red chandelier, mirrors and black feathers. As there are only seats for two clients, you know the service will be attentive. Head here with a friend to get a manicure before a big night out. You can also design your own perfume for £15 – to buy it, prices start from £45.

TOOTING BEC LIDO

- ❶ Tooting Bec Road, SW16 1UT
- ⊕ Tel: 020 8871 7198 (summer), 07985 141 532 (winter); www.wandsworth.gov.uk
- ◑ Tooting Bec, then bus 249, 319
- ▦ From Whitsun (the seventh Sun after Easter) to 31 Aug 6am–8pm (last ticket 7.30pm); 1–30 Sep 6am–5pm (last ticket 4.30pm)
- ❹ £4.75 all day in summer; £25 SLSC membership and annual lido pass £100

The 90-metre pool at Tooting Bec is one of Europe's biggest freshwater lidos. You may recognize it from the film *Snatch*. The lido has been criticized for its dubious levels of hygiene, but remains popular because it's fun and cheap. During the winter, it's closed to the public, but you can still swim here if you're a member of the South London Swimming Club (www.slsc.org.uk).

▼ EAST

BRICK LANE BIKES

- *118 Bethnal Green Road, E2 6DG*
- *Tel: 020 7033 9053; www.bricklanebikes.co.uk*
- *Liverpool Street, then bus 8*

As well as selling new and used bicycles, BLB repair bikes in their on-site workshop. They specialize in vintage Italian racers, track bikes and fixed-wheel bikes. They can also design track bikes and fixed-wheel bikes to your specifications.

BRITANNIA LEISURE CENTRE CLIMBING CENTRE

- *40 Hyde Road, Hackney, N1 5JU*
- *Tel: 020 7729 4485; www.climblondon.co.uk*
- *Essex Road BR, then bus 67*
- *Climbing: £6.50 per session for experienced climbers*

At the time of writing, this small climbing centre offered climbing sessions on Tuesdays at 7pm for experienced climbers. A refurbishment is planned.

THE CIRCUS SPACE

- *Coronet Street, Shoreditch, N1 6HD*
- *Tel: 020 7729 9522; www.thecircusspace.co.uk*
- *Old Street*
- *Half day classes £55; full day classes £99; six drop-in classes over three months £78*

When this power station was built in 1896, we bet no one guessed it would, one day, house a circus school. Now children and adults can try circus tricks, acrobatics and dance – you can even do a degree in Circus Arts. Learn to fly on a trapeze, walk on a tightrope, do backflips and somersaults and climb silks. There is also a Wild West course: students learn how to crack a whip, lasso a stallion (an imaginary one) and throw knives. Workshops start from £5, for juggling.

CLUB AQUARIUM

- *256–64 Old Street, EC1V 9DD*
- *Tel: 020 7253 3558; www.clubaquarium.co.uk*
- *Old Street*

What makes this pool unique is its location: it's in a nightclub (see p.188). But don't expect glamour. Apart from a glitzy mirror and withering palm tree, it resembles a leisure centre. The pool is 1.5 metres deep, and there's a jacuzzi, too.

DOCKLANDS SAILING AND WATERSPORTS CENTRE

- *235a Westferry Road, Millwall Dock, Isle of Dogs, E14 3QS*
- *Tel: 020 7537 2626; www.dswc.org*
- *Crossharbour DLR*
- *Adult day membership £10; Adult annual membership £110*

This watersports centre is on the banks of the River Thames and has the added bonus of being next to the Millwall Outer Dock, so beginners can learn in the sheltered 25-acre expanse. The centre has dinghy, yachting and powerboat courses for all levels, and windsurfing and kayaking lessons for beginners. It also offers canoeing, rowing and swimming lessons. From April to September, the centre organizes informal twilight racing events on Wednesday evenings; the £20 ticket includes live music, a barbecue and a beer after the race.

EAST HAM CLIMBING WALL

- ❶ 324 Barking Road, East Ham, E6 2RT
- ⊕ Tel: 020 8548 5850; www.climblondon.co.uk
- ⊖ East Ham
- ❹ £17.50 instructed climbing session; £8.30 per visit for experienced climbers

This climbing centre has over 50 routes across its two walls. It offers courses for beginners to advanced – beginners must first have an induction session.

E REJUVENATION CENTRE

- ❶ 132 Commercial Street, E1 6NG
- ⊕ Tel: 020 7650 0718; www.therejuvenationcentre.com
- ⊖ Liverpool Street

Each of the five treatment rooms here is designed according to the principles of feng shui, so there are rooms dedicated to fire, wood, metal, earth and water. There are also three massage rooms.

LCB

- ❶ 121 Bethnal Green Road, E2 7DG
- ⊕ Tel: 020 7739 3839; www.lcbsurf.co.uk
- ⊖ Liverpool Street, then bus 8; Old Street

Going on a beach holiday? Buy handmade surfboards, wetsuits, T-shirts and other surfing paraphernalia here. Surf-film nights and acoustic music events are also held once a month, usually in summer. The owners arrange surf trips, too.

THE LEE VALLEY CANOE & CYCLE CENTRE

- ❶ The Water's Edge, Stone Bridge Lock, Tottenham, N17 0XD
- ⊕ Tel: 07747 873 831; www.lvcc.biz, www.leevalleypark.org.uk
- ⊖ Tottenham Hale BR, then bus 192
- ❹ £8 per person for single kayak, per hour (£12 per two hours); £12 two-person canoe, per hour (£16 per two hours); £25 per person for a two-hour lesson

On the next warm weekend, hire a canoe or kayak and paddle up the marshes in this vast urban park. You'll pass grassy reservoir banks and colourful narrow boats, and the water's clear enough to spot fish swimming below you. Better still, contact the centre directly and enquire about sunrise and sunset canoe hire – nothing beats gliding through the calm waters while the sky is pastel pink.

LEE VALLEY ICE CENTRE

- *Lea Bridge Road, Leyton, E10 7QL*
- *Tel: 020 8533 3154; www.leevalleypark.org.uk*
- *Clapton BR, then bus 48, 55, N55, 56*
- *£6.60 public skating*

Since Torvill and Dean opened this ice rink in January 1984, it's been a popular ice-skating venue – ITV's *Dancing on Ice* was filmed here. It is open to the public everyday, and organizes figure skating and synchronized skating lessons. It is also an ice-hockey venue, and hosts ice shows each Christmas. The rink can fit up to 800 people at any one time, with an additional 750 spectators.

LEE VALLEY RIDING CENTRE

- *Lea Bridge Road, Leyton, E10 7QL*
- *Tel: 020 8556 2629; www.leevalleypark.org.uk*
- *Leyton, then bus 55; Walthamstow Central, then bus 48*
- *£25 per one-hour 'have a go' lessons (up to eight students); £38 per 30-minute private lesson; £350 per 12-week course*

Learn to ride at this 25-acre riding school, set within the boundaries of the tranquil Lee Valley nature reserve. The centre provides lessons for beginners and those with disabilities, and lessons in show jumping and dressage for more advanced riders. Learners can practise in the indoor arena or in the two flood-lit outdoor arenas. There are 50 horses and ponies.

LONDON BUDDHIST CENTRE

- *51 Roman Road, E2 0HU*
- *Tel: 0845 458 4716; www.lbc.org.uk*
- *Bethnal Green*
- *£1 drop-in meditation classes; £55–395 retreats*

This Buddhist centre opened in 1978 in an old Victorian fire station. It runs drop-in classes Monday to Saturday for as little as £1, in which you can de-stress and calm down by learning how to meditate or learn about Buddhist principles. The centre also runs regular events, such as poetry evenings, creative-writing workshops and themed retreats in Suffolk.

LONDON FIELDS LIDO

- *London Fields Park, London Fields Westside, Hackney, E8 3EU*
- *Tel: 020 7254 9038*
- *London Fields BR*
- *£4*

This lido first opened in April 1932, then closed during World War II, reopened in 1951, only to close again in 1986. It was resurrected for the second time in October 2006 by Hackney Council, after the council pumped in £2.5 million to return the derelict 50-metre pool into an art deco icon. The pool is heated.

MILE END CLIMBING WALL

- *Haverfield Road, E3 5BE*
- *Tel: 020 8980 0289; www.mileendwall.org.uk*
- *Mile End*
- *£5 registration, then £7 per visit (includes shoe hire); £35 monthly pass*

Housed in a former pipe-engineering works within Mile End Park, this climbing wall has been open to the public since 1986. Courses for beginners or semi-professionals can be arranged on the vast 1,500-square-metre indoor climbing space. Climbers can practise on 6.5-metre-high walls, which have eight top rope routes. More advanced climbers can climb without a rope on the centre's six lead climbing routes, or build the strength in their fingers and arms on a series of rungs in the board room. Fans of bouldering can climb on their 3.5-metre-high wall, or in their 'monkey house', so-called because you can climb across the roof. The centre also runs courses off-site in the UK and the French Alps.

MILE END PARK

- *Arches 422–4, Mile End Park, Burdett Road, E3 4AA*
- *Tel: 020 7538 5195; www.revolutionkarting.com*
- *Mile End*
- *£20 per person for 16 laps round a go-kart track*

If Amsterdam is too clichéd and Vegas out of your price range, then stags should consider go-karting at the electric go-kart track in Mile End Park. Make a day of it and visit the Xtreme Sports Centre next to the go-kart track. Here you can rollerblade, skateboard, snakeboard or turn a few tricks on your BMX. Children will love the park's facilities, too – the Adventure Park, designed for 11–17 year olds, has two basketball hoops, and the Youth Outreach Centre next door organizes cycling, canoeing and orienteering. Elsewhere in the park is a fitness centre, which has a gym, dance studio, sauna and swimming pools.

PIMPS & PINUPS

- *14 Lamb Street, Spitalfields, E1 6EA*
- *Tel: 020 7426 2121; www.pimpsandpinups.com*
- *Liverpool Street*

Treat yourself to a retro experience as well as a retro hairstyle at this stylish hairdressing salon, which has a neon sign, Hollywood-style lightbulbs round each mirror and comfy reclining chairs – a 1920s blowdry for an 'up-do' will set you back £40. A glass of wine or beer is on the house.

SPA LONDON

- *York Hall Leisure Centre, Old Ford Road, Bethnal Green, E2 9PJ*
- *Tel: 020 8709 5845; www.spa-london.org*
- *Bethnal Green, Cambridge Heath BR*
- *Facials from £35; treatments from £35; massage from £31; threading from £7*
- *Sun: mixed; Mon, Thur: men; Tues, Wed, Fri, Sat: women*

The York Hall and baths were built in 1929, and many of the original features can still be seen. The spa has a hammam, or heated seated area, the original Turkish baths (hot, dry rooms) and an ice fountain – you rub the ice flakes over your body. The spa offers over 50 treatments, including massage, facials and body scrubs. There's also a plunge pool and a gym.

TIMUNA SEA

- 🛈 *121 Cannon Workshops, Cannon Drive, E14 4AS*
- ☎ *Tel: 020 7719 9444; www.timunasea.com*
- 🚇 *West India Quay DLR*
- 💷 *£250 open water plus £150 dives; £235 advanced includes dives; £250 rescue diver includes dives; £400 dive master excluding dives*

This is five-star PADI dive centre that provides scuba-diving tuition for beginners and advanced levels in the Tiller Centre swimming pool on the Isle of Dogs. The centre teaches basic open-water qualifications, as well as advanced open-water, rescue diver and dive master. If you'd rather do your qualifying dives in a more glamorous location, you can complete your qualification on trips abroad. Timuna Sea organizes open-water trips to Micronesia and Egypt. The centre sells beachwear all year round, as well as selling and repairing diving equipment.

TURKISH BATHS

- 🛈 *1–11 Ironmonger Row, EC1V 3QF*
- ☎ *Tel: 020 7253 4011*
- 🚇 *Old Street*
- 💷 *£8 entrance to baths, includes swim; £8 olive oil scrubs; £12 sea salt scrub*

These baths opened in 1931, and many of the original features remain, such as patterned tiles. The baths consist of a steam room, three hot rooms and an icy plunge pool. You can also have 30-minute body-scrub treatments while resting on a marble slab. Guests usually bathe naked, except for on Mondays, when the baths are mixed. It is men-only on Tuesdays, Thursdays and Saturdays, and women-only on Sundays.

RING THE BELLS OF LONDON

★ CAMPANOLOGY CLASSES

- 🛈 *Various venues. Office: University of London Society of Change Ringers, c/o St Olave's Church, 8 Hart St, EC3R 7NB*
- ☎ *Tel: 020 8642 2400; www.ulscr.org.uk, www.cccbr.org.uk*

Ever wanted an unusual skill? Then take up campanology, the art of bell ringing. It's practised in churches across London and one-to-one tuition or beginners' classes are usually free. Anyone can ring bells, regardless of their age or physical ability, although having triceps of steel would help.

▼ WEST

BLINK

- *House of Fraser, Westfield, Ariel Way, W12 7SL*
- *Tel: 020 8765 3297; www.blinkbrowbar.com*
- *Wood Lane, White City*
- *£17 for eyebrow threading*

This eyebrow bar offers a walk-in service, so you can have tidy brows (or hair-free chins, for that matter) within 15 minutes. The therapists use a threading technique, popular in India, which involves twisting cotton and rolling it across the skin, catching stray hairs and ripping them out – ouch. A 5p donation from each threading appointment goes towards helping street children in Delhi.

HERSHESONS BLOWDRY BAR

- *Westfield, Ariel Way, W12 7GD*
- *Tel: 020 8743 0868; www.hershesonsblowdrybar.com*
- *Wood Lane, White City*
- *£22 per 30-minute blowdry*

This 'blowdry bar' has a menu of eight different blowdries, from the Alice in Wonderland look (soft waves) to the B52, or Amy Winehouse-look. But there's nothing old-fashioned about the decor: the open-plan room has high, lofty ceilings, hanging lights and an exposed air-conditioning unit.

HYDRO HEALING

- *216a Kensington Park Road, Notting Hill, W11 1NR*
- *Tel: 020 7727 2570; www.hydrohealing.com*
- *Ladbroke Grove*
- *£70 one-hour treatment; £65 one-hour massage; £80 one-hour colonic hydrotherapy*

This centre also offers iridology treatments, which is the scientific study of the iris of the eye. Using a magnifying glass and professional iris camera, the iridologist will assess your health in the same way that reflexologists check your well-being by assessing your feet. You can also opt for a massage on heated water cushions, or the slightly less glamorous treatment of colonic hydrotherapy.

OLD DEER PARK

- *Twickenham Road, Richmond, Surrey TW9 2SF*
- *Tel: 020 8940 0561; www.springhealth.net*
- *Richmond BR*
- *£3.85 all day, May–Sep*
- Lido: Apr–Oct

There are two 33-metre-long pools in the park; a heated indoor one and an out-door one. Indoor swimmers can still see the park through three all-glass walls. Those prepared to brave the lido will be relieved to know it's also heated.

RESOURCES

This selection of resources is not exhaustive, but it will give you sound advice, helpful blogs and websites and some handy phone numbers you can rely on — whatever your query.

Books

▶ **Andrew Duncan's Favourite London Walks**, *Andrew Duncan, RRP £14.99*
Whether you're in London for a short trip or the city is the only home you've known, one of the 50 walks described in this book will surely appeal to you. This walking guide covers everything from strolls up the high street and down intriguing alleys to long country walks through quaint villages.

▶ **Eccentric London,**
Tom Quinn and Ricky Leaver RRP, £9.99
If you're curious about London's history, but are tired of reading about the plague and the Great Fire, then this book focuses on places and periods you'll be less familiar with. *Eccentric London* is full of little-known facts with which you can impress (or irritate) friends. Try this one: anyone who has been made a freeman of the City of London can insist on being hanged with a silken rope, or drive sheep over London Bridge whenever they choose, as neither statute has ever been overturned.

▶ **The Essential Guide to London's Best Food Shops**, *Antonio Carluccio, RRP £10.99*
A comprehensive guide to sourcing the best ingredients available in London's food halls, specialist shops, markets and mail-order services.

▶ **Haunted London,**
Richard Jones, RRP £9.99
If you've been intrigued by the haunted tales in this almanac, then you may well want to delve deeper into London's supernatural side. This book, illustrated with full-colour photographs, takes you through the city's spookiest streets, documenting ghostly sightings along the way.

▶ **London's Best Pubs,**
Peter Haydon RRP, £14.99
You might be planning a pub crawl for your mate's stag do or a quiet drink with the in-laws, or perhaps you live outside the city and want to make the most of your weekend in London. Either way, this book documents London's pubs so rigorously you'll wish you had the job of the author, Peter Haydon. The illustrated book is divided by area, each with its own map, with historical anecdotes and the lowdown on the cask ales on offer.

▶ **Uncovering Jack the Ripper's London,**
Richard Jones, RRP £14.99
This book looks at Victorian London's fear of Jack the Ripper, brought to life with previously unpublished documents and photographs. Jones examines the social conditions in the East End at the time of the murders and the hostile relationship between the press and police.

▶ **Walking Secret London,**
Andrew Duncan, RRP £10.99
Discover the city's most fascinating secrets – both above and below ground – with this unusual collection of walks.

Blogs

▶ **www.derelictlondon.com**
This blog by Paul Talling documents derelict London through a series of graphic photographs.

▶ **www.thegreenwichphantom.co.uk**
A lively account covering anything remotely connected to Greenwich, from free things to do and events to books and places of interest.

▶ *www.deptforddame.blogspot.com*
Information on the comings and goings of Deptford, with lots of links to other south London-related blogs, such as Nunhead Ramblings, Blackheath Bugle and Transpontine.

▶ *www.faded-london.blogspot.com*
This blogger puts an interesting spin on the bits of London most of us wouldn't give the time of day to.

▶ *www.london-underground.blogspot.com*
Musings on the city's tube system.

▶ *www.diamondgeezer.blogspot.com*
This diamond geezer explores some of London's less well-known boroughs.

▶ *www.londondailyphoto.blogspot.com*
A collection of photos from around the capital – some better than others.

▶ *www.londonist.com*
Informative and accurate, this blog covers everything from politics and arts to food and drink – with an emphasis on the offbeat.

Websites
Eating Out
The following websites allow you to quickly hunt for the details of a restaurant you know by name, or lets you search for recommended restaurants by cuisine, area or occasion.

▶ *www.classiccafes.co.uk*
▶ *www.london-eating.co.uk*
▶ *www.squaremeal.co.uk*
▶ *www.londonrestaurantsguide.com*
▶ *www.bestlondonrestaurants.co.uk*
▶ *www.london-restaurants.com*

Nightlife and Music
The websites below give you the low-down on London's upmarket cocktail bars, old man's boozers, dives with character and buzzing gay clubs.

▶ *www.london-drinking.com*
▶ *www.trustedplaces.com*
▶ *www.citypublife.co.uk*
▶ *www.scene-out.com*

Shopping
The following websites will point you in the right direction for the shop you want – whether you're looking for a new set of golf clubs, a designer handbag or a wooden birdcage.

▶ *www.streetsensation.co.uk* – explore London street by street.

www.towerhamlets.gov.uk – lists the East End's markets.

▶ *www.wineanorak.com* – a compact rundown of the city's wine shops.

▶ *www.farmshopping.net* – this site dedicates itself to 'farm shops and pick-your-own farms selling local food in London and within 10 miles of the M25'.

▶ *www.lfm.org.uk* – a comprehensive list of 15 of the city's farmer's markets, as well as a map and directions.

▶ *www.farmersmarkets.net* – another good bet for London's farmer's markets.

▶ *www.wendyfairmarkets.com* – info on little-known farmer's markets in the Home Counties, plus the one in Wembley.

Walking and cycling
London is so much smaller than you think, but you only realise this once you set off on foot or by bike. If you're a walkaphobe, the websites below will get you started:

▶ *www.tfl.gov.uk/legiblelondon* – find the quickest way to get where you need to be along with information on sights you'll see along the way.

▶ *www.londoncyclesport.com* – for dedicated, competitive London cyclists.

▶ *www.walklondon.org.uk* – for details of a specific walk or inspiration for walks such as The Capital Ring (*see* p.203).

RESOURCES

▶ *www.walkit.com/london* – find out the quickest route from A to B, plus how long it'll take you if you walk quickly, at a medium pace or slowly, and how many calories you'll burn along the way.

▶ *www.londonwalks.com* – walking tours of London, some of which are themed.

London lifestyle
The sites below cover everything from which gigs are playing this weekend and what exhibitions are on to walking routes and what you can do for free.

▶ *www.london-ers.com*

▶ *www.londonisfree.com*

▶ *www.londonforfree.net*

▶ *www.hidden-london.com*

▶ *www.visitlondon.com*

▶ *www.londontown.com*

▶ *www.timeout.com*

▶ *www.viewlondon.co.uk*

▶ *www.allinlondon.co.uk*

▶ *www.virtual-london.com*

▶ *www.london.gov.uk*

▶ *www.lecool.com*

▶ *www.run-riot.com*

▶ *www.first4london.com*

Everyday life
When all your mates offer to help you move house and give you a full introduction to the city, but they don't really mean it; you're on your own. But the websites below can help.

▶ *www.livinginlondon.net* – helps you choose which borough to live in.

▶ *www.moveflat.com* – if you're moving house...

▶ *www.spareroom.com* – another helpful moving-house website

▶ *www.mr-skill.co.uk* – whether you need

a shower cubicle fitted or floating shelves put up in your front room, post the job you want done and London's builders will come to you. Then just pick the quote that suits you best.

▶ *www.talkonthetube.com* – a site dedicated to encouraging miserable Londoners to talk to one another on the tube – or at least smile.

▶ *www.secret-london.co.uk* – a fantastic website with details of the city's hidden gardens, along with suggested walks and London trivia.

▶ *www.tntonline.co.uk* – aimed at Antipodean expats living in London.

▶ *www.stuckinlondon.com* – aimed at expats living in London.

▶ *www.tfl.gov.uk* – Transport for London – 020 7222 1234 – save it in your phone!

▶ *www.urban75.org* – join like-minded activists on their next march to protest about issues you care about.

▶ *www.cinemasinlondon.co.uk* – film buffs will love this one – as well as listings cinemas across the city, it gives information on their history and cheap deals.

▶ *www.opensquares.org* – brief notes on London's secret gardens.

▶ *www.gingerbeer.co.uk* – for London's lesbian community.

▶ *www.eastdulwichforum.co.uk* – information on the East Dulwich community.

▶ *www.shoreditchlife.com* – information on places of interest in Shoreditch.

▶ *www.n16mag.com* – information on boozers, eateries and shops in Stoke Newington.

Council contacts
Council staff are a mixed bag – some are enormously helpful, the rest, well, take a deep breath and count to 10... As with the staff, council websites vary; whereas

238

some offer little more than online complaint forms or information on your local recycling scheme, some detail events for the months ahead long before anyone else. They're also handy if you're looking for information on parks and outdoor markets that no one else seems to know, or if you need to know how to find your local hospital.

▶ *www.cityoflondon.gov.uk* – City of London 020 7606 3030

▶ *www.westminster.gov.uk* – City of Westminster 020 7641 6000

▶ *www.barking-dagenham.gov.uk* – London Borough of Barking and Dagenham 020 8215 3000

▶ *www.barnet.gov.uk* – London Borough of Barnet 020 8359 2000

▶ *www.bexley.gov.uk* – London Borough of Bexley 020 8303 7777

▶ *www.brent.gov.uk* – London Borough of Brent 020 8937 1200

▶ *www.bromley.gov.uk* – London Borough of Bromley 020 8464 3333

▶ *www.camden.gov.uk* – London Borough of Camden 020 7278 4444

▶ *www.croydon.gov.uk* – London Borough of Croydon 020 8726 6000

▶ *www.ealing.gov.uk* – London Borough of Ealing 020 8825 5000

▶ *www.enfield.gov.uk* – London Borough of Enfield 020 8379 1000

▶ *www.greenwich.gov.uk* – London Borough of Greenwich 020 8854 8888

▶ *www.hackney.gov.uk* – London Borough of Hackney 020 8356 3000

▶ *www.lbhf.gov.uk* – London Borough of Hammersmith & Fulham 020 8748 3020

▶ *www.haringey.gov.uk* – London Borough of Haringey 020 8489 0000

▶ *www.harrow.gov.uk* – London Borough of Harrow 020 8863 5611

▶ *www.havering.gov.uk* – London Borough of Havering 01708 434 343

▶ *www.hillingdon.gov.uk* – London Borough of Hillingdon 01895 250 111

▶ *www.hounslow.gov.uk* – London Borough of Hounslow 020 8583 2000

▶ *www.islington.gov.uk* – London Borough of Islington 020 7527 2000

▶ *www.rbkc.gov.uk* – Royal Borough of Kensington and Chelsea 020 7361 3000

▶ *www.kingston.gov.uk* – Royal Borough of Kingston upon Thames 020 8547 5757

▶ *www.lambeth.gov.uk* – London Borough of Lambeth 020 7926 1000

▶ *www.lewisham.gov.uk* – London Borough of Lewisham 020 8314 6000

▶ *www.merton.gov.uk* – London Borough of Merton 020 8274 4901

▶ *www.newham.gov.uk* – London Borough of Newham 020 8430 2000

▶ *www.redbridge.gov.uk* – London Borough of Redbridge 020 8554 5000

▶ *www.richmond.gov.uk* – London Borough of Richmond upon Thames 020 8891 1411

▶ *www.southwark.gov.uk* – London Borough of Southwark 020 7525 5000

▶ *www.sutton.gov.uk* – London Borough of Sutton 020 8770 5000

▶ *www.towerhamlets.gov.uk* – London Borough of Tower Hamlets 020 7364 5000

▶ *www.walthamforest.gov.uk* – London Borough of Waltham Forest 020 8496 3000

▶ *www.wandsworth.gov.uk* – London Borough of Wandsworth 020 8871 6000

This edition published in 2009 by
New Holland Publishers (UK) Ltd
London • Cape Town • Sydney • Auckland
www.newhollandpublishers.com

Garfield House, 86–88 Edgware Road, London W2 2EA

80 McKenzie Street, Cape Town 8001, South Africa

Unit 1, 66 Gibbes Street, Chatswood, NSW 2067, Australia

218 Lake Road, Northcote, Auckland, New Zealand

ISBN 978 1 84773 542 3

Design: Lucy Parissi
Senior Editor: Louise Coe
Production: Marion Storz
Editorial Direction: Rosemary Wilkinson
Printed and bound in India by Replika Press Pvt Ltd
Cover reproduction by Pica Digital Pte Ltd, Singapore

NOTE
The information in this book was as accurate as possible at the time of going to
press. Events, dates, prices, locations and other features may have changed from
the details provided.